*Men in Midlife Crisis* is a must read for every Christian. Dr. Jim Conway has walked through this issue with integrity. His seminars, retreats, and books have touched the souls of countless thousands. God will use this book to help you or someone you love.

Earl Henslin, Psy.D., author, international speaker,
and president of Henslin and Associates

Conway does far more than trace the roots of midlife crises. He offers concrete, tested counsel from Scripture, psychology, and his own ministry.

Dr. Vernon Grounds, president emeritus,
Denver Seminary

This book has been a help to me even though I'm a bit past midlife . . . and I've given several copies to younger friends.

Kenneth N. Taylor, author, publisher, and
translator of *The Living Bible*

God used you to save our marriage. . . . Now four years later, we are helping others and still passing around your books. Thank you, thank you!

Cindy Hageman, reader,
Florida

## Books by Jim and Sally Conway

*Men in Midlife Crisis* Jim Conway

*Your Husband's Midlife Crisis* Sally Conway

*Women in Midlife Crisis* Jim and Sally Conway

*Maximize Your Midlife* Jim and Sally Conway

*Your Marriage Can Survive Midlife Crisis* Jim and Sally Conway

*Making Real Friends in a Phony World* Jim Conway

*Trusting God in a Family Crisis* Becki Conway Sanders and Jim and Sally Conway

*Menopause* Sally Conway

*Adult Children of Legal or Emotional Divorce* Jim Conway

*Traits of a Lasting Marriage* Jim and Sally Conway

*When a Mate Wants Out* Jim and Sally Conway

*Sexual Harassment No More* Jim and Sally Conway

*Pure Pleasure: Making Your Marriage a Great Affair* Bill and Pam Farrel and Jim and Sally Conway

*Moving on After He Moves Out* Jim and Sally Conway

The Conways have over one million books in print in English and several other languages.

# MEN IN MIDLIFE CRISIS

## JIM CONWAY

**Chariot VICTOR**
PUBLISHING
A DIVISION OF COOK COMMUNICATIONS

Victor Books is an imprint of ChariotVictor Publishing, a division of
Cook Communications, Colorado Springs, Colorado 80918
Cook Communications, Paris, Ontario
Kingsway Communications, Eastbourne, England

MEN IN MIDLIFE CRISIS
© 1978, 1997 by Jim Conway

Scripture quotations, unless otherwise noted, are from *The Living Bible*, ©
1971, Tyndale House Publishers, Wheaton, IL 60189. Used by permission.
Other Scripture quotations are from *New American Standard Bible*, © the
Lockman Foundation 1960, 1962, 1963, 1968, 1971, 1972, 1973, 1975,
1977; and *Holy Bible, New Living Translation* (NLT), Copyright © 1996
Tyndale Charitable Trust.  All Rights Reserved.

Edited by LoraBeth Norton and Julie Smith
Designed by Bill Gray

Printed in Canada
First printing revised edition, 1997

    3  4  5  Printing/Year  01  00

Library of Congress  Cataloging-in-Publication Data
Conway, Jim.
    Men in midlife crisis / by Jim Conway.
    p. cm.
    Includes bibliographical references.
    ISBN:1-56476-698-5
    1. Middle aged men—Religious life. 2. Middle aged men—psychology.
3. Midlife crisis—Religious aspects—Christianity.
I. Title.
BV4579.5.C63    1997
248.8' 42—dc21                                    97-29004
                                                      CIP

## To my wife, Sally,

Who for all my writing was my
Researcher,
Editor,
Typist, and
Friendly Critic;
And who for all of our marriage was my
Encourager,
Lover, and
Closest Friend.

Sally Christon Conway
1934–1997

# CONTENTS

# Foreword

Born out of the crucible of personal experience, this book brings front and center a problem evangelicals have previously ignored. With candor, insight, sensitivity, and compassion, Pastor Conway explores the multi-causal complexity of this life-upsetting trauma. But he does far more than trace the roots of midlife crises. He offers concrete, tested counsel from Scripture, psychology, and his own ministry.

More than that, he holds out realistic assurance that a man can emerge from his struggle with self-doubt, vocational despair, and existential darkness a stronger, deeper person who in human weakness has discovered the resources of God's power.

VERNON GROUNDS
President Emeritus
Denver Seminary
Denver, Colorado

# The more things change, the more they are the same.

**What's the same?**

When this book was orginally published in 1978, I thought that since midlife crisis was a new issue it would disappear as people came to understand it. But this has not been the case. Current letters to our Midlife Dimensions office carry the same intensity of pain and confusion; the writers express the same feeling of being "lepers" in the Christian community.

In one of the first 1978 letters, a woman included a note from her husband. In part it said:

> I'm leaving and will not return of my own free will. I am going to make what's left of my life what I want it to be. Enclosed is a power of attorney so that you may sign my name legally to any documents necessary. I trust you not to do me wrong with it. I have left signed checks to pay off employees.
>
> Tell the kids I'm sorry and I love them dearly—I'm crying as I write this—but it has been over between us for a long time and I want out. I sincerely hope you continue in the business. It is truly your life interest—please do stay in it.

P. S. Please don't try to find me because if you do, I will only have to move somewhere else.

P.P.S. The tax stuff is on my desk. (Daughter's name) can have my stereo, (Son's name) can have my hunting and fishing gear when he is old enough.

This man was not just leaving his wife and family—his note was almost his last will. The letters we get today are just as desperate. We hear the same story again and again: my husband was a stable man, attending church, involved in the community, then suddenly he quit his work and ran off with a younger woman.

Wives describe other changes such as depression, anger, abuse, and even incestuous relationships with children. Our office receives thousands of letters, E-mail messages, and telephone calls every year. The volume is more than twenty times what it was in the early eighties. People seem to reach out to us as their last hope for help with their midlife crisis.

In 1978, the publisher said this book would go out of print in three years and not sell more than five thousand copies. Today hundreds of thousands of books are in print, and *Men in Midlife Crisis* has been printed in several languages. We hear from people around the world who have read one of our books, connected to our Web page, or attended a conference. Midlife crisis is not going away!

## What's different?

The largest segment of the U.S. population, "baby boomers," are in midlife. They are the first generation whose parents felt guilty if they didn't give them everything; consequently, boomers have grown up expecting it all. But there isn't room for everybody to be company president, drive a "Beamer," live in a gated pool community, and have a condo in Palm Springs and another in Vail. There just isn't enough to go around.

There's a deep sense of failure in the lives of many boomers. Now they must make painful choices to simplify their lives, often triggering a full-blown midlife crisis.

The media have changed. In the seventies, the computer was a professional tool used only by business and government. The PC wasn't on everyone's desk. There was a Web network, but it only linked educational institutions for research purposes. Now home access to the Internet is a reality, with all of the benefits and moral dangers.

Morals in the U.S. are very different. On the "Net" it's possible to connect to hundreds of pornographic sites, even sites where live models take off their clothing or stroke themselves in any way the client asks. The paying client, who may live in Toronto, London, or Sydney, types the instructions while the model in southern California does as she's instructed. This remote sexual experience has been described as the ultimate safe sex.

But TV is not to be left out; it seems to be competing with the Internet to see which can be the most sexually explicit. Twenty years ago sexual intercourse was obliquely referred to, now during prime time you can enter a TV bedroom as two people roll around nude, "making love." In the spring of 1997, Pamela Anderson Lee, the busty "Baywatch" babe, was the host of "Saturday Night Live." On live television, she told her audience that it was necessary to get their attention. So she took off her top. To make sure she had their attention, she took off the rest of her clothes. The sad thing was that her stripping—with hardly any "tease"—was not even noticed as a moral issue.

What's the same and what has changed? With midlife crisis I guess it's true—"the more things change, the more they are the same."

JIM CONWAY
President
Midlife Dimensions
Fullerton, CA, 1997

# Not All the King's Horses . . .

My depression had grown all through the spring, summer, and fall. By October it had reached giant proportions. I would often stare out the window, or simply sit in a chair gazing into space. Several times I went for long drives in the car, on bike rides, or on long walks. I had literally come to the bottom of me. I was ready to chuck everything. Repeatedly I had fantasies of getting on a sailboat and sailing to some unknown destination where no one knew me and where I carried no responsibility for anyone in my church or my family.

By mid-November the depression had grown to unbelievable proportions. Since spring my wife, Sally, and I had been researching this book. I had hoped by taking November off, I could spend a great deal of time on the final draft, but now I was ready to throw everything away.

On a cold, wintry night, I went for a long walk and made some decisions. I would resign as pastor of the church, write a letter to my graduate school telling them I was dropping my doctoral program, and write my publishers that I no longer would be writing. I also would legally turn everything over to Sally, take only our old Olds Cutlass, and start driving south. For me, it was all over. I had had it with people, with responsibility, with society, and even with God, who had been such a close friend all of my adult life. He now seemed to be distant and uninterested in the agony through which I was going.

You see, this book is about me as well as about other men in midlife. I felt like the proverbial Humpty Dumpty who had just crashed off the wall—and all the king's horses and all the king's men couldn't possibly put my life back together again. All I could do was cry out in desperation the words of a psalm I had learned many years ago:

> Come, Lord, and show me your mercy, for I am helpless, overwhelmed, in deep distress; my problems go from bad to worse. Oh, save me from them all! See my sorrows; feel my pain; forgive my sins.

> Psalm 25:16-18

# PART 1
# It's For Real

# 1

# The Crisis

I HAD NOT PREVIOUSLY MET the woman sitting across the desk from me. She had been referred by another woman whose husband was going through a midlife crisis. She had hardly introduced herself before she began to cry with great convulsive sobs. It was as if I were watching her disintegrate before my eyes.

After several minutes she looked up, mascara running down her puffy cheeks, the hair around her face wet with tears, and a clump of wadded Kleenex in her lap. The story about her confusing relationship with her husband poured out.

They had been married more than fifteen years. All this time he had been an ideal husband and father, kind, thankful, gentle, and thoughtful. He enjoyed spending time with the children. He was a man oriented to his career, moving steadily toward his ultimate goal of being a congressman.

Then the change came. He had taken a short-term job in another state, and the family had joined him for the summer. When the summer ended and it was time for the family to go home, the wife began to realize that he was not simply sending them home—he was sending them away.

Then his personality changed. He couldn't stand being around his wife or being touched by her. Almost anything she said made him angry. He felt he was being exploited and misunderstood by his family. It was as though everything in his life had suddenly gone sour.

Several days after his wife saw me, he came to my office. He was suspicious and feared that as a pastor-counselor, I might heap guilt on him for the change in his life. As he began to trust me, he shared that nothing really seemed worthwhile anymore. He wasn't moving fast enough toward his career goal, and his marriage was tasteless and dull. Even the tennis he had taken up was only a momentary diversion from the oppressive boredom of his life.

The only thing that seemed to give life to him was a young woman he had met. She was in her twenties, and she seemed able to take him back to his own young adulthood. They did fun things together—picnicking, lying out under the stars, walking along the beach. She read poetry to him. And her touch—it made him feel so alive! She was so warm and real. She understood him. They could talk about all kinds of things. He felt so free, so good, as if his life finally had meaning. Sex was not a duty or a chore—it was exhilarating and life-giving.

I asked him why he had come to see me—apparently this new love was providing all of the things he wanted in life. Then he shared the other part of his life—his children. He couldn't forget them. He wanted to be their father. He wanted to be with them. The trouble was his wife—if only he could have the children and get rid of his wife. That would solve all of his problems.

Over the following months there were short times of separation, but always he was inexorably drawn back to his family. He was exhilarated when he was with his girlfriend, yet he seemed to need the ties with his wife and family. Here was a man, as the old seventies song says, "torn between two lovers, feeling like a fool." He was torn between two lives, two lifestyles, two directions, two ages. This man was in a full-blown "midlife crisis."

## Danger Ahead

The man approaching midlife has strange and difficult times ahead of him. He might negotiate this walk along the unfamiliar top of the brick wall with little trouble—but many men in midlife feel more like Humpty Dumpty.

The midlife crisis is a time of high risk for marriages. It's a time of potential career disruption. There is depression, anger, frustration, and rebellion. The crisis is a pervasive thing that seems to affect not only the physical, but also the social, cultural, spiritual, and occupational parts of a man's life.

It's as if a man reaches the peak of a mountain. Then he looks back over his past steps and forward to what lies ahead. He also looks at himself and asks, "Now that I've climbed the mountain, am I any different for it? Do I feel fulfilled? Have I achieved what I wanted to achieve?"

His evaluation of his past accomplishments, hopes, and dreams will determine whether his life ahead will be an exhilarating challenge to him, or simply a demoralizing distance that he must drearily traverse. In either case, he is at a time of trauma, because his emotions, as never before, are highly involved.

## Opportunity Also

The Chinese have a picture-word for crisis. This word *crisis* is really two words combined—"danger" and "opportunity."

CRISIS          DANGER     OPPORTUNITY

A midlife crisis is really an opportunity to fulfill all of the potential of our personality. It's an opportunity to look at reality, get rid of unnecessary junk that may have limited our lives, and make full use of our experience and expertise. What a waste if we do not make positive changes. Sadly, at retirement some of us realize that we have been living the same dumb life for the last twenty years—when we could have changed!

## He's a Pioneer

In the 1930s Walter Pitkin made publishing history with a best-seller, *Life Begins at Forty,* which introduced a new era in life.[1] He points out that it was not until the twentieth century that people began to live through what we now call the middle years. In prehistoric times man lived an average of about eighteen years. Fossil remains indicate that only a few lived beyond forty. Even as recently as 1900, life expectancy was about forty-eight for a man and fifty-one for a woman. In 1900 only 10 percent of the population was "middle-aged." Today the average adult person in the labor force is over forty-five. The

United States population increased almost 100 percent in the twentieth century, but midlife people increased over 200 percent.

Midlife crisis is a developmental crisis that is relatively new in our history. As we have worked with people around the world, we have found that stress at midlife is only a problem in developed countries. Starving people are worried about their next meal—not self-actualization.

## He Awakens to a Surprise

A man in midlife has crossed an age barrier that influences the way he is viewed at work, by his family, and by society in general. Much is known about child, adolescent, and young-adult development—and libraries are loaded with books on gerontology. Unfortunately, there seems to be little information about the adult in the long era between the early twenties and retirement. The person in midlife is surprised by a developmental crisis he was not expecting, and there is little written material to help.

In the early fifties Dr. Edmund Bergler, one of the pioneers who identified the male midlife crisis, wrote a book, *The Revolt of the Middle-Aged Man*. In it he recorded a comment from a wife who was surprised by the drastic change in her husband. "I believe my husband is either disintegrating or going crazy. My husband has always been a reliable, satisfied, solid person, with a good sense of humor, and a sense of duty. All at once, in the last few months, his whole personality has changed. All he does is rebel and attack. He attacks marriage, myself, even his profession. He is rambunctious, cantankerous, unruly, practically unmanageable. I don't know for sure, but I suspect there is a girl. His constant furies and his attacks on everybody and everything seem to use up all his ener-gy, at least as far as I am concerned. There is nothing he approves of anymore."[2]

## His Inner Feelings

There is no sudden biological event that causes these emotional changes, nothing at least comparable to the female menopause (the ending of the monthly menstrual cycle). A man does, however, have some of the same psy-chological feelings of menopausal women—depression, anxiety, irritability, fatigue, self-pity, and overall unhap-piness with life.

In the novel *Herzog* by Saul Bellow we can catch the feeling of the man in midlife crisis. Herzog is overcome with a desperate need to explain life and put it into per-spective. He begins to consider the value of his entire life and concludes that he has mismanaged everything—his life is literally ruined. He sees himself as having failed with both of his wives, his son and daughter, his parents, his country, his brothers and sisters, his friends, and even his own soul. Previously, the occupations of living life had kept him busy. But now his life is disintegrating into hopeless despair.[3]

As another man put it, "If I had my life to live over again, I'd be a failure. I'd be better off, because then I wouldn't have as much to lose as I do now."[4] Or, as Byron expressed it in his poem, "On This Day I Complete My Thirty-Sixth Year":

My days are in the yellow leaf;
    The flowers and fruits of Love are gone;

The worm, the canker, and the grief
> Are mine alone!

As you talk to men and women in their forties, you get the distinct impression that the men are far more unhappy than the women. Women seem to be a bit more future-oriented, whereas men in midlife seem to feel that the best was in the past.

Our society quite clearly lays out the path that the young adult male is expected to follow. He should get started in a career, marry, establish a home, then move up the ladder of success. By age forty many men have accomplished all of these goals. So it seems from forty on, it's all downhill. Yet they have twenty-five to thirty good, productive years left. They ask, "Where do I go from here—all society has expected me to accomplish I've already done?"

## He's Depressed

Depression is one of two major emotional feelings prevalent in the man at midlife. True depression incapacitates a person. He feels worthless and hopeless, often complaining of fatigue and experiencing real or imaginary physical disorders.

He is suspended in a time warp where he feels there are no answers or solutions. He is like a rabbit caught in a trap, with the options of waiting for the hunter to kill him or to chew off his own leg and escape into life maimed. The hopelessness of his choices cause the midlife man to be intensely depressed, immobilized by fear; he distorts reality and reacts in irrational panic.

## Magnificent Martyr

Self-pity is the second emotional theme of the midlife man. When the TV show "Male Menopause" examined the midlife crisis, John J. O'Connor, television critic for *The New York Times*, commented on the program, "The monotonous tone throughout is one of self-pity."[5]

The man at midlife feels sorry for himself because he feels trapped. He must now act his age, do his duty. He is tied to a treadmill. He must provide for his family and fill innumerable positions in society. Yet he is the target of indignation because he is aging, nagged to do his duties—and all of the time he is unable to tell anyone he is desperately bewildered inside.

He wonders what hit him and if life is worth living. He may finally rebel against all of this and abandon the two things he thinks are causing his problems—his wife and his work. He will later learn that abandoning these was not a good solution, and then his new disillusionment will produce a giant martyr complex. He will be a man with self-pity written across his forehead in neon lights.

## Trapped in Silence

Years ago *The New York Times* ran an anonymous but pointed letter which read in part, "I was forty years old and my husband forty-six when the eccentric behavior began. An otherwise reasonable and family-loving man suffered, not depression as we understood it, but rage, fatigue, incommunicability, suspicion, hostility. But every incident was my fault supposedly. I was the woman and I was alleged to be in the change of life. Unfortunately, doctors, psychiatrists, *men in general, have kept it all under the rug where they have swept it themselves.* They are in terror of the truth of acknowledging a condition which affects their behavior beyond their control, but which they readily ascribe to women without mercy [italics mine]."

It is extremely painful for a man to talk about his problems. Over the years women have been the first ones to come to my office for help with a marital problem. The wife pushes her husband to seek help. He is always the one dragging his feet. Our culture conditions men not to share their troubles. They are the leaders. They are strong. They are not supposed to cry, feel pain, or hurt. They are not supposed to be frustrated, confused, or disappointed with life. To admit there is a problem often destroys that quality of "man" within a man. The man in midlife crisis would rather grin and bear it—tough it out. He would rather take his lumps than share with anyone.

This silence is tragic. A line in Vachel Lindsay's poem "The Leaden-Eyed" says, "Not that they die, but that they die like sheep."[6] Sadly, men run away rather than face their problems and seek help. It's time for men to stop rolling over and playing dead, or walking off silently to the slaughter of midlife crisis. They need to share their feelings with people around them, with each other, and with God. It's time for Christians in general and the church in particular to acknowledge that there is a developmental crisis of gigantic proportions that needs our sympathetic understanding and support.

### Awareness Is a Beginning

Not only are men unwilling to talk about midlife crisis, but they often don't realize what is happening. They may deliberately ignore it, or even worse, reject the reality that aging is taking place. A common saying expresses some of this midlife stress, "A young man lives through his body, an old man lives against it."

The midlife developmental transition is intertwined with all of a man's life—all he's done and thought in the past and everything he will do, think, and become in the future. It will not simply go away by being ignored or rejected. A midlife man is not the same person he was at twenty-five, nor are his cultural surroundings the same. Someone put it another way, "We spend about one-quarter of our lives growing up and three-quarters growing old."[7]

Instead of ignoring or rejecting the midlife process, it should be viewed as perhaps the most exciting time in life. I agree with the authors who wrote, "No other decade is more intriguing, complex, interesting, and unsettled. Its characteristics are change, flux, crisis, growth, and intense challenges. Other than childhood, no period has a greater impact on the balance of our lives, for at no other time is anxiety coupled with so great a possibility for fulfillment."[8]

### He Is Not Alone

Because men do not share their feelings, they are unaware that other men at this age are having similar struggles. The truth is that nearly all men at midlife experience some trauma. At one point or another they may all feel like a fallen Humpty Dumpty, smashed and forever beyond repair. The intensity and duration of each man's time may vary, but the crisis comes to the white-collar as well as the blue-collar worker, to the married and the single, to the Christian as well as to the unbeliever. The crisis has been documented by experts, observed by counselors and psychoanalysts, but it is the experience of the man in isolation that is so tragic. A man must face it frankly if he is to find any hope or help for the future.

> Show me the path where I should go, O Lord; point out the right road for me to walk. Lead me; teach me; for you are the God who gives me salvation. I have no hope except in you.
>
> Psalm 25:4-5

# 2

# Expert Opinions

IT IS TREMENDOUSLY ENCOURAGING that an increasing number of specialists in the area of adult development have explored the problems of men at midlife. Scores of magazine and newspaper articles, as well as journal articles and movies, have not only made midlife crisis a topic of contemporary conversation, but also have pointed out that a real problem does exist— men in midlife do need help.

## When Does the Crisis Come?

Experts disagree on what years should be identified as the midlife years or when the crisis is most likely to take place. Carl Jung places the height of the midlife trauma between thirty-five and forty.[1] In 1968 Lee Stockford presented findings based on three studies involving more than 2,100 men and women. His research indicated that 80 percent of the executives aged thirty-four to forty-two were hit by this crisis.[2] In the late seventies, Dr. Daniel Levinson, a Yale researcher who had been involved in an extensive study of the midlife male, put the midlife decade at thirty-five to forty-five.[3] Gail Sheehy in *Passages* echoes Levinson's view.[4] Others, however, put the midlife reevaluation time in the fifties.

In a *New Choice* magazine article entitled "Is There Really A Male Menopause?" experts debate the subject. "While scientists disagree about male menopause, the ultimate experts on the subjects—middle-aged men themselves—express few doubts that it exists. I talked to a dozen men, ranging in age from forty-five to seventy, about their experience. Many shared sixty-year-old song-writer and piano player Dave Frishberg's sentiment: 'Gee, I hope there's such a thing as male menopause.' Long pause. 'Because if there isn't . . . what was that?' "[5]

In a real sense, the midlife crisis is not so much a matter of a man's chronological age as it is his state of mind. The goals chosen and how he handled earlier developmental problems will help determine whether he will arrive early or late at the midlife crisis and how intense the evaluation period will be.

## Is There a Male Menopause?

People have suggested that since men experience the similar emotions of self-pity, gloom, unhappiness, depression, and irritability that women feel at menopause, perhaps there is some hormonal change in men—a male menopause. The evidence we have says no. There is no common biological cause in a man that causes this emotional change. If, however, we are talking about male menopause as a "turning point," then such a thing does take place.

The problem is that most men are so sure they're not going to experience any midlife reassessment that they have a false sense of security. Most men never believe it will happen to them, in spite of all the information about the commonness of a midlife crisis.

An extensive study in *Transitions Through Adult Life* reports: "Farrell and Resenberg help a great deal with clearing up the confusion over the midlife experience. Although only twelve percent of the persons they studied really had what might be called an overt midlife crisis, another fifty-six percent were hiding it. That means that a majority are experiencing a distinct crisis during those years."[6]

## Second Childhood

The man who is not expecting anything to happen to him as he moves along through life is startled to find that in midlife he begins to act somewhat like an adolescent. He finds himself acting in the same bizarre ways as his teenage child.

Reassessment is the prevailing theme of the midlife crisis. He asks questions about values—"Who am I? What do I want to be? Does my work have value? Am I accomplishing anything?" He also asks questions about his marriage, job, friendships, and social commitments. These are the same general questions his teenager is asking: "Who am I? Who will I be? What should my values be? What will my life work be? Who will my friends be? Whom will I marry? What part will God have in my life?" Basically both generations are asking, "What will I do when I grow up?"

## Three Major Forces

The midlife crisis is not caused by one problem that

can be resolved with a simplistic answer. It's not going to go away with two aspirin and a good night's sleep. Nor is it going to go away by simply telling the man to read his Bible more, believe God, or stop worrying.

Three major forces converge on a man at this time in his life:

First, some biological changes do take place. He is losing physical energy and muscle tone. His body weight is shifting to his middle, and he is losing his hair. Death suddenly becomes more of a reality.

The second force is psychological—his ego or his self-image may be hit hard. He begins to view himself as less of a man because he may not be as physically strong as he used to be. He may be having trouble or dissatisfaction at work. Many men draw ego strength from career accomplishments. Maybe he realizes that he's not going to meet all his goals, or perhaps he has met them and says, "So what?"

The third major area affected at midlife is his social life. The world clearly tells him that there isn't meaningful life after forty and he can't get a job after forty-five or fifty. Television commercials continue to convince him that youth is good, age is bad. Because he feels rejected by society, he begins to reevaluate his life in social areas—his relationship to his wife, his children, his career, his friends, the world around him, and even God.

### The Crisis Is Inevitable

By now the picture may be so black and dismal that our hero is crying, "How in the world can I get out of this? Stop the merry-go-round and let me off." Or, "God, why in the world did You make me so that this kind of pressure would hit?"

There is a growing opinion among sociologists, psychologists, psychiatrists, and other professionals that all men are going to go through the crisis to some degree. Every man will come through it with either a positive outlook for the future or a dismal view marked by despair. We need to see that a midlife transition is a natural developmental stage that is unavoidable.

Escaping the midlife developmental crisis is about as likely as a child escaping adolescence. A teenager may put off facing this developmental phase, but sooner or later he must answer those questions of who he is and what he wants to do in life. The man in midlife may suppress the reassessment of his life for a while, but he must face it eventually.

One major difference between the teen and the man in midlife crisis is that the teen *wants* to get older, while the man in midlife crisis wants to stay young. Before a midlife crisis, it is possible to think of yourself as young. After you have successfully dealt with the developmental problems of midlife, you will be able to comfortably accept yourself as no longer young, yet having a valuable contribution to make that the young do not have.

### A Dangerous Time for Others

When the teenager is going through his teen evaluation, his emotional gyrations, alternating directions, and changing values don't really affect many people other than his immediate family. He may decide to drop out, fool around with sex or drugs, and/or put God on a shelf for a while. He may become antisocial, irritable, and depressed. His parents, because they are older and a bit more secure, understand what the adolescent is going through. They are able to remain relatively objective, cool, and collected in most situations. They realize this is a passing phase, and soon the young person will emerge into young adulthood.

However, the man in the midlife crisis who begins to do the same things as the teenager causes terrifying havoc in his family, his business, and his community. For example, if he has an extramarital affair, a great many futures hinge on what happens with that affair. He is no longer a teenager trying to learn a little bit about sex. Now he is a man with a wife and children who depend on his stability. He may hold positions in the community or his church. He also is a man whose business or political future may be affected by the sexual affair.

Atlanta psychiatrist and author Frank Pittman says, "When they look in the mirror, they look more like their fathers every day. Every day, they are going to become older, fatter, balder, weaker, and less important to the world."

Pittman, who has written *Man Enough*, goes on to say, "When middle-aged men go messing around, they're not really looking for new partners, they're looking for reassurance of their potency."[7]

The man in midlife crisis has more social expertise, power, and freedom than the adolescent. For those reasons his hostility or rebellion may be extremely dangerous to every other person involved with him.

## His Psychological Clock Is Out of Whack

Something is wrong with the clock of the man in midlife crisis. In fact, on many occasions he seems totally disconnected from time. We often generalize about people at different ages. Youth, for example, is thought to look more toward the future, ignoring the past. Grandparents, on the other hand, look backward. The man at midlife seems to be most concerned with *now*. When he looks to the future, he only sees old age creeping in on him and the inevitability of death. He fears losing his job, his productivity, influence, impact, and life itself. When he looks to the past, he sees only a long list of unfulfilled goals and dreams, so he desperately, almost in panic, wants to live life *now*.

There is, however, a problem. He is often so preoccupied with his past failures and future fears that he is unable to enjoy the *now*. Even though he feels an urgency to make something happen before it is too late, he fails to enjoy life as it comes. He doesn't enjoy his wife and family, his work, God, or the world around him. He is at the time in life when he should be enjoying his position, family, and achievements—but to him they all stink.

## Fact Or Fantasy

The pressure of time running out forces him into a brutal race with the fantasies he dreamed in his youth or young adulthood. "Someday" he was to become king of this or that. "Someday" he was to be a millionaire, a sports hero, an actor, poet, singer, or writer. "Someday" he was going to be a great lover. "Someday" he was going to be rich and famous. But suddenly *now* is upon him. He's reached midlife, and he begins to realize that the future is here—that all he is ever going to achieve must happen "now!" It's got to happen by forty, or at least by forty-five.

Sadly, his young-adult dreams and fantasies are confronted with the reality about his job—he is never going to become the boss or the president. He has a house in the suburbs, but he is never going to be a millionaire. He can watch a lot of football on Sunday afternoon—but he is never going to be a professional quarterback.

Even the men who actually reach the top in their work and who have arrived at all their goals aren't as happy as they thought they'd be. For the first time he compares his fantasies, which have motivated him the past twenty years, with the facts of his life—and he is depressed.

Dr. Ernest van den Haag, a psychoanalyst and a psychologist, says, "This crisis consists in the clash between your fantasies and reality. You begin to have a more realistic conception of yourself." Dr. van den Haag points out that the difference between the crisis in the teenage boy and in the midlife man is that the teen has not tested his abilities and is looking forward to the future with optimism, expecting his fantasies to be fulfilled. "When you have reached middle age, if you are realistic, you see the limitations of your career. And that is for most people rather difficult to take."[8]

It is the comparison of dreams versus the accomplishments that cause men in midlife crisis to be depressed. Only as a man can successfully face the facts of who he is and what he can do, will he be able to graciously move to the next era in life.

### Search for a Spiritual Answer

I've watched a number of men struggling with midlife crisis come to a point of blaming God for what is taking place. Carl Jung, the famous psychologist, found that the root of mental illness among all his patients over the age of thirty-five was a loss of spiritual moorings. It is heartbreaking for a man who has been a leader in the church and who has provided spiritual stability for both young and old to suddenly throw God overboard as he struggles with guilt, anger, depression, and confusion. Throwing God away will only increase a man's sense of instability.

I stand silently before the Lord, waiting for him to rescue me. For salvation comes from him alone. Yes, he alone is my Rock, my rescuer, defense and fortress. Why then should I be tense with fear when troubles come?

Psalm 62:1-2

# 3

# Believe Me, It Really Happens

I TOLD YOU EARLIER THAT I write as one who has experienced a midlife crisis. I'd like to share my story, believing that if you know something about me, this book may mean more to you.

## What I Do

At the time of my midlife crisis, I was the senior pastor of a large church on the edge of a university campus. I spent a lot of time counseling students and families from the church as well as people from the community. I was writing a monthly magazine column, answering emotional and spiritual questions from students. Previous to my midlife crisis I had pastored two other churches. At that time I had two master's degrees and was working on a doctorate.

My wife, Sally, loved me deeply and had made me more than I ever thought I could be. During my midlife crisis our daughters Barbara and Brenda were in college, and Becki was in high school. Our family has always enjoyed traveling. We vacationed in many parts of the

United States, camping most of the time. Sally and I had been overseas several times to minister in various countries. We have been around the world twice. Our three daughters accompanied us on one trip to South America.

## Who I Am

The above information is only a series of facts, but it doesn't really tell you too much about who I am inside. I like people, and I like to be needed. I also enjoy being alone. I like the woods, and I like to see things grow. I am turned on by the first sprouts of daffodils or fat buds on trees. I can sit for hours watching water. We have a sixteen-foot catamaran, and I enjoy sailing when the wind is blowing hard and I'm able to fly one hull out of the water. I like the challenge of my skill against the unpredictability of the wind.

I am a fairly creative person. When I'm speaking at conferences, I occasionally do unusual things to stimulate people into sensing the relevancy of God's involvement in our lives. Sometimes I get into trouble by doing things that are too different.

As a teen I had an extremely low self-image. In those years I felt unsuccessful in every area of my life. Academically, I barely made it. Teachers graciously passed me along. There were 614 people in my high-school graduating class, and I ranked below 612. The principal told my father that he shouldn't waste his money sending me to college because I would never make it. My counselors advised me to go to a trade school where I could use my hands—they meant that nothing was alive above my shoulders.

In high school I was a loner. I had very few friends, and those friends were older than I. I ran track, hoping somehow to gain approval from a cute girl. Unfortunately, even in that area I was not very successful. Every time I think of my adolescent years, I'm reminded of the story of the man who went to a psychiatrist and told him how inadequate he felt. He listed in detail all the areas that caused him to feel inferior. After his sad tale of woe, the psychiatrist looked at him and said, "Man, you shouldn't just *feel* inadequate—you *are* inadequate!"

My life began to change drastically when I went to college. I had become a Christian the summer before college, and God, through the Bible, began to build my self-image with promise after promise of His love, care, and direction. He showed me that "I can do everything God asks me to with the help of Christ who gives me the strength and power" (Phil. 4:13).

The second greatest thing that happened to me was meeting Sally. She loved me as I was and believed I could be more than I was. We were married after my college graduation. I am also a workaholic. I tend to work hard—so that people will love me. Even though I have felt a definite call from God into full-time ministry, and I love doing God's work, it's easy for me to be caught in the trap of wanting man's approval instead of only God's.

I also tend to be very sensitive. I feel deeply, especially for other people who have been ripped off by life. Yet it was not until I was in my midthirties that I began to let my emotions show publicly as I spoke.

Frequently I have been so deeply touched while speaking that I am unable to continue. Several times I have broken down in tears. At first, these were very humiliating experiences for me, but I've come to see that it has helped other people, especially men, to express their emotions.

43

## Why a Book on Midlife?

"You're pastoring a university church filled with young people. You write for a youth magazine. So why are you doing a book about midlife crisis? It seems you ought to be writing a book about the college age." My friend's comment contained some truth, but as you already have perceived, I decided to write about midlife crisis not only to benefit others, but also as a way to work through my own crisis.

To me, midlife crisis wasn't simply an academic problem. It wasn't that I was a writer looking for a new topic. This was a personal battle. My midlife crisis came upon me as a very shocking experience. I was totally unprepared. I had watched the problem in the lives of other men, but I never anticipated it would happen to me. I thought they were just weak men who couldn't get it all together.

I remember my father at this age. He was also a workaholic, but he suddenly stopped working as much and bought an airplane. After he learned to fly, he quite often would leave work in the middle of the day to go flying. At the time I thought he was only taking up a hobby, but now I see he was wrestling with meaning and direction in his life. He also was catching up on feeling deprived and overworked.

About the same time, my father's brother, a partner in their business, sold his half of the business, sold his house, moved his family from Cleveland to Florida, and started an entirely different business. He seemed to be saying that he was getting older, and life was too short to spend it all in cold, smoky Cleveland.

During my seminary days there was a midlife pastor and his wife who had a troubled marriage. There were rumors of an affair. He later left the church and was divorced. That gifted preacher went into selling real estate.

Many of my friends from college and seminary years have gone through midlife struggles. Some of them left their churches to start new careers, while others exist in dull marriages. But a wise group of them used the midlife adjustment period to focus their lives and have become increasingly productive.

Over the past years thousands of couples struggling with the various agonies of a man's midlife crisis have come to Sally and me for help. Their pain created a deep desire within us to help people successfully navigate the midlife years.

## Dissatisfaction with My Job

My own midlife crisis did not come suddenly, nor did it touch all areas of my life at the same time. It started with a growing unhappiness with work. When I got into my sixth year at church, I began to feel that I was simply repeating the work of the previous five years. Nothing new was happening. I began to ask questions: "Why am I doing this? How long will I continue this pattern?" Previously, the ministry had been the magnet of my life. I literally ate, drank, slept, and played with a consciousness of what I could do to make a greater spiritual impact in the lives of people. I dreamed about what I could do to cause the church I was pastoring to be more effective in its outreach into the community.

But suddenly, I wanted to escape work. I didn't like

being in the office. It often was a tedious chore to counsel troubled people. I was glad to get out of extra meetings. I wanted more and more time for myself. I began to use the TV to stop myself from thinking about my pastoral responsibilities. But the questions kept crying out for an answer. "Who am I? What do I want to do with the rest of my life? What is important?"

## The Chicks Are Leaving the Nest

When our oldest daughter, Barbara, went off to Taylor University, I couldn't believe that I was old enough for this to happen. We were a very tightly knit family, yet Barbara was leaving my life. This was the beginning of a new era that I didn't like. I cried as we left her at college, and for months afterward as I walked into her room—now strangely silent and dreadfully barren—tears welled up inside me.

I felt a strong anger about living in a society that drags kids off to college, where they'll likely meet and marry a stranger. Then they'll live a thousand miles away and our only communications will be limited to the telephone and letters. It was as if my leg had been amputated. All of my mind said my daughter should be here in her room—but she was gone.

Two years later the process happened again with our second daughter, Brenda. You would think by now I would have accepted the change in my life. But with two-thirds of the chicks gone, the frustration only intensified. There were still so many things I wanted to do with my daughters, so many things I wanted to teach them, so many plans we had not carried out. Again I felt as though I were being maimed. "God, it's unfair! Life is unfair."

## The Emotional Drain . . . the Physical Toll

The church was growing very rapidly. In a four-year period before my midlife crisis, the attendance had climbed from 350 to more than 1,200 people. Even though the staff had increased, my workload continued to sky-rocket. It was normal for me to work seventy to eighty hours a week, with many weeks going over a hundred hours. I spent as much as thirty-five to forty hours a week in private counseling with people of the church and community.

Each spring was getting worse. I gradually wore down through the school year, so that by springtime I was totally exhausted. Finally, I collapsed in the office from physical and emotional fatigue and had to be hauled off to the emergency room. When I was home I turned off the phone, yet I experienced guilt because I was supposed to be serving people. Hadn't Jesus set the pattern by encouraging the disciples to serve each other and not expect to be served? Now I had guilt in addition to my exhaustion.

Super-busy people don't have time for a late-night date, and certainly not for a weekend away as a couple. They are so drained by other people that they don't have the emotional capacity to give to a mate. I put off cultivating our marriage. I was too tired to talk, to listen, to carry responsibilities. In fact, I was too tired to even care as Sally went through her own midlife crisis. Marriage, for me, became increasingly monotonous. I was too preoccupied trying to keep the church and myself going. I couldn't worry about the emptiness I felt toward our marriage.

Our two oldest daughters had each had infectious mononucleosis. Then I developed the same symptoms. It was a chore to drag my body around. By June I was in bed with a severe case of mono, along with some liver dysfunction. I was flat on my back for two weeks. I was gone from the church much of the summer, resting and recuperating.

Suddenly, school was about to begin. It was time for me to jump into the demanding fall schedule, but I was still physically shot and needed extra sleep. As the new semester started, I tried to keep a full schedule, but I found it increasingly difficult to help people with their troubles. I simply didn't have anything to give to people.

By October, any administrative decisions I had to make for the church were unbearable. People's problems caused me great anguish. I finally asked the church board for a leave of absence without pay for the month of November so I could rest. The board asked the people of the church to pray for me—and to leave me alone.

In the middle of one November night I decided to drive south, to escape it all—to run away. I was in the grip of a full-fledged, life-shattering midlife crisis.

> Oh, for wings like a dove, to fly away and rest! I would fly to the far off deserts and stay there. I would flee to some refuge from all this storm.
>
> Psalm 55:6-8

# PART 2
# Inside The Man

# 4

# The Cultural Squeeze

OUR CULTURE CAUSES A GREAT deal of stress on the man at midlife. Some of this has resulted from a change in lifestyle. For example in the U.S. during the early 1990s, 90 percent of the people lived on farms while only 10 percent lived in cities. Today that percentage has reversed. In the early 1900s, people expected to live all of their lives in the same community. They expected to hand their farms from one generation to another. Neighbors and friends would be lifelong companions. Today our society is extremely mobile, with more than one in every five households moving to a new location every year. Adapting to new surroundings and friends has become a way of life.

When I pastored a church in the Wheaton, Illinois area, I visited a new family who had moved into our community. The wife apologized for the appearance of the uncut lawn, the weeds in the flower bed, and the bare walls inside the house. She told me that many of their boxes were unpacked. I didn't think any of this was abnormal for a family beginning to settle in a new community. But she went on to explain that she had no intention of maintaining the yard or putting any pictures on the wall. In fact, one of the bedrooms would be used to store many of the items that would not be unpacked.

Her husband was in middle management of a growing corporation, and over the last ten years their family had moved at least once a year. It seemed a waste of time to put pictures on the wall only to take them down in a short while. I was even more sad to learn that she didn't want to get involved with any church or with any neighbors in the community—it would only cause heartache when it was time to leave.

## New Technologies

Not only are we a nation on the move, but new technology and the knowledge explosion are causing rapid job obsolescence. New technology forces workers into job changes. Some predict that a young man may have to plan on at least five to seven major job shifts in his lifetime.

Machines and computers increasingly threaten men, who view themselves as only operators. How does a man cope with his own identity when a computer takes over the operation of his machine? "The repetitively perfect operating of the machine, with tolerances and quality control far beyond those of people, leaves the man who operates a machine with a frightening sense of being expendable."[1]

## The Knowledge Explosion

Technology and knowledge have advanced together, resulting in a knowledge explosion. Knowledge didn't begin to grow rapidly until the fifteenth century with the invention of Gutenberg's movable type. From one thousand new books a year in the sixteenth century, we have progressed to more than one thousand new print books a week in our time. Books and articles are also increasingly available to download from the Internet. The explosion of knowledge has caused greater specialization. But the more specialized a man is, the harder it may be for him to adapt, and the more likely he is to become unneeded.

## A World Economy

I've been overseas several times. On one trip around the world, I bought a special souvenir from each country. I chose items that couldn't be purchased in the United States—jewelry from Thailand, wood carvings from India and the Philippines, a Greek handbag. Some of these things we proudly displayed in our dining room china cabinet. Now we can buy most of them at discount drugstores. A man can't settle comfortably in his small secure little job, or in his own community, or even in his own nation. We are forced to think and to compete globally.

Peter Drucker confirms this observation: "There has emerged a world economy in which common information generates the same economic appetites, aspirations, and demands—cutting across national boundaries and languages."[2]

## Can a Man Adapt?

The easiest culture to live in is a culture that is not changing too rapidly, especially from external events. Yet midlife man is facing a rapidly changing culture whose drastic changes are the very hindrance to his flexibility.

In a rapidly changing culture, we must have the ability to change. I've observed that a man who has had a close relationship with his parents is more likely to be flexible and able to change. However, many men who are now in their forties may not be too adaptable, because they were raised by a father who was highly oriented toward work and felt his family responsibility was only to provide a financial income—not an emotional income.

There is a deep "father-hunger" in our world. The Promise Keepers movement is evidence of this deep desire among men to connect in a rapidly changing and confusing world. A man in midlife may not be as emotionally flexible as he might have been if he had been better connected to his father. But even if the connection doesn't start until midlife, it can still result in a powerful positive effect.

## Cynicism

In the late sixties and early seventies the university campuses spawned great turmoil, yet offered hope. Young people believed they could change the world. Students on the university campus today have settled into a quiet cynicism that says, "You can't fight the system, but you can passively resist it."

Many people are disenchanted with government and cynical about its ability to perform. Politicians are frightened because they are dealing with voters who are totally unpredictable, who don't respond to old slogans, political lines, old liberalism, or old conservatism.

The midlife man has been hoping that everything would be figured out by this time in his life. But instead he finds himself caught in a society of cynicism and confusion.

## Caught Between Generations

Midlife today is not defined by what it is but by what is *in between*. The man at midlife is caught between his adolescent children and his aging parents. The aging parents need attention because of their age, and the children need attention because they are teens or starting college or jobs.

Values about age are also changing. The man at midlife was brought up by parents who believed that children should respect their parents, and in most cases his parents lived to please *their* parents. However, we live in a society of the child-centered family. Our children tend to come first. We work hard at pleasing *them*. We take our children's failures and limitations as an indication of our inadequacy, not theirs! We truly believe that it's possible to be a perfect parent.

We are a generation caught between the world that valued the aged for their wisdom and the world now that values only youth. One of the highest compliments that can be given to a midlife man is to say that he doesn't look his age.

Robert Raines describes this feeling of being caught in the middle:

Middle-agers are beautiful!
    aren't we, Lord?
I feel for us
    too radical for our parents
    too reactionary for our kids
    supposedly in the prime of life
        like prime rib
        everybody eating off me
           devouring me
        nobody thanking me

> appreciating me
> but still hanging in there
>     communicating with my parents
>     in touch with my kids
> and getting more in touch
>     with myself
> and that's all good
>     thanks for making it good,
> and
>     could you make it a little better?[3]

## The Young Adult Cult

In many cultures of the world, the young are offered sympathy for being young. The older you are, the more enthusiastically you are greeted. In old China, for example, age is equated with wisdom. Who you are is valued more than what you do. In our society we tend to reverse the order. We value productivity, not the quality of life. We are drawn more and more to worshipping the quick, bright, the new—youth.

Years ago anthropologist Margaret Mead said, "I would expect to find depression among late-middle-aged men in societies where strength is important. But, if old age means having wisdom and skills that don't require physical strength, that's fine. The Australian aboriginal men, when they grow older, had all the ceremonial wisdom and so got most of the younger women, and it isn't reported to have depressed them."[4]

American men at midlife feel frustrated because our society communicates that young adulthood is the most valuable and desirable age. Yet obviously, we are no longer young adults. It is easy to conclude, therefore, that we are neither valuable nor desirable.

Recently I watched all the television advertisements between two programs. Six of the seven ads used youth to sell their products. You never see a fifty-year-old woman who is fifty pounds overweight leaning on a new sports car and saying in a sexy voice, "This is the car you need to feel like a real man." Using youth to sell products sends a demoralizing and humiliating message that nothing good ever happens to anyone over thirty.

"Men feel they need to look fresher, younger, and more masculine," says Tim Sproule, one of seven plastic surgeons at Scarborough General Hospital. "They're not interested in looking thirty, but looking a fit fifty. They want the flab gone." Roughly 20 percent of Sproule's patients are men.[5]

John Revson, a cosmetic executive, noted twenty years ago that the fastest growing part of his industry was sales to men who were apparently trying to maintain youth and compete with the young adults. "Middle-aged men today are buying 'male cosmetics' . . . because they're looking for that fountain of youth."[6]

### Only Young Is Fun

Men are weary of having the young adult culture rammed down their throats. The youth cult tends to compel a man to do everything possible to stop the aging process. For a number of years I had been jokingly telling people that I was twenty-eight years old. In my mind that was an optimum time—a man has accumulated a little bit of experience and education and still maintains the physical vigor and energy of the twenties. The problem came when I introduced my oldest daughter, who was twenty-two.

No man will successfully make it through the midlife transition until he can comfortably accept his aging and let go of the fantasy of being twenty-eight—or whatever is your favorite age. As the young adult is increasingly worshipped, the rest of life is devalued. The young then become "our venerable youth." We live in a society where older people have nothing to live for and younger people have nothing to grow up for.

### Change Is on the Way—Perhaps

Ralph Barton Perry wrote in his *Plea for an Age Movement* that we should teach the world to admire wrinkles, experience, and character.[7] Encouragingly, there is some evidence that young people are turning toward older people and their wisdom. Certainly as the boomers become old they will demand respect because of the massive size of their group. Older people who have something to say and who understand the young person's situation are now being sought instead of being avoided as they were during the difficult days of the sixties. This may indicate a slight shift toward utilizing the wisdom and experience of people in the middle and later years of life.

### Too Much Pressure

People between thirty-five and fifty-five comprise the largest block of our population and occupy the positions of power. They make the decisions, but they also pay the bills and carry the major responsibility for the other two generations in our society.

Meanwhile, pressures come from the community.

Magazine articles, doctors, and wives nag the man in midlife to slow down and relax, but he finds his telephone ringing all the time. He is asked to support this cause, be on that board, be involved in this fund-raising campaign. A leader is needed for the youth group, someone with his travel experience is wanted to speak at school—and on and on and on.

As the pressures mounted on me during my midlife crisis, the Board of Leadership of our church asked people to divert their requests for help to other members of the staff. After one of these announcements in the morning service, two university students asked me if there was a time during the week when the three of us could meet to pray that God would enable me to have more time to relax. As kindly as possible I suggested they pray in their own rooms and allow me to have that time to myself.

It's easy for a man in midlife to be conditioned to follow the expectations of other people. In the past, if you wanted to succeed, you did what your boss suggested. If you wanted to be respected in the community, you served on various committees. If you wanted to be considered spiritual, you got involved in every program of the church. The problem with living this pattern is that you end up with a life directed by others rather than by your own choices based on the unique creation God has made you to be.

### Family Pressures

Family responsibilities also put pressure on the midlife man. At midlife he must maintain a large home for the children and all their stuff and activities—plus the extra cars, braces, special sports equipment, and fees for camps, sports events, and proms. At the same time, he must provide money for a college education and for launching his children into their own careers. In addition he may have financial responsibilities for his aging parents. And yes, he's supposed to be preparing for his own retirement.

Shortly after Sally and I were married, we started seminary in Denver. As we moved to the Mile-High City, all of our possessions fit into a small four-by-four trailer. But our last move to California required a sixty-five-foot truck plus three cars, one of which towed my sixteen-foot "midlife crisis" sailboat. I wonder sometimes how in the world we accumulated all this "junk" and what a waste of money it is to maintain it.

All my life I have worried over whether there will be enough money, watching each month as hundreds of dollars melt away like butter on a hot griddle. The midlife man is constantly told that he should prepare financially for the future, but there never seems to be anything left over at the end of the month.

## Work Pressures

Work is also a problem to the man in midlife. Let's not delude ourselves—we're not as fast as we used to be, nor do we have our youthful stamina. When I play racquetball, my mind says, "Reach! Stretch! Get that ball!" But my body says, "Who are you kidding?" I also cannot stand the long work hours I used to be able to take. Nor does my body spring back as quickly when I'm up late at night.

My doctor has often urged me to slow down. I told

him the problem is that I know what it takes to succeed at my job. It takes lots of energy, creativity, training, and just plain hours of work. To cut back on my time from eighty hours a week to forty would mean the job just wouldn't get done.

The truth is, we live in a competitive world. If I can't cut it, there are dozens of younger men who can. All of the above stresses affect my job, and ultimately, how people view my effectiveness.

There is a concept in business called the "Peter Principle"—a man will be advanced in his work and be given greater and greater responsibility until he literally becomes incompetent as he is pushed beyond his ability. Sadly, most businesses then dump the man rather than move him back to the level of his competence.

The midlife man has been following the "Peter Principle" for ten to fifteen years as he worked for success and continually extended himself. His body and mind have been able to carry that pressure up to now. But by midlife, two forces may converge at work. He may have been pushed to a level of responsibility that is beyond him, thus causing frustration. Second, his body is probably slowing down and unable to stand the stress. His job, therefore, usually becomes increasingly dissatisfying.

### Just a Machine

One result of all this pressure is extreme frustration. He may find himself living by other people's goals and feel angry at them. He may also feel angry at himself for allowing himself to be manipulated. But he cannot change now. He is too deeply committed with responsibilities. Everyone seems to be taking from his life. A president of a small corporation told me, "If I did what I wanted to do, I would have to lose everything, go back to school and start all over. I'd like to do that, but I'm too old and I have too many people depending on me."

During my midlife crisis, I said to Sally, "I feel like a vending machine. Someone pushes a button, and out comes a sermon or an article. Someone pushes another button for a solution to a personal or administrative problem. The family pushes buttons, and out come dollars or time. The community pushes other buttons, and I show up at meetings, sign petitions, and take stands." It's easy for a man at midlife to feel that he is trapped with obligations to everyone. And the frustration is—he can't get out! In my twenties, he thinks, I handled all these demands with enthusiasm, but now they are draining away my life.

The second result of work pressure is a feeling of inadequacy. A man's body is slowing down. If he compares himself to some of the young men coming up in the organization, his inadequacy will be intensified. When he begins to look around at the job market, he realizes there's a great deal of age discrimination. The number of jobs available to him, which produce the money he needs for his time in life, are shriveling.

A pastor friend said to me, "You know, I'm really fortunate to have been called to this church, because I'm now over fifty. Most churches want a man between thirty-five and forty-five." In addition the midlife man may feel inadequate because of the knowledge explosion. The younger men may seem to have brighter, newer ideas. They know how to run the computers—they even know how to program their VCRs. They must be good!

The third result of work pressure is fatigue. Our midlife man is tired of trying to keep up with the demands of the community. He's had it with the increasing pressure at work. He's simply tired of having a tired body. The man in midlife doesn't have time to pursue art or music. He doesn't have time for contemplation, watching things grow, looking at a sunset. He's like a hamster, running on the little wheel in his cage—he has to keep running to keep his balance.

One man who was struggling with the pressures of life said, "I feel a weakening of the need to be a great man and an increasing feeling of let's just get through this the best way we can. Never mind hitting any home runs. Let's just get through the ball game without getting beaned."[8]

> But I am a worm, not a man, scorned and despised by my own people and by all mankind. Everyone who sees me mocks and sneers and shrugs. . . . "Is this the one who claims the Lord delights in him? We'll believe it when we see God rescue him!"
>
> Psalm 22:6-8

## For Further Reading

*What Makes a Man?* by Bill McCartney and others (Colorado Springs: Navpress, 1992).

# 5

# Second Adolescence

"ASK A BUNCH OF PROSPEROUS, fortyish white guys from Connecticut to meet and talk about midlife crisis, and they dance around the subject as though you had inquired about their experiences with sexual impotence."[1]

Midlife crisis? The men, gathered in a focus group conducted for *Fortune* by Yankelovich Partners, could be remarkably compassionate about the subject, but generally they regarded midlife crises as vaguely embarrassing things that other people—men and women—occasionally have. Says Al, a financial projects wholesaler, "Midlife crisis is a label you put on other people doing bizarre behavior. But you never anticipate that you will do it."[2]

But some midlife men do act strangely, sometimes even irrationally. "Men are more drastic, more irrational," Al continues. "Men buy Porsches, disappear to Florida, shack up with chippies, and come back six weeks later."[3]

To understand the man in midlife crisis, it's helpful to start with something known—teenage behavior, moods, and thinking. The comparison of a teen with the midlife man will help us to understand a man in midlife crisis.

The teenage boy is moving from childhood into that long era of success-oriented, active young adult life. The man at midlife is moving from that active, aggressive period of young adulthood to the long plateau of the middle years.

Like the teenager, the man in midlife crisis has three basic areas that cause him difficulty.

### The Midlife Man's Body

First, they both are trying to handle the physical changes. The teenager is rapidly growing taller and filling out. He has trouble controlling his exciting sex drive, and he is embarrassed by acne and his changing voice. At times he doesn't seem to belong to his body with its strange hormones.

The man in his forties is also having physical problems. His weight is beginning to shift toward the trunk of his body. His muscles no longer have the tone they once had. His skin is beginning to sag. He is losing that beautiful hair. He runs out for a pass in a game of backyard football with his son and almost drops from exhaustion. He fears a decrease in his sexual capacity, which may cause temporary impotence. And, insult of insults, he may also have some acne problems.

### The Midlife Man's Feelings

The second area of problems is psychological. Sometimes the adolescent has expanding aggressive energies. His moods swing from great joy to restlessness, to gloom, or to downright depression. The teenager is known for grumbling. He complains about school, parents, his old computer—in fact, very few things in life really satisfy him. The teen has some problem putting things into perspective. He can't really get a grasp on the childhood from which he came, and he has trouble clearly seeing the future. He is extremely introspective—he sits with his headphones on, totally alone in another world.

The man in the midlife crisis wrestles with astoundingly similar problems. His son, for example, may be asking, "What is sex all about?" The father, worried because it takes him longer to achieve an erection, is asking, "How soon will I lose it?" At midlife, physical and emotional fatigue may cause him to feel he is becoming impotent, and sex may occupy many of his thoughts. The midlife man also is wrestling with aggressive feelings toward the young men who may replace him at work. He has angry, moody feelings toward society, his family, and even God for putting so much pressure on him—and for making life what it is.

Similar to the teenager, the midlife man has giant mood swings. At one point things are going along quite well, the next thing you know, he is in his car, driving off somewhere "to be alone." There may be times of great productivity, and other times of only lethargy.

The teenager grumbles about everything in life. The man in midlife grumbles about everything in life—his children, wife, job, work around the house, taxes, politics, every duty and responsibilities. All of life seems to be sour. Similarly to his teenage son, this man has lost perspective. He thinks that the crisis he is experiencing is the sum total of his life. He can't see it as a temporary developmental time of passage from his earlier, young-adult life. He cannot seem to accept the plateau ahead of him.

Lost in his present crisis, he becomes adolescent in his introspection, totally absorbed within himself, and almost oblivious to the world around him as he stares into space.

### The Midlife Man's Friends

A third area of trouble for both the teenager and the man at midlife is social relationships. One day parents see the deep relationship between their son and another friend, and the next day the two are not speaking. The man at midlife also has problems socially. For a while his friends really take it on the chin. Sometimes he is very rude, with no time for people. He defiantly declares, "I want to be with people—I want to be with—when I want to be with them."

He is quite often disenchanted with the world around him. He may have been deeply committed to big business, but now he is disgusted with the selfish, dollar-oriented direction of his company, and he is not shy in telling them so. There are times when he enjoys being with his wife, then suddenly he can't stand to touch her. He simply wants to escape everything and everybody. In short, he may become very antisocial.

### Identity Crisis

The teen and the man at midlife are having identity crises. Each is asking, "Who am I? What are my values? What do I want to do with my life?" The difference, however, is the boy is asking questions looking toward the future, while the father is asking the questions looking at the past as well as toward the future. Fried says of this crisis, "Where forty and fourteen differ, of course, is that this is the second time around for the adult. What he is involved in is not so much a quest for identity, as an inquest."[4]

Sometimes the teenager is quite angry at the environment that has made him the way he is—his world, parents, and God. The man in his forties cannot totally blame the environment for the person he is now. And deep within himself he realizes that he is the result of the choices he has made. This reality intensifies his anger.

One man expressed his unhappiness this way: "Sure, I feel trapped. Why shouldn't I? Twenty-five years ago a dumb eighteen-year-old college kid made up his mind that I was going to be a dentist. So now here I am, a dentist. I'm stuck. What I want to know is, who told that kid he could decide what I was going to have to do for the rest of my life?"[5]

## The Crisis Is Necessary

We all know that adolescence is an important part of life development. This is the time when the teen will try out new attitudes, behaviors, and ways of thinking, and establish a philosophy of life. Successful parents have learned it is important to encourage this process and provide the necessary support so the young person can successfully navigate these difficult waters.

The man in his forties also needs to be encouraged to face similar issues. People need to stand alongside in support. Encourage the man not to run from the stress, but to let the developmental process mature him for the next stage in life.

The adolescent and the man in midlife will change as they pass through their respective crises. They will not entirely be the same men they were before. These are the two key times in life when the clay will be "thrown" repeatedly on the potter's wheel and the pot formed again and again—until the potter gets exactly his desired creation.

Each of them will relinquish some of their old patterns of life, and some of the old ways of viewing themselves and the world. The Bible says, "It's like this: When I was a child, I spoke and thought and reasoned as a child does. But when I grew up, I put away childish things" (1 Cor. 13:11 NLT).

The midlife dad has at least one advantage over his son. He can now evaluate all of his life and set new directions from a broad base of skills, status, power, and experience. His son does not have those abilities.

There is, however, one danger the man at midlife faces that the adolescent doesn't. The man in his forties is going through this complex developmental change unable to escape the day-to-day responsibilities. His teenage son can plop on the headphones and step into another world without hurting other people. The man at midlife must care for a family, maintain his productivity at work, pay bills, repair appliances, continue community contacts—in short, it is almost impossible for him simply to run away. He must deal with real life around him while he struggles with the turmoil inside.

> I keep thinking of the good old days of the past, long since ended. Then my nights were filled with joyous songs. I search my soul and meditate upon the difference now.

> I think of God and moan, overwhelmed with longing for his help. I cannot sleep until you act. I am too distressed even to pray!
>
> Psalm 77:5-6, 3-4

# 6

# The Enemy Horde

AVERY CORMAN WROTE *The Old Neighborhood*, a story of a man in midlife crisis. "As a young man, Steve Robbins left his neighborhood to be a success. He has become one of the best advertising copywriters in the field. He has a beautiful, successful wife, and two lovely daughters. He has achieved everything he thought he wanted.

"Yet, at forty-five, Steve Robbins finds that the life he had so desperately wanted is meaningless. His relationship with his career-minded wife is less a marriage than a corporation. His children are independent and growing away from him. His career has turned into a monotonous game of being clever. Where once he would have given anything to create an award-winning advertising campaign, he would now trade all his success for a soda at Fisher's candy store."[1]

The man at midlife now identifies four major enemies in his life.

## Enemy #1

The first foe is his body. It is aging, slowing down, and losing youthful appeal. When he was younger, women looked at him admiringly. Now they don't look at him at all. If only he could do something about his body!

He is angry that he does not have the energy and stamina of his earlier days. He has trouble accepting the fact that his muscles are getting flabby, he is gaining weight, he is losing his hair, wrinkles are appearing, and his mighty chest only looks good if he holds his breath (but he has to breathe, so his stomach flops out like Santa's "bowl full of jelly").

## Enemy #2

The second enemy is his work. How in the world did he ever get trapped in this job? Why would anyone in his right mind want to be president of Amalgamated Widget? What good is a widget anyway? Yes, he wants to be famous, but not for this. He wants to do something significant for the world—bring peace, happiness, and hope to people—not build widgets!

Or maybe he hasn't made it to the presidency, and now he sees he never will. He is on a treadmill, grinding through the boring daily routine in order to meet his heavy financial obligations. Instead of an exciting challenge, work has become oppressive.

## Enemy #3

The third enemy is his wife and family. You see, if it weren't for his massive domestic responsibilities, he'd give up his job immediately. He's hated it for years anyway, but it provides the money he needs for his house, three cars, and cottage on the lake—not to mention keeping the kids in college and taking vacations to various parts of the country.

If he didn't have all of these family responsibilities, he could give up his job and do something more simple. He could live off the land. If he weren't married, he could just be a beach bum. He could get on a motorcycle with a couple of sleeping bags, a tent, and a young woman—and start roaming the country.

## The Ultimate Enemy

The fourth enemy is God. The midlife man pictures God as leaning over the banister of heaven, grinning fiendishly and pointing a long, bony finger as He says, "You despicable, disgraceful person! You are the worst possible example of a mature man. You are selfish, filled with lust—you are so disgusting that I want to spew you out of my mouth!"

The man in midlife views God not only as an enemy, but as an *unfair* enemy. He says to God, "You made me this way. You gave me these drives and interests. You knew all about the midlife change coming to my life. You are the one who allowed the human body to age and finally die. You are the one who ultimately is to blame for the mess I'm in now!"

This blaming of God is much the same as the account of Adam in the Bible as he expressed his animosity to God in the Garden of Eden. After Adam and Eve had disobeyed, God came to talk with them. Let me paraphrase the event:

God said, "Adam, where are you?"

Adam responded, "I'm over here, hiding behind this tree. "

"Why are you hiding, Adam?"

Adam replied, "Well, you see, God, I'm naked."

God asked, "Who told you that you were naked? Have you eaten fruit from the tree I warned you about?"

Adam, realizing that he was found out, began to shift the blame.

"The woman—it was that woman You gave me! And it's not only her fault, God. You were the one involved in creation. You knew that this was going to happen. Therefore, it's *Your* fault."

Sadly, the man in midlife crisis adds God, as an "unfair enemy," to his list of other enemies.

> Who will protect me from the wicked? Who will be my shield? I would have died unless the Lord had helped me. I screamed, "I'm slipping, Lord!" and he was kind and saved me. Lord, when doubts fill my mind, when my heart is in turmoil, quiet me and give me renewed hope and cheer.
>
> Psalm 94:16-19

# PART 3
# Dead-end Roads

# 7

# Depression

THE MAN IN MIDLIFE CRISIS will try many different solutions to reduce tension in his life. Most of the methods he'll use in the early days of the crisis are escape-oriented. These tactics are not real solutions and many times will only compound his problems.

He's like a little boy lost in a crowd at a shopping center. He goes one direction, thinking he sees legs that look familiar, only to find they are not those of his parents. He turns another direction, but again finds it doesn't lead him to his parents, and he is more lost than ever.

Because the midlife man thinks other people are causing his problems, he uses tactics to eliminate those enemies from his life. He will probably try several dead-end roads before he begins to realize that the causes of the crisis are primarily inside himself—not external. Often he needs to be frustrated by trying several of his escape solutions before he can look at himself, and life, realistically.

## Feeling Down

One of the most common responses of the man strug-gling with a midlife crisis is depression. It's the easiest escape and the one that comes most naturally. It's the log-ical progression of all the events we've looked at in the previous chapters. Depression is the natural outcome of the forces pressing on his life. And why not, with pres-sures like these:

- •My company is downsizing.
- •My wife makes more money than I do.
- •I'm forty and I haven't made it yet.
- •I'm forty and I've made it . . . but is this all there is?

The anger, frustration, bitterness, and self-pity build-ing within him lead to depression.

At work he stares at his papers, or idly watches his machine do its job. He only does his job if he is prodded by someone. He isn't thinking about anything in particu-lar, he just feels crummy and depressed. His productivi-ty drops off. If he works in a creative/think business, he loses his capacity for creativity. He is short-tempered with everyone. People who work under him say he is very difficult to please and, he always finds small things wrong with the way they do their job.

At home he seems to have dropped out. If he was a handyman, he doesn't do the little things around the house and yard he used to do. Sometimes he only sits in a chair gazing out the window or listening endlessly to music or staring at television. He avoids conversation. He dodges leadership and problem-solving. His temper flares at his wife and children, "I just want to be left alone! Can't you understand that?" Of course his mar-riage suffers. He talks only about surface topics. As for sex, well, it's usually, "Not tonight, dear, I'm too tired."

## The New Face of Depression

"From men's magazines, to psychological journals, to radio talk shows, the same tale is being told. More and more successful professional men in their thirties and forties are suffering depression." The rate of depression has risen sharply in men during the nineties—faster than in women, according to Ronald Kessler, sociology professor at the University of Michigan. "In the 1970s studies found women three times as likely to be depressed. In the 1980s the ratio changed to 2.4 to 1. New surveys have found the tightest ratio: 1.7 to 1."[1]

Another social worker reports, "Baby boomers grew up with the idea of limitless possibilities." Lately she has been seeing male clients who have "found the possibilities were limited, and their expectations cannot be met." Frequently the midlife man doesn't know why he is depressed. He will frequently tell a counselor or friend that he doesn't know what's wrong—and he doesn't.[2]

Depression spills over into social relationships. The midlife man withdraws from late-night coffees, card games, movies, or dinners with friends from church. He explains to his wife that he doesn't want to be around people. Repeatedly he is off on long walks, bike rides, a drive in the car, or endless hours surfing the Net.

Many such men, when asked to describe their feelings about work, marriage, and life in general, say they are bored. They feel that life is a farce, a dumb thing they're forced to continue doing. The word bore means "to make something empty," and this is what has happened in the midlife man's job, marriage, and friendships—in short, all of his life is "empty."

## Causes of Depression

Depression doesn't just happen! It's not enough just to say, "I'm bored." That only identifies your situation. To get help you need to identify the source of the problem and specifically look at the losses you have experienced. Psychological depression is always connected to a loss. Let's look at some of these loss areas.

*Relational loss*—Death of a mate, divorce, or a lost romance. Depression can occur whenever there is a breakdown in or a termination of any interpersonal relationship. Depression should be expected because of these kinds of losses.

*Loss of material things*—Sally and I were vacationing in the Tahitian Islands for a second honeymoon in celebration of our twenty-fifth wedding anniversary. We had loaded a few things into a small outrigger canoe and were paddling from our hotel to an island about half a mile offshore. We had gone only about 150 yards when we made a slight readjustment of our weight in the canoe. To our absolute amazement, the canoe started to tip over. The outrigger pontoon that was to keep the canoe balanced was waterlogged and absolutely worthless. We seemed to be acting out a slow-motion movie as it slowly settled deeper and deeper into the water until finally we and the contents of our canoe had slipped into the Pacific.

I had a brand-new Olympus OM 1 camera with a 1:2 lens. It went straight to the bottom of seventy-five feet of salt water. It was difficult for me to shake off the gnawing depression—that terrible down feeling. If you lose something tangible which you value, you likely will feel depressed for a period of time. It's normal.

*Time loss*—"How can my children suddenly be going

off to college?" You can't go back and relive the years. But it can be depressing to feel that we are losing "the best years of our lives."

*Lost opportunities*—A job you didn't take, an investment overlooked, or time you should have spent connecting to your dad. "Why do I feel so depressed? I feel like I'm going crazy."

*Loss of control or choice*—If we go for prolonged periods of time with too many demands on our time and energy without a break for restoration, we can become depressed. When every hour of every day, day after day, is determined for us, we may feel dejected and weighed down without realizing why. If we have neither voice nor choice in decisions which affect us, we may feel depressed.

Loss, then, in any area of life, may cause us to have feelings of depression. We must identify the sources of loss and make necessary adjustments—then the depression will lift and we can move on with living.[3]

## Early Challenges

When a man is in his twenties he has goals, things to accomplish, mountains to climb. There are exciting new things to learn, skills to master, and relationships to develop. In my twenties I set goals for my life. I didn't sit down and write my complete list of priorities in one day. But as I went through college, and came to understand myself and God, certain targets began to crystallize in my mind. I wanted to succeed in college and to overcome the educational inadequacy of my earlier years. I wanted to become more acceptable to other people socially. I had a goal of finding the right wife and raising a warm family who would love each other and God. I wanted to ably explain the Scriptures and God to people and to be an effective counselor.

Another goal was to become a good public speaker, being able to move people with words. I wanted to pastor a large church (in my thinking then, a church over one thousand was large). I wanted to travel around the world. I even had goals of being on radio and television and writing books and magazine articles. These goals certainly would provide a lifetime of challenge.

But by my early forties, all of the goals I envisioned in my early twenties had been fulfilled—except being the president of a college or seminary. I was depressed and bored—I had run out of goals. For me to successfully come through my midlife crisis, I needed to enlarge some of the old goals and allow God to lead me into new goals for the long, productive midlife era ahead.

### Midlife Man in the Psalms

The man in midlife crisis who sinks into depression identifies very closely with the writer of Psalm 102 (quoted here from *The Living Bible*). Whoever wrote that psalm was certainly familiar with anxiety and was able to spell out in brief form some of the causes of his own personal depression.

Shortness of life was one cause. "For my days disappear like smoke. My life is passing swiftly as the evening shadows. I am withering like grass. He has cut me down in middle life, shortening my days" (vss. 3, 11, 23). It seems that all of us try to resist the process of aging and death.

*Poor health* is another problem. "My health is broken"

(vs. 3). In the midyears, physical health becomes an increasing problem. These are the years of the heart attack, the time when diabetes increases, and when a tumor in the prostate may be discovered. In short, the body is beginning to show some clear signs of poor health.

The writer of Psalm 102 says that he is *emotionally unable to cope*, and this also produces depression. He says, "My heart is sick" (vs. 4), and he uses the illustration of grass that is trampled and withered. This is a pre-ulcer state of mind. He is unable to handle the problems of life, and the unresolved problems in turn increase his inability to handle problems. Emotional stress is cyclical. It is like a giant whirlpool, sucking ever downward and increasing in intensity.

The psalmist also says that *loss of appetite* depresses him. "My food is tasteless, I have lost my appetite" (vs. 4). Literally, food becomes unimportant. The King James Version says, "I forget to eat my bread." The writer is preoccupied with his problems and so loses his appetite. Weight loss is very common during times of great anxiety. The result of the loss of appetite is that "I am reduced to skin and bones" (vs. 5). Not eating or not eating the right food only compounds the problem and increases anxiety and depression.

Loneliness is another reason for the psalmist's depression. "I am like a vulture in a far-off wilderness, or like an owl alone in the desert. I lie awake, lonely as a solitary sparrow on the roof" (vss. 6-7). Each of these birds describes a special kind of loneliness. The vulture represents the loneliness just before death. The owl is pictured alone, hooting from an isolated branch by himself at night. Troubled people frequently have trouble being alone at night. The psalmist carefully identifies the sparrow as a "solitary sparrow" alone on the roof. Sparrows are ordinarily in groups. But this one sits awake by himself on the roof.

The psalmist also says that he is depressed because he is *mocked by his enemies*: "My enemies taunt me day after day and curse at me" (vs. 8). Success brings with it not only a feeling of having arrived, but also an unmentioned fear that other people are waiting for you to fail. The higher you move up the ladder of success, the smaller the number of people ahead of you, and greater the number beneath you who may be looking for opportunities to peck you to death.

The psalmist writes that *humiliation—a loss of poise, control, and stability* is another reason for his depression. This man sits and weeps in utter mourning and humiliation. As he lifts a cup of water to his lips, his tears drop into the cup. He is a broken man with a life out of control.

Next, the psalmist lists the problem of not being recognized by the world. His life is coming to an end. He has done nothing of significance. "My life is passing swiftly as the evening shadows. I am withering like grass, while you, Lord, are a famous King forever. Your fame will endure to every generation" (vss. 11-12). The psalmist paints a contrasting picture: I am a passing, finite, frail, dying human who has accomplished nothing. But You, God, are secure, famous, and everyone from generation to generation will continue to remember You. The man's life is short and limited. Soon he will die. But God is well known to the world and continues to outlive one generation after another.

*Impending death* is another source of his depression: "He has cut me down in middle life, shortening my days" (vs. 23). A young man sees life as endless. Even though he knows that death will come someday, he always feels it will come to someone else. But the man in midlife sees death as a near reality. He realizes his days are numbered, and each time the sun rises and sets, another segment of his life has been cut off.

The troubled human personality gravitates toward depression. The difficulty is that the "depression solution" is not effective, because many of the problems do not have human solutions. There is no way that the psalmist can lengthen his life, avoid death, or in his own strength become famous, or change the mind of an enemy, or eliminate a physical health problem.

## Will Alcohol Answer?

The problem with depression is that it is essentially a vacuum—not an answer. Our lives won't tolerate a vacuum, and sooner or later something else will rush in to fill that emptiness. All too often it is alcohol. Alcoholism is one of the country's major health problems, affecting more than eighty million people, if we include both alcoholics and those who live and work with them. It's not only a nationwide problem, but it is a major problem for people in midlife. Alcoholism increases 50 percent among people in the forty-to-sixty age bracket compared to those in their thirties.

Alcoholism is a self-defeating process that affects a man's output at work, his relationships at home, and his contacts with other people. He feels he is escaping his problems, but they are only intensified. Just beneath the surface of our personalities lies a great deal of immaturity, anger, and resentment carefully kept in check—but alcohol releases these inhibitions. Remarks released by alcohol which are spoken at work, home, or social gatherings will drive away the very people who could be the most help to the midlife man.

Because the man at midlife is struggling with questions of his sexual prowess, he sometimes feels that alcohol will enable him to express himself more adequately sexually. The truth is just the opposite. Alcohol tends to diminish sexual potency and make the man less effective.

Alcohol also works against him physically. He is already feeling tired and run-down. He needs a different kind of diet to build his body. Alcohol adds to his physical depletion.

## Anger, Rage, And Guilt

The man in midlife who tries the alcohol solution is also emotionally miserable. Alcohol reinforces low self-esteem and self-pity. Alcohol pushes the man toward self-punishment, resentment, and an inclination to project blame for his troubles toward other people. He becomes impatient, irritable, anxious, stubborn, and jealous. Alcohol is used to forget troubles, but it's also a drug to cover the strong emotional feelings of anger and rage.

The man at midlife is suddenly becoming aware of several losses in his life—youth, success at work, connection with his children, his own aging parents, and his stale marriage. In addition, he thought he would outgrow the damage from his dysfunctional family. He thought he would be farther along in life—that he would be happy! But he's not!

"The faster he runs, the behinder he gets." So he throws up his hands in anger and then reaches for the bottle to control the disappointments, anger, maybe even the rage he feels.

Now the midlife man has another problem—guilt. He kicks himself for being out of control, for drinking, for not being able to "fix his life." But this type of guilt is only a symptom of his failing attempt to escape his midlife crisis through depression and alcohol.

Alcohol is not really an answer. It just exaggerates the problems, isolates a man from people, intensifies his feeling of guilt, and works hand-in-hand with depression. Hiding in alcohol is like getting into quicksand—it only sucks a man deeper and deeper into a midlife crisis and farther away from people, God, and real solutions.

## God Is A Friend

Look again at Psalm 102. We can find real help for depression by involving God. To begin with, as the psalmist indicates, God is concerned. "He will listen to the prayers of the destitute, for he is never too busy to heed their requests" (vs. 17). God knows we are weak and needy, and He loves us. The Bible says that Jesus was tempted in all ways like we are and understands us. "But Jesus the Son of God is our great High Priest who has gone to heaven itself to help us; therefore let us never stop trusting him. This High Priest of ours understands our weaknesses, since he had the same temptations we do, though he never once gave way to them and sinned. So let us come boldly to the very throne of God and stay there to receive his mercy and to find grace to help us in our times of need" (Heb. 4:14-16).

The writer of Psalm 102 bares his heart in his struggle with depression, but he also points us to God who understands. I believe there was no mistake that God placed the words of Psalm 102 (the anguish of a man at midlife) next to the comfort and encouragement of Psalm 103, which shows the heart concern of God as people struggle with problems.

> He forgives all my sins. He heals me. He ransoms me from hell. He surrounds me with lovingkindness and tender mercies. He fills my life with good things! My youth is renewed like the eagle's!
>
> He is merciful and tender toward those who don't deserve it; he is slow to get angry and full of kindness and love. He never bears a grudge, nor remains angry forever. He has not punished us as we deserve for all our sins, for his mercy toward those who fear and honor him is as great as the height of the heavens above the earth.
>
> He has removed our sins as far away from us as the east is from the west. He is like a father to us, tender and sympathetic to those who reverence him. For he knows we are but dust, and that our days are few and brief, like grass, like flowers, blown by the wind and gone forever.
>
> Psalm 103:3-5, 8-15 NLT

The answer is to allow God to define who we should be and what we should be doing with our lives, days, and hours, goals, and future aspirations. Also, you will need to forgive—your employer, your mate, parents, children, even your culture. You may rage at God, "Didn't You create us and cause us to age?" Ultimately you will also need to forgive God. Lewis Smedes has written a most helpful book, Forgive and Forget. He shows how to do more than try to forget past pain—he will help you to really release the pain.[4] The Bible says, "Give all your worries and cares to God, for He cares about what happens to you" (1 Peter 5:7 NLT).

## Hope and Help

Archibald Hart, dean and professor of psychology at the Graduate School of Psychology, Fuller Theological Seminary, has written an extremely helpful book entitled *Dark Clouds, Silver Linings*, in which he says, "Depression is an epidemic. One of every eighteen adults—about ten million of us—suffers from depression. A problem that seems to be on the rise. As a culture we may well have our own emotional "Great Depression."[5]

Dr. Hart, in a very practical and down-to-earth manner, talks about depression—how it starts, some of the childhood contributions and developments, and how anger, inferiority, and guilt are involved in depression. He also helps people understand the causes of depression, as well as the difference between real and false guilt. He gives sane and helpful suggestions for people who are wrestling with depression. Most important, he says there is hope and help for the man in midlife in the throes of depression.

Depression may become a temporary escape to provide momentary relief from the pain at midlife—but it is only a brief painkiller. When you have a toothache, you must deal with the infected tooth.

> I waited patiently for God to help me; then he listened and heard my cry. He lifted me out of the pit of despair, out from the bog and the mire, and set my feet

on a hard, firm path and steadied me as I walked along. He has given me a new song to sing, of praises to our God.

Psalm 40:1-3

## Defining Depression
Here are the hallmarks of depression as defined by the American Psychiatric Association:
- Noticeable change of appetite or sleeping patterns
- Loss of interest in activities previously enjoyed
- Fatigue, loss of energy
- Feelings of worthlessness and hopelessness
- Feelings of inappropriate guilt
- Inability to concentrate or think; indecisiveness
- Recurring thoughts of death or suicide
- Overwhelming feelings of sadness and grief
- Headaches or stomachaches

If you have four or more of these symptoms for more than two weeks, seek help.

## For Further Reading
*The Angry Man* by David Stoop and Stephen Arterburn (Dallas: Word Publishing, 1991).

*The Faces of Rage* by David Damico (Colorado Springs: Navpress, 1992).

*Good Guilt, Bad Guilt* by Becca Cowan Johnson (Downers Grove, IL: InterVarsity Press, 1996).

*Love's Unseen Enemy* by Dr. Les Parrott II (Grand Rapids, MI: Zondervan, 1994).

# 8

# A New Shell

The time for wild kisses goes fast and it's
Time for Sanka
Already?—*Judith Viorst*

ABOUT A YEAR AGO I saw a picture of people from my era who had gathered for a college reunion. What a shock! These people had lost their hair—and their shapes. The women didn't look sexy. The men who had been athletic and really "big" with the college women looked tired, conservative, and just plain old. I thought, *Wow! I'm glad I'm not like those old people.* And then I had a second thought: *I'm glad I wasn't there to have my picture taken.*

## A New Body

To put it very bluntly, the man's body at midlife is beginning to show visible signs of crumbling. Like an ancient building, the roof is in trouble, mortar is coming out of the joints, the floors are sagging, and the doors creak. To make matters worse, there is a large conspiracy continually telling us that outward appearance and productivity are the only things that count.

Suddenly, people you thought were your friends are enemies. You casually ask your dentist about a problem with a tooth and he says, "Well, for a man of your age . . ." If you suggest to the barber that he comb your hair to cover the bald spot, he says, "When you hit forty, you have to expect a bald spot."

Biologically speaking, we spend the last three-quarters of our lives aging. The fastest growth takes place in the unborn child. Growth is rapid in the infant and the young child, but it's progressively slower until about age twenty-one. Growth then turns toward decline. The man in his twenties and thirties is not much aware of it, but he is slowing down, even as he jokingly passes it off.

When he hits forty, however, he begins to identify his body as an enemy who is making him look old. He frantically attempts to change his appearance—to win the battle with age and stay perpetually young. When a man looks good and knows it, he feels great. His morale soars and even more serious problems become manageable. So a man believes that if he can only change his body, get the muscle tone back, and reduce the flab, he's going to solve his midlife crisis.

Midlife men, traditionally dubious of plastic surgery, are paying for the cosmetic resculpting of their bodies in ever growing numbers. Males were 5 percent to 10 percent of the cosmetic surgery clientele a decade ago. Now in many practices one out of every four to five patients is a man.[1] "Men are also getting 30 percent of nose jobs, and 17 percent of facelifts."[2]

His attempt to create a new body is not all negative. If he can get his body into better shape, it will improve his self-image, increase his confidence with people, perhaps prevent a heart attack, and also help some of his problems with stamina.

## Beauty Is Good

Joyce Brothers, well-known psychologist, points out that "beautiful people have beautiful personalities. We consistently judge them to be more sensitive, kind, intelligent, interesting, sociable, and exciting than less attractive people."

Dr. Brothers goes on to speak of a study made in a school among kindergartners and teachers regarding the people to whom they were most often attracted: "They [the children] picked the most attractive children as their favorites. Their teachers did likewise, and considered the less attractive children more likely to be troublemakers." She continues, "When we grow up, for both men and women, higher salary levels and greater advancement have a high correlation with pleasant looks, at all ages and in all fields."[3]

## Fat Is Bad

Years ago, *The New York Times* reported an interesting study by Robert Half, the president of a chain of employment agencies. He evaluated the salaries of fifteen thousand agency executives. Among the executives who earned the highest salaries, only 9 percent were more than ten pounds overweight. But executives who earned medium to lower salaries were more than ten pounds overweight. Mr. Half commented that his offices received thousands of requests for thin people, but the only request they had ever had for a fat man came from a company that made clothing for overweight men.[4]

The side benefits of an improved body are extremely great. As the midlife man gets his body in shape, he will be less likely to experience heart attack or stroke. Greater physical activity also tends to decrease depression, and he will be able to handle greater pressure. He will feel better about himself as he takes off pounds. But a man must not believe if he gets his body back into shape that he is going to erase the years and suddenly regain his youth. The truth is—he is not going to be young again.

## A New Wardrobe

It is true that our society is contriving to make youth last for all of life. So a man not only fights to make his body look younger, but he also packages himself to look younger. The way we look does have a direct bearing upon the way we feel about ourselves. We can't erase age, but by wearing current styles we may feel better about ourselves. Wearing current styles also helps people view us as worthwhile. So, even though the initial motivation may be wrong, the outcome will have a small positive effect in helping a man through his midlife crisis.

## Gray Hair on That Manly Chest

There is a definite difference between trying to dress in current styles and trying to look like a twenty-year-old who just came off the beach. There is nothing quite so comical as a fifty-year-old man in too-tight pants, with carefully dyed but thin hair combed down over his forehead, a shirt unbuttoned to his waist, and a chain hanging on his gray chest hair.

A young clothing salesman in a men's store commented about the tastes of his midlife customers. "I've seen it a thousand times. They try to be cool when they're pushing fifty. They want style. They come in here wearing conservative cuts, dark gray and blue, and they walk out with the look of a college guy. I had one guy in here this morning—looked like a VP. He was in a gray flannel suit, white shirt, cuff links. You'll never believe me when I tell you he walks out of here in a turtleneck and a wild jacket I couldn't unload on a college guy at half the price. He asks me how does he look. You make a four hundred buck sale, and the guy is standing there with a paunch, gray hair, bags under his eyes, and what do you say? You tell me."[5]

## A New Lifestyle

So our man has trimmed down his weight, got his muscles back into shape, and is wearing current style clothing. All of these are a part of his changing lifestyle. He seems ready now to do what he wants to do and to be himself. He may spend less time at his work and more time in leisure activities. New hobbies and activities become important to him. And he may even trade in his four-door brown Buick for a red sports car.

His attempt at this new lifestyle may cause people around him to say he's entering his second childhood. He's living a lifestyle that in some ways is "catch-up"— doing the things he didn't get to do in his teens and twenties.

A friend who pastored an extremely successful, large, multi-staffed church, decided he had had it. The church seemed to be moving too slowly, and no one really wanted to do anything creative. He was tired of the lethargy of boards and committees, so he decided to drop out. He resigned from the church, moved to another part of the country, and went back to school.

He also felt he needed time away from his family, so he bought a big Harley motorcycle and all the gear. Then he set off across the country at his own pace, stopping wherever he wanted for as long as he wanted, doing his own thing. He traveled about three-quarters of the way across the United States before he returned to his family and his studies.

The Frenchman Paul Gauguin is another example of a man who changed directions in midlife. Gauguin worked for a stock brokerage firm in Paris from 1871 to 1883, and was also an amateur painter. He kept dreaming of how wonderful it would be to live in the peaceful South Sea islands of Tahiti, to spend his time painting, and be free from the struggle for money. After several years of dreaming, Gauguin did move to Tahiti and became a world-famous artist.

## College Friends

When I was in college, I had three very close friends. Each of us sensed that God had called us into the ministry. We talked and prayed about our daily lives, as well as our futures. We hitchhiked together, shared our meager financial resources, helped each other with studies, and shared the joys and sadness of each other's love lives. When college was over, three of us went on to seminaries and eventually into local churches. The fourth friend pastored a church after college graduation and then became a Youth for Christ director.

At midlife, three of the four of us were going through crisis times. The fourth man did not experience the same crisis. The death of his wife when he was in his early thirties accelerated the whole process of midlife assessment for him. He married a second wife ten years younger, and he did not go through what the other three of us experienced.

The other three of us have been involved in a succession of successful pastorates. But at midlife, each grew restless. One of the guys left a long pastorate and moved to a new church. There he unwillingly put up with the politicking and intrachurch conflicts. He abruptly resigned, moved to another state, and started doctoral studies. He and his wife are presently involved in counseling married couples and pastoring a new church. Their lifestyle has been sharply altered. They seem more relaxed and less pressured by the expectations of people.

The second man pastored churches where his salary was always less than adequate, even though the churches were relatively large. His wife had to work most of the time. He had very successful ministries, earning recognition from church leaders as well as business and community people. He began to feel a growing urgency to enjoy a few of the financial benefits of his business friends. Was it really fair that he should be serving God, ministering unselfishly to people, while his family lived near poverty? This growing dissatisfaction led him out of the ministry, into an affair, and into business.

## Sailboat or Motorcycle?

I am the fourth of our group, and my lifestyle also changed. Previously, I had no time for recreation or days off, because there was a world to be won for Christ and an endless stream of people to be helped. Then I began to have the urge to get away occasionally. At Sally's urging, I bought a used sixteen-foot catamaran and began to sail. My view of work changed so that work became one of many things I did, rather than the only thing.

During a flight layover in a large city, I called one of my seminary friends to see how he was doing. As we talked, I shared with him that I was in the process of writing a book on men at midlife. He laughed loudly. "You can use me as a prime example of a change in lifestyle," he said. I was surprised, because he was always fastidiously dressed, careful about how people saw him, and extremely well controlled. Now he owned a motorcycle and was riding back and forth to his church. He felt comfortable wearing jeans and his leather jacket to the church office. In general, he was following a new easygoing style of living.

Since our conversation, he has resigned from his very large thriving church, which he had built from scratch. He was ready for a different kind of ministry and accepted a teaching position at a graduate school. Even though his salary is reduced, the benefits of this new challenge and the reduced pressure far outweigh his lessened income.

### A Young Lifestyle

Perhaps the most basic need of the midlife man is to convince himself and the world around him that he is still young. He enlists the help of all the experts to maintain his youthful appearance. Bags under his eyes can be removed, double chins can disappear, his face can be lifted, his nose can be modified, and hair can be transplanted to the top of his head.

If a man's purpose in all these changes is to turn the clock back and recapture lost years, he is destined for disappointment. The solutions will be incomplete. A *Fortune* cover story illustrates the massive shift in male vanity. "American men are refusing to age gracefully. Science has teamed up with cosmetology to give men new and potent weapons to combat ugliness. Grooming products for males, depending on how that category is defined, now generate as much as $3.3 billion in sales. Conservative estimates predict that spending will increase eleven percent in three years."[6]

These changes can have a positive effect on a man's self-image and lead to a positive resolution of his midlife crisis. But the changes must be more than a panic-stricken grab to remain young forever. If each lifestyle change is done in the context of who he is and what he wants to be, the new exercises, diet, medical checkups, loss of weight, clothes, and a more realistic lifestyle will become part of a positive solution in his midlife crisis.

## Over the Ocean Blue

The story of a lifestyle change that grabs me most is the story of Robert Manry, recorded in his book, Tinkerbelle. The story is close to me because Manry lived in Cleveland, Ohio, where I was raised. As a boy I delivered the Cleveland *Plain Dealer*; Robert Manry worked for the *Plain Dealer* as an unimportant copy editor. At forty-seven, Manry decided he had to do some things with his life that were fun. He never dreamed his actions would lead to a total change in his lifestyle.

Manry was a little nuts about sailing, and that's the second reason I'm attracted to his story. Sailors are essentially dreamers, and it's easy for me to identify with his dreams to sail across the Atlantic Ocean. A friend of his who owned a twenty-five-foot boat asked Manry if he would sail with him across the Atlantic. Manry leaped at the opportunity and began to plan for all that was involved in making the trip.

Shortly before they were to set out on the voyage, Manry's friend backed out. Manry's dreams were on the verge of being shattered. But secretly he began to make plans for the trip alone in *Tinkerbelle*, his own 13-1/2-foot boat. For the next several months, he quietly prepared and equipped his boat for the trip. Only his wife and a few close friends knew he was going to try to cross the Atlantic in this small boat.

On June 1, 1965, Manry, in his little white boat with the red sail, left Falmouth, Massachusetts, bound for Falmouth, England, three thousand miles away. He spent the next seventy-eight days on the high seas with all of the joys and terrors of sailing. He was swept overboard, experienced fear, hallucinations, and loneliness. He almost turned back. Finally, he arrived at his destination and was greeted by nearly fifty thousand people. Those people were not there to see history being made, they were there because they identified with Manry's dream. Manry told the world, "The voyage was something I simply had to do."[7]

The notoriety and new sources of income cut Manry free from the bondage he had experienced as a mundane copy editor. For the rest of his life, he lived his new lifestyle that came about as he was willing to live out one of his dreams.

A man's changed lifestyle may be triggered by wonderful dreams of faraway places or experiences he wants to have before he dies. He may change because he feels deprived, frustrated, or even depressed. Colonel Edward E. "Buzz" Aldrin, Jr., the second human to step on the moon, shared some of the positive results during his midlife transition and depression. "My depression forced me, at the age of forty-one, to stop and for the first time examine my life. The circumstances that brought about my study were extreme, but I now look upon this experience as one of the most valuable things I have done. It taught me to live again, at an age when it is very possible to begin anew."[8] Aldrin left the Air Force and began ranching in California.

Don't just settle for a new body—go for some of your dreams!

> Never envy the wicked! Soon they fade away like grass and disappear. Trust in the Lord instead. Be kind and good to others; then you will live safely here in the land and prosper, feeding in safety.
>
> Be delighted with the Lord. Then he will give you all your heart's desires. Commit everything you do to the Lord. Trust him to help you do it and he will.
>
> Psalm 37:1-5

# 9

# Early Retirement

GENE THARPE, WRITING in the *Atlanta Constitution*, says, "More than half of America's workers are in their thirties and forties, and for these baby boomers, reality is coming home. They are facing midlife, the years when personal horizons squeeze tighter, and limits appear on life and career, causing burnout, frustration, aggravation and stress-related illnesses such as hypertension."[1]

## The Bliss of Dropping Out

Again and again I hear midlife men talk about the sheer joy of quitting their work. Many men feel their work consumes so much of their time and energy that they don't have time to establish their own identity.

One of my fantasies has been to gain increasing expertise with sailboats in the forty-foot class and then set out on a cruise of the Caribbean Islands. No timetable! Simply go from one small island's secluded cove to another, living from the sea and foods of the islands. And above all, living without a razor.

Rust Hills, in *How to Retire at Forty-One*, says with

tongue in cheek that there are four absolute prerequisites if you are going to retire early. "First and foremost is that you be forty-one and have a job to retire from. Second, you should be somewhat fed up with your work. Third, you should have done fairly well when you were working so you won't feel your retreat is some kind of a defeat. Fourth, you should have some idea of how you are going to use all of the time that will suddenly become available."[2]

Hills decided to leave his publishing job so he could retreat to his oceanside place called Coveside. He felt he simply could not go on as he was and needed some time to think for at least a year or two.

Sometimes a person doesn't really retire, but only changes jobs at midlife. Hills jokingly writes that this is cheating. He says, "These people aren't *retiring* at all, they're just *switching*. It's like a good second marriage.[3]

### Early Out

Most men feel valuable and worthwhile only because they work. At the same time they feel work is oppressive. But early retirement has its own stresses, especially for the man who has been working frantically before he decides to drop out. It's almost like trying to get unhooked from a drug addiction. There can be violent emotional convulsions and erratic responses, because the man no longer has the structure provided by his work routine.

The man who takes early retirement sometimes experiences the same emotional stress that working people have over long holidays such as Christmas or New Year's. When they don't work over an extended holiday, they quite often get the blues because they feel worthless. Early retirement may cause a man to feel the Christmas neurosis blues all year long.

## The Guru of No Work

Thoreau and his early retirement are thought of by many people as the ideal experience. At one time he was so admired that his observations on work and play were displayed on the advertising cards of the New York City Transit Authority. One read, "The mass of men lead lives of quiet desperation. What is called resignation is confirmed desperation. From the desperate city you go into the desperate country."[4]

Thoreau has been idealized by many as having carried out the perfect way to live—dropping out and doing his own thing. Even though Thoreau's pursuits were unlike most men's occupations, he never did truly drop out. He never was able to do nothing. Thoreau was always at work. He was an amateur naturalist. He wrote books, gave lectures, traveled, and studied. Thoreau could be occupied for hours in simple observation of the life going on in his pond just beneath the ice. Yes, he had dropped out from society, in a sense, but he had not dropped out from life. He had only changed jobs.

## Real Fears

Fear sometimes is the real pressure that drives a midlife man to think of early retirement. He is afraid of the young men coming up within the company. He is afraid he is going to be displaced and his information and expertise outmoded, so he opts to retire early. It's not necessarily because he doesn't enjoy his job, he's just afraid he is going to be kicked out.

Certainly there are real fears stemming from our rapidly changing society. But a man's decision to quit his job and drop out is simply another escape. Yes, there are temporary benefits. He will probably be more rested and will have an opportunity to think through who he is. But it certainly will not be a satisfying long-range solution.

For most men in our society, their occupation—in an office, factory, or working at home with a computer—is where they gain identity and self-esteem. Fully 70 to 80 percent of a man's identity is his job. When a man drops out, he has to establish an entirely new identity and activities to provide a new positive self-image. Unless he does this, his so-called solution will only dig his hole deeper.

> In my distress I prayed to the Lord and he answered me and rescued me. He is for me! How can I be afraid? What can mere man do to me? The Lord is on my side, he will help me. . . . It is better to trust the Lord than to put confidence in men.
>
> Psalm 118:5-8 NLT

# 10

# The Affair

THE FRENCH HAVE A WORD for it: *de'mon de midi*; the "devil" that gets into men at the "noonday" of their lives when their wives have perhaps grown matronly. The Germans have a word for it, too: *Torschlusspanik*, "closed-door panic"; the pursuit of young women by middle-aged men seeking a final fling "before the gates close."[1]

Of all the solutions that the man in midlife may try, the affair is the one most talked about. The midlife affair is the subject of radio and television programs, magazine articles, and movies. Publishers, writers, and producers justify themselves by saying they are only presenting what the public wants.

### Is Everybody Doing It?

Barbara Fried, in her book *The Middle-Age Crisis*, talks about twelve marriages of midlife people she knew at a seaside colony one summer. One or both of the partners in the marriages were having extramarital affairs. One woman summarized what was happening. "Well, I look at it this way. There was a year when it seemed that everybody I knew, including me, was getting married, and now there's another year when it seems everybody I know, including me, is getting divorced."[2]

Morton Hunt, who did extensive research on the sexual habits of Americans, says bluntly: "Many people cheat—some a little, some a lot; most who don't would like to but are afraid; neither the actual nor the would-be cheaters admit the truth or defend their views except to a few confidants; and practically all of them teach their children the accepted traditional code, though they know they neither believe in it themselves nor expect that their children will do so when they grow up."[3]

Family breakup through divorce has been at epidemic proportions for decades. In some major urban areas of our country, the number of divorces granted in a year is greater than the number of marriages performed. The man in midlife is in an extremely precarious position. His insides cry out for a change in his lifestyle, plus he lives in a society in which it appears that "everybody is doing it." The man in midlife crisis is ripe for an affair.

## Why David Got into Trouble

David's midlife affair with Bathsheba is probably the best-known story of adultery in the Bible. His affair followed a pattern similar to the affairs of men at midlife today. "In the spring of the following year," the story goes, "at the time when wars begin, David sent Joab and the Israeli army to destroy the Ammonites. . . . But David stayed in Jerusalem. One night he couldn't get to sleep and went for a stroll on the roof of the palace" (2 Sam. 11:1-2).

David was a man at midlife who now was too valuable to be leading the army as he did when he was
younger. Joab, one of his officers, encouraged him to stay
at home. When the battle was secure, he could "bring the
rest of the army and finish the job, so that you will get the
credit for the victory instead of me" (2 Sam. 12:28).

## Physical Strength—Bane or Blessing?

David had lived all of his life by his physical power. As
a young man tending sheep, he had fought off wild lions
and bears. When he was only a teenager, he had his
famous confrontation with the giant Goliath. Goliath's
sword, taken as a trophy after that victory, became the
symbol to David and to the nation of David's physical
prowess.

After he was anointed to be king while yet in his teens,
he was deprived from assuming the throne by the insane-
ly jealous King Saul. For the next ten years, through his
late teens and into his twenties, David was forced to live
in the mountains and caves, depending upon his physical ability, wit, and power for survival.

David's success after he did assume the throne led him
inexorably to administrative duties. His success made
him more and more valuable and pulled him increasingly from the physical style of life that had given him meaning for so many years. David was a man emotionally set
up for an affair. His inability to sleep perhaps had a direct
connection with what was happening inside of him at
this age, as he was increasingly forced to assume different roles.

## David's Discontent

Why does a man get into affairs? Invariably, it is a group of circumstances that set him up for an affair. Like David, he thinks of the affair as a way to satisfy his discontent. In the midst of a great deal of internal turmoil and dissatisfaction with life, it's easy for a midlife man to think back over his life and remember the kinds of things that gave him pleasure and satisfaction in the past. A new girlfriend did it when he was a teenager. Why shouldn't it happen again? After all, romance dispelled monotony, emptiness, boredom, and depression.

He remembers what it was like to look into the eyes of someone who was looking intently at him. He recalls the thrill of the first touch of her hand. He remembers how satisfying it was to talk to another person for endless hours. Certainly that same sparkle would happen again. He really believes that "love conquers all"—even his internal discontent.

Sometimes the man in midlife senses an awakening sexual drive. Some people suggest this may be caused by hormonal changes. Others feel if a man thinks he is losing his potency, he becomes a victim of fantasizing and daydreaming—"What would it be like?"

For the midlife man who wonders, "What would it be like with another woman . . . with another intoxicating look . . . her flirty whisper," the Internet is the perfect trap for his wandering lust.

An article entitled "Internet Infidelity" tells of Jim, a fifty-something man who filed for divorce, ending a thirty-year marriage. After the divorce, Jim's grown children searched his computer and found what had been keeping Dad up late at night—and what had triggered the divorce. Vestiges of erased files told a tale of the life he lived in the on-line chat rooms. In graphic and explicit detail they had undressed each other. They further described how they would have sex with each other.[4]

Fantasizing prepares the man for the affair. The Bible tells us, "For as he thinks within himself, so he is" (Prov. 23:7 NASB). The man at midlife, however, rationalizes that he deserves a little happiness, a little fling. So he justifies his fantasizing as totally acceptable. He may even convince himself that by having an affair, he will become a more effective husband and a better lover.

The concept "virtual reality" was launched in 1989 by Jaron Lanier and has become a common expression, along with "cyberspace," "Internet," and hundreds of other "Web" terms and abbreviations. Virtual reality—the process of making something seem so real that our normal senses are fooled—includes an aspect of hallucination. It's the same principle used by phone-sex women: words, heavy breathing, and voice tones to convey an idea, a mood—a reality that doesn't exist.[5]

VR causes the Internet affair to appear real, so much so that marriages are breaking up as "Net" junkies run off to find their keyboard virtual lovers. Books, radio, drama, and *Playboy* magazine all count on the human mind to fill in the gaps and make partial truth appear to be tangible truth.

Face it, guys. "Miss October," the *Playboy* college beauty from the Midwest, is not really undressing in your bedroom. In fact, if you met her on an airplane, she wouldn't give you the time of day. But neither would the late-night Internet sex bomb really go to bed with you unless you paid. It's a dream world—but a powerful one built on the vacuums in our own minds and experience.

Perhaps the most common cause for the midlife affair

is a desperate urgency to solve the trauma of lost youth and masculinity. One man told me, "When I used to meet a good-looking young woman on the street, there was a sort of spark between us—a message that we both found the other attractive. Now they don't even acknowledge my existence—they look at me as if I'm a telephone pole."

## The Available Mistress

The man in midlife crisis is an unhappy man. He has a spiritual and emotional vacuum in his personality. Something or someone has to meet the needs of this man, and most surely someone will. Unfortunately, there are women who also have problems and are looking for solutions to their troubles.

The unhappy man in midlife doesn't set out in a careful search for the best possible person to meet the needs of his life. Statistics show that he starts an affair with someone who is readily available. This is the reason for the office romance. There is opportunity, a shared work experience, and a degree of trust and mutual respect. It is convenient to share common anxieties and stresses. The affair generally starts out with a simple sharing of problems. Then the relationship deepens and moves toward a physical context.

This same sharing and building of trust is happening in chat rooms on the Internet. The article "Virtual Liaison," which appeared in *The Orange County Register*, asked the question, "Is a sexual encounter on-line an act of adultery?" When is it adultery—a flirtatious smile, an intimate dinner, a hug, a kiss, petting, or is it when there has been sexual penetration? "No question that virtual infidelity can lead to the real thing. Everyone has a story about people who met on the Net, had passionate conversations and cybersex, then moved on to real-life adulterous liaisons. Author Tom Clancy's wife is suing him for divorce because of what happened between him and a woman he met on-line."[6]

The Internet is forcing people to rethink what is sex—can it be just passion created by words in a cyberspace chat room? Or are these virtual reality experiences becoming real-life affairs which are drawing people away from working on their marriage?

## A Vacuum Is Dangerous

Over the years I have counseled many men and women involved in affairs. Always there has been a vacuum, an unhappiness, that prepared them for the affair. Then someone has been readily available. The relationship started with light social discussions that became more meaningful as the couple spent more time together.

A dentist begins to spend time with his hygienist, talking about the work at the office and his own personal life. A businessman finds it convenient to talk to one of the women who works in his company. A neighbor begins to talk to his neighbor, and they share some basics about gardening. A deacon in the church decides to carry out the spiritual ministry of helping widows and so begins doing some of the maintenance around a widow's house. A minister begins to chat on-line with a friendly woman—someone he can talk to who is not in his church.

The list is almost endless, but the patterns are always the same. An emotional-spiritual vacuum attracts other persons who also have a vacuum. Their deep, caring relationship leads to an emotional and physical affair. Typically they already know each other and have a close, convenient opportunity to share their experiences.

David's affair followed the same pattern. The Bible says, "One night he couldn't get to sleep and went for a stroll on the roof of the palace. As he looked out over the city, he noticed a woman of unusual beauty taking her evening bath. He sent to find out who she was and was told that she was Bathsheba" (2 Sam. 11:2-3).

David had been exposed to many women. In fact, he had a harem of beautiful women living in the palace. Why was this woman different? Because David was different! David was emotionally prepared for an affair—and Bathsheba just happened to be available.

### The Affair and the Marriage

Affairs seem to take one of three general directions. One, the man has an affair or a series of affairs, decides that's not what he wants, and settles down again with his wife in a more successful marriage than he had experienced before.

Two, the man has an affair, comes back to his wife, but doesn't resolve the problems that caused the marital vacuum in the first place, or she will not really forgive him. The marriage may be reestablished, but it is not secure, and in coming months or years it breaks apart again. Sometimes this is the final break, other times it is only one of a series of breaks.

The third outcome is that a man decides the new woman is superior to his wife, so he files for a divorce. Or the wife may decide that she cannot live with a man who has had an affair, and she files for a divorce.

## How Society Views the Affair

Society offers a strange and mixed bag of responses. On the one hand, people seem fascinated with affairs, but they are extremely judgmental of anyone who gets caught. Society also feels that if a man in his twenties is fooling around sexually, married or unmarried, he is cool and normal, but at forty-five, a man should remember he is a family man.

Over the years some writers have proposed a free-love approach to marriage. They argue that only cultural prejudice ties sex to love and marriage—and sexual fidelity is essentially a property right and therefore dehumanizing. If a marriage is to survive, they reason, the partners must go outside for a broader experience, enrichment, and growth. Marriage counselors, on the other hand, generally have found that free love only creates more problems.

God, who has a fair degree of insight into people because He is their Creator, planned that husband and wife should have a commitment *only* to each other all through their lives. When we divorce sex from love and commitment, sex loses its ability to satisfy. In our book *Pure Pleasure* we point out that some men in our society have become increasingly jaded and need more sex and novelty to satisfy their distorted personalities.[7]

From the beginning of life, a child connects the sensory good feelings of the mother's breast with his feeling of being loved. As he grows, he learns that his coming into the world was part of the expression of his mother and father loving each other and committing themselves to stay together to care for him. In adulthood there are deep-seated, unconscious convictions that sex is related to commitment.

## The Lover Wants Commitment

People don't really get what they hope for in an affair. One or perhaps both partners originally thought the affair would be just a passing thing, providing some physical release and an opportunity to share happiness. Most men think of an affair as a weekend vacation, not a move to Europe. However, the more time they spend together, the more a need for commitment grows.

I know two different young women in affairs who were each angry at their lovers because these men continued to have sexual relationships with their wives! The men couldn't understand what was happening—these young women were asking for commitment. I have also watched the pattern in reverse, where a man becomes furious when his mistress has an occasional *extra affair* in the middle of the affair he is having with her. He tries to get her to stop. He wants to own her and force her to be committed only to him.

## Everyone Is *Not* Doing It

If we truly believed the media information, it would be easy to conclude that every man in midlife, age thirty-five to fifty-five, is involved in an affair. That is not at all the case.

A study done by Chicago social scientist Tom W. Smith disputes the popular notion that "everyone is doing it." He says, "There are probably more scientifically worthless 'facts' on extramarital relations than on any other facet of human behavior."[8]

He was very critical of Morton Hunt, Shere Hite, and Joyce Brothers who have reported that as many as 70 percent of married people commit adultery.

"The best estimates are that 3 to 4 percent of currently married people have a sexual partner besides their spouse in a given year."[9]

Dr. Harry J. Johnson in *Executive Lifestyles* has noticed that as income rises, the tendency for affairs increases. Thirty-two percent of the men in the higher brackets were involved in affairs.[10]

## Bathsheba Had Problems

David's affair with Bathsheba appeared to be a one-night stand. David saw this attractive female body and wanted it—not her—it. Perhaps he felt that the novelty would relieve some of the pressures he felt. "Then David sent for her and when she came he slept with her. . . . Then she returned home" (2 Sam. 11: 4).

As I mentioned earlier, David was prepared for the affair. But so was Bathsheba. Her husband was off at war. She was alone. Needs in her life were going unmet. It was not simply that the king was calling for her. She was making herself available to him. After all, she was taking her bath close to his bedroom rooftop view. This also fits the pattern—the woman who is available for the affair has some emotional needs in her own life that she is seeking to satisfy.

## Neurotics Attract Neurotics

The young woman who gets into an affair with a midlife man typically has at least one of the following problems—a lack of connection with her parents, especially her father; sexual molestation as a child; an extremely low self-image; psychological immaturity.

The affair between a midlife man and a younger

woman is almost always marked by an emotionally needy young woman. If a young woman is partially emotionally stable, she automatically avoids the midlife man's hopeless troubles and the problems inherent in a relationship with him. The midlife man who is looking for a better relationship than his present marriage is fighting insurmountable odds.

## Affairs Produce Stress

Most midlife men involved in an affair think they are reducing their pain with this new woman, but only find an intensified pressure. Even though they say there is a great spark and newness they have not felt for years, they are not really facing the increased internal pressure of trying to live two lives.

Some men try to handle the conflicting emotions by becoming a Dr. Jekyll and Mr. Hyde. They take on one lifestyle with their wife and totally block out the other life. When they are with their mistress, they become another person, mentally blotting out the life with their wife. By these mental gymnastics the midlife man hopes he will not be forced to choose one or the other. He hopes he can live without unifying his two personalities.

## How Did He Get So Involved?

Soon the affair grows beyond his original expectations. It was supposed to be a brief, casual, bright interlude in his life—a vacation. But now it has become something more. She wants more from him—commitment.

It was so in David's case. He had counted on a one-night stand, but then a note was placed in his hands by a messenger. His heart must have skipped several beats and his face turned white as he read that Bathsheba was pregnant. The one-night stand had become drastically more serious than the casual event he had planned.

Now there is an additional conflict. It is fairly common knowledge that "men give love to get sex" and "women give sex to get love." So the man in an affair must convince the woman that he really cares for her in order to have a satisfying sexual relationship. One of the basic premises of a "good affair" is that he is not buying a woman, he is developing a relationship—which may lead into a sexual contact. For most women, a live, vital, enthusiastic sexual relationship is only possible if they feel a deep sense of acceptance and warmth. Otherwise, they feel they are nothing more than a streetwalker.

The midlife man likely will be preoccupied with this new relationship. Affairs, virtual or real, take a great deal of daydream time and money. In fact, the affair may be draining more energy away from his marriage and family than he wants. He only wanted a brief affair, a few nights at an out-of-town motel, a little late-night lusting on his computer, just a little sex and understanding—but it has grown beyond his original plan.

## Destructive Risks

The risks of an affair—in any form—are enormous. Marriage, children, extended family, friends, work performance, even volunteer organizations, all take a hit from the fallout of the affair.

But the midlife man is so driven that he doesn't care about any of the costs. He only wonders, "Where can I find safe sex?" Where—a bar, a topless club, with one of the women at the office, maybe the woman in the church choir, or why not the neighbor?

In his desperation he pushes out of his mind the knowledge that sexually transmitted diseases (STDs) are so very common. A male doctor (OBGYN) in Orange County, California told a woman patient he was trying to reassure that 60 percent of the women in his practice had some type of STD. But it won't happen to our midlife man. He'll use a condom—although most men hate them and often at the last minute decide to risk an STD.

But greater than all of these potential physical hazards is the damage to the two people involved in the affair. They start to live a distorted lifestyle of lies, secret meetings, and trying to remember which excuse they used last time. They begin to change reality within themselves—ultimately lying to themselves.

### Rejection and No Erection

On top of all this there are the great risks involved for the midlife man who pursues a younger woman. She may reject him for a younger man. Society may reject him, even though society is preoccupied and tantalized by such affairs. Then there is the constant awareness that the affair is a violation of God's truth.

And horror of horrors, he may have psychological damage if he is unable to perform sexually. One man asked me about his mistress, "Why can't I keep my erection when I'm with Lisa?" He was worried about losing his potency. With his wife he had no sexual problems at all. Another man told me the opposite was happening to him. As soon as he started the affair, he was not able to have sex with his wife. Both of these men were experiencing psychological damage caused by affairs.

Years ago Gail Sheehy wrote in Passages about the two risks that the midlife man may face: "Today the silvery-sideburned sexual hunter finds himself in competition with younger men who can pick up from one good porn film the technique it took their elders years to acquire. And among the current generation of young women, he is apt to find an aggressive bluntness that is positively shriveling in bed."[11]

## The Mistress Suffers

There is also the risk of damage for the mistress. I knew two young women, both in their early thirties, who were trying to work through such damage. Both of these women had abortions, along with a great deal of emotional and spiritual trauma. Neither of them wanted the abortion but felt it was the only way to keep their "love" relationship. Tragically, neither of these women married the man in their affair, but only experienced hurt and distress as the relationships fell apart. One of them later was unable to have children.

## The Affair Collapses

Another major problem is that an affair needs security to continue. Yet by its very definition, it is a liaison that lacks security. People having an affair cannot allow that relationship to develop beyond the superficial. They have very limited activities, are ashamed to let the community know about their affair, and they feel guilty before God. After all, you can't take your lover to church, introduce her to your small Bible group, or even take her home to meet Mom. You might talk secretly at a private little restaurant, and then go to bed. But the scope of your affair is extremely narrow, and the secrecy will ultimately destroy the affair.

The midlife man is trying to escape the monotony and boredom of his marriage. But he soon finds that he has reproduced the same tediousness in the affair. The new monotony is even more intense, because the affair doesn't have the potential to grow into a broad relationship providing variety, sparkle, and ultimate security. Quite often when the affair becomes publicly known, the couple tries to build a broader relationship. Sadly they discover that in the light of day they don't like each other.

Bernice Neugarten, former professor of human development at the University of Chicago, studied the lives of midlife people for over twenty years. She says that intimacy can be quickly attained. But people are looking for something more than immediate intimacy. "You can go to bed with someone," she says, "but that somehow doesn't dismiss the need for the long-standing relationship—you still want to go home to someone who has known you for twenty-five years."[12]

> There was a time when I wouldn't admit what a sinner I was. But my dishonesty made me miserable and filled my days with frustration. All day and all night your hand was heavy on me. My strength evaporated like water on a sunny day until I finally admitted all my sins to you and stopped trying to hide them. I said to myself, "I will confess them to the Lord." And you forgave me! All my guilt is gone.
>
> Psalm 32:3-5 NLT

# 1 1

# Escaping the Affair

AT FIRST THE AFFAIR SEEMS to be so great. This wonderful woman is available, and she seems to meet the midlife man's needs. For perhaps the first time since he was dating his wife, he feels as if he is living in absolute bliss. But a change is in the wind. Because of increasing dissatisfaction with this new woman's habits, and the demands she puts on him, the affair begins to disintegrate. The midlife man now is looking for a way out, and the affair moves toward disengagement.

David first attempted to solve his problem with Bathsheba by ordering her husband Uriah to return home from battle. He hoped that while Uriah was home, they would have sexual intercourse, thus solving David's problem. Uriah would believe the child was his, and David could easily disengage from the affair.

But the Bible tells us that Uriah didn't go home: "He stayed that night at the gateway of the palace with the other servants of the king" (2 Sam. 11: 9 ). The next day David learned that Uriah hadn't gone home nor slept with his wife. When David called Uriah and asked him why not, Uriah responded that he couldn't go home and sleep with his wife when his men were out facing the battle. David then invited him to dinner, got him drunk, hoping this would prepare him to go home and sleep with his wife. But again Uriah refused and slept at the entry to the palace.

### Disengaging Is Difficult

The process of becoming detached from the affair is extremely complicated, and many people get hurt. In David's case, he wrote a letter the next morning to Joab, the commander of the army, instructing him to "put Uriah at the front of the hottest part of the battle—and then pull back and leave him there to die! So Joab assigned Uriah to a spot close to the besieged city where he knew that the enemies' best men were fighting; and Uriah was killed along with several other Israeli soldiers" (2 Sam. 11: 15-17).

David's attempt to disengage from the affair had now led him into a murder conspiracy, and to the actual death of Uriah and other innocent men who were with Uriah.

### What Will Help Disengagement?

Disconnecting is generally painful for most men. I remember an old movie in which a midlife man had taken his mistress on a vacation. While there he ran into a close friend who also knew his wife. The man in midlife introduced his young mistress as his secretary who had dropped by for the afternoon to take dictation and have dinner with him.

Later that evening the friend confronted the man and said, "You must make a break!"

"But how can I make a break?" the man asked.

Then the friend gave him the crucial information. "You must create a situation that makes each of you so dissatisfied with the relationship that you won't keep hanging onto the affair."

The movie depicts the trapped feeling many people experience in an affair. After a while most men having an affair want out—but don't know how to get out. They experience great stress because they are unable to disengage.

## Confront the Unreality

All affairs are illusions! It may be a secret meeting in an out-of-the-way motel, a weekend "business trip," a late-night steamy session in the chat room on the Internet, sexual fantasizing over a *Playboy* centerfold, or just plain lusting over a woman at the office. All these are unreal fantasies! It's the falseness that keeps the affair going. Tragically, some men become so connected to the unreal fantasy world that they become addicted to it.

A few years ago Sally and I had the great adventure of rafting for a week down the rapids of the Colorado River. One of the rapids fell thirty-seven feet. Wow, that was heart stopping—and it was real! We also explored an out-of-the-way waterfall, slid down rushing streams without a raft, ate fresh pink trout, and slept out under the stars for six nights on a sandbar with the sound of the rushing river only yards away.

Now which is better? Taking a trip down the Colorado in person—or viewing it on a CD-ROM on your computer? You can get the information about the river from the computer—but you can't really experience the river. The same is true with an affair. When you turn off the computer, close the magazine, turn off the porn Playboy channel, you are still left with only your false world and your lonely life. Even if you start a motel romance, the next day she puts on her clothes and walks out the door. She is not yours—she is only a fantasy!

What you really want is a loving wife who is a great companion for all of your life. You want great sex without guilt, warm arms to hug you as you drop off to sleep, and a smiling face in the morning to remind you that God has given you this special woman—and you have the rest of your lives to share.

Go for the *real*—not the affair!

## False Objections

The major problem in disengagement is that there is no easy way to become disentangled. Everyone gets hurt in the process. The unwillingness to be hurt, or to hurt someone else, often keeps people in a relationship far beyond the initial reasons that drew them together.

I have received the strangest excuses as I've encouraged midlife men to break off the affair. Many are religious men who have made a personal commitment to God. It's often confusing and pathetically laughable to hear their moral dilemma. They are committing adultery—yet they seem so spiritually concerned.

> "Well, you see, I have led this woman to a personal relationship with Christ, and I feel I would be abandoning her spiritually if I would leave her."

> "I've become so attached to her children, and they treat me as their father. I would hurt the children if I left."

"I just can't tell her I don't love her anymore—
she would be shattered."

"I've taken her into my business, and the only
way out is to fire her or buy out her shares."

I have helped both Christians and non-Christians
through the painful disengagement process. *None* of
these people has been willing to disengage simply
because of the clear moral teaching of Scripture—"You
must not commit adultery." Nor have any of these
midlife men been convinced to disengage because of
obligations to their families or previous commitments. It
is my experience that people are only ready to disengage
from an affair if the dissatisfaction level rises high
enough so that the couple feels there is greater stress and
less satisfaction than what they had hoped for.

## Healing After the Affair

During the last stages of an affair, and certainly afterward, emotions such as guilt and anger must be worked
through. Often the healing should include not only the
two people in the affair, but also other members of the
family and friends.

David thought he had solved his problem by arranging for Bathsheba's husband to be killed and then by
making her one of his wives. But David still had a great
deal of guilt to be settled. He wrote Psalm 32 soon after
his affair: "There was a time when I wouldn't admit what
a sinner I was. But my dishonesty made me miserable
and filled my days with frustration. All day and all night
your hand was heavy on me. My strength evaporated
like water on a sunny day until I finally admitted all my
sins to you and stopped trying to hide them. I said to

myself, 'I will confess them to the Lord.' And you forgave me! All my guilt is gone" (Ps. 32:3-5).

## The Healing of Guilt

David couldn't seem to work through his guilt by himself. It was necessary for God to send Nathan the prophet. When Nathan confronted him, David was then able to say, "I have sinned against the Lord." Nathan's reply from God was, "Yes, but the Lord has forgiven you, and you won't die for this sin. But you have given great opportunity to the enemies of the Lord to despise and blaspheme him, so your child shall die" (2 Sam. 12:13-14).

For David to return to a state of emotional and spiritual health, he had to work through the guilt by first owning it as his responsibility, and then confessing it to God. Furthermore, he also had to accept the forgiveness God offered and realize he was cleansed and forgiven. In Psalm 32:7-8 David accepts forgiveness from God, and God again directs his life: "You are my hiding place from every storm of life; you even keep me from getting into trouble! You surround me with songs of victory. I will instruct you (says the Lord) and guide you along the best pathway for your life; I will advise you and watch your progress" (Ps. 32:7-8).

## Accepting Forgiveness

After an affair, many people find it difficult to forgive themselves. They may be willing to acknowledge the problem and be able to confess it to God and to others. They may also know intellectually they are forgiven by God. But until they can emotionally accept God's forgiveness and forgive themselves, they will not experience total healing.

A man recovering from an affair should read through the Psalms of the Old Testament and consciously visualize God speaking directly to him. It's also a help to read the four Gospels in the New Testament, watching specifically the way Jesus worked with people. Then remember Jesus' words, "Anyone who has seen me has seen the Father!" (John 14:9).

As we understand the life, ministry, and kindness of Jesus, we see an expression of God's concern for men. Repeatedly, Jesus is shown as caring for people who were the moral rejects of society. He offered them forgiveness, love, and acceptance. He invited them to become part of his family. The Scripture says it in a nutshell: "So if the Son sets you free, you will indeed be free" (John 8:36). David accepted God's deep forgiveness for his several sins related to his affair with Bathsheba. It is also what every midlife man in an affair needs to experience.

## The Healing of Others

David was not alone in this affair. Nor was Bathsheba the only other person. Several others were hurt. In David's case, the child born to Bathsheba died shortly after birth, and there was the shame which the enemies of God used as an opportunity to mock God.

The children of a man involved in a midlife affair also need healing. Sociologists now estimate that between twenty-five and fifty million children will be raised by one parent during the first eighteen years of their life because of divorce. Whether or not the affair leads to a divorce, the midlife affair is especially hard on adolescent children, who are learning from their parents the concepts of sexuality, care, love, and commitment. My ten-year research on the effects of divorce discovered that these children tend to experience an increased level of vulnerability to stress, feelings of emptiness, uncontrollable rage, worry, isolation, and bitterness. They also feel insecure, are controllers, frequently are immoral, and have trouble themselves with marital commitment.[1]

Teenagers often feel betrayed because a parent who has led them in one direction is himself moving in a different direction. Their concepts of love and trust are often shattered. They may look at love now as a weapon to be used against people. Or they may see love as a trap and determine never to be ensnared.

The wife also needs healing following an affair. Her greatest fear may have been being replaced by another woman. Her self-image has taken a beating. She might experience a time of being bitterly immobilized by terror. The closer the couple were to each other before the affair, the more destructive the affair will be to both partners.

It will help if the wife can keep perspective and realize this affair is probably just that—a temporary affair that will soon be over. If she can temporarily put up with his craziness and work at areas in her life that need improvement, then she will be able to accelerate the healing in both of them.

But it's painful for a wife to put up with all this deception. In the article "Confessions of An Internet Widow," Cotton Ward quotes a woman who pinpoints the pain caused by a "Net" affair: "The worst thing was that he was using the computer all through the night. Now I know he was chatting to her while I was falling asleep, waiting for him to come to bed."[2]

This short-range affair probably was brought to the surface by anxieties the midlife man had—his fading youth, fear about sexuality, concern about work, or just the impending awareness of death. It will help her to realize he must work through these problems. The affair was the wrong way to do it, but the affair will lose its power as the problems begin to be resolved.

Our society teaches men to be strong and have no needs. Yet many midlife men have a great deal of stress. Often they are about to come unglued, and need to talk with someone. Our culture also conditions men not to be close friends with other men—at least not to the extent of a deep sharing of intimate problems. Men have been trained from childhood to be open with their mothers but not with their fathers.

The natural outlet for the man in our society, therefore, is to seek a female to share his concerns. If the wife can understand her husband's need at this time, she can gently start to talk about his feelings as she draws her husband out. She can also encourage his male friends to connect with him in greater depth.

The wife also must realize she is in competition with the other woman. It is an unfair competition—but nevertheless it is a competition. The other woman never talks about problems, such as the appliances to be repaired or mounting bills. She doesn't nag or scold. She always seems to have a listening ear, to be patient, and understanding. She also admires, appreciates, and flatters him.

The other woman is a sharp contrast to the pressure a husband is experiencing at home. If his wife realizes the contrast, she can alter the way she relates to her husband.

She can build his ego as a man, a businessman, a father, and as a husband. Hopefully he will begin to see his wife as a helpful friend who appreciates him—not just as the one making demands on his life.

## Counseling Can Help

There are causes for this change in her husband's behavior. A counselor can give her insight on the dynamics of their relationship. The counselor may be able to point out areas in which she can improve. He may help her to discover causes for stress in the marriage. As she understands her husband and the dynamics of their marriage, she may find her husband willing to become involved in counseling.

It takes a number of months, perhaps years, for a man to work through his midlife crisis. If the wife uses this time to develop her own life, as well as the marriage, it will give her a sense of achievement and diminish her own self-pity. She will become a stronger, more effective person with a greater sense of purpose when the midlife stress period has ended.

Wives react many different ways when they find out a husband has been unfaithful. Sometimes Christian women condemn and hold up the moral standard of the Bible—faithfulness and no adultery. Without question, adultery is wrong! Too often, however, when the wife discovers infidelity, she reacts with natural hurt and uses the moral teaching of the Bible as a club on her husband and a shield against her pain. Sadly, in some cases the biblical standards act as a security blanket to cover the guilt she feels for contributing to the causes of the infidelity.

When an affair is discovered, understanding and forgiveness—not condemnation—are most needed. The couple must then talk to each other and find the causes and the solutions, so the marriage can become a new and stronger relationship with greater communication and care.

## Honesty Can Help

Honesty always comes up as we talk about the healing after an affair. There is probably no general statement that can be made, such as, "Tell everything—in every detail," or "Tell nothing." Each couple and each situation will have to be treated individually. Ideally, it would be good if a couple were strong enough to share what had happened without further damage. In reality, many people cannot stand that kind of truth. Judith Viorst writes about making her husband promise to always tell the full truth in all cases, no matter how unpleasant—and then she wonders, "How come he thought I meant it?"[3]

Many people say they want the truth, but in reality, they don't know how much of the truth they can stand. After a man has confessed his affair to his wife, she may be able to forgive—but she'll never be able to forget. It's not only the shock of truth, but living with it years after.

Often midlife couples who are having marital stress honestly don't want to tell each other how they feel. They are afraid to rock the boat. As one man told me, "I'm not telling my wife how I feel toward any other women, or our marriage—and she's not pushing me to talk about it either." Neither do they share with friends—they carry the pain silently. Each one of them, however, is crying on the inside. They each have decided to carry on life as usual. This couple's choice not to talk pushes them further apart. Each concludes they really have nothing in common—so why stay together?

## Fear Won't Help

The fear of making things worse by honesty is the real fear. If, however, there is forgiveness and continued communication and affirmation of each other, then the marriage can stand a great degree of honesty.

A midlife pastor friend shared with me the increasing problem he was having with lust. He was repeatedly fantasizing about other women. The problem became so bad that he decided to talk to a Christian psychologist. The psychologist told him the next time they got together he wanted him to have told his wife about his lust problem. My friend asked, "How in the world can I share my lust problem with my wife? Do I just walk up to her and say, 'You know, I'm really turned on by Mary Jane. I keep dreaming about being in bed with her.' When do I share this with her? At night, when I'm snuggling with her? Over a cup of coffee at breakfast? How can I share something as threatening as lust with my wife?"

When he went back to the psychologist, my friend told him that he had tried, but he simply could not do it. The words just got stuck in his mouth. The psychologist said he didn't want to see him again until he had shared this with his wife. So the man finally took his wife out to dinner, and after they had a delightful meal and talked about a lot of other nice things, he told her that there was something he wanted to tell her.

After several minutes of beating around the bush, he finally blurted out, "This might surprise you, but I'm really attracted to other women. They really turn me on."

His wife smiled pleasantly and said, "So what else is new?"

He couldn't believe she knew he was attracted to other women. And beyond that, he couldn't believe she would understand. As they talked, they came to realize that each of them was attracted and sexually aroused by other people. Out of that discussion, they recommitted themselves to total fidelity to each other.

A man in counseling shared with his counselor his wife's strength when she discovered his affair, saying, "I'll never forget how Alice behaved when my sordid little affair with the girl at the office blew up in her face. I knew it must be hurting her terribly—but she didn't whine and she didn't lash out. She sat me down, looked me straight in the eyes, and asked me where she had gone wrong and what this girl had she didn't. From that moment the other girl didn't have a chance."[4]

## The Private Self

Each one of us has a private self we never really share with anyone—except perhaps God. It isn't wrong to have a private self. Yet if we allow the private self to become an excuse or an escape from the growth of marital intimacy, then it will inevitably drive the couple apart.

Many, if not most marriages, start on the basis of dishonesty. From the beginning the couple hide thoughts and habits they are afraid will hurt the other person, or might cause the other person not to like them. Many marriages exist for years behind this unfortunate black curtain of fear and dishonesty.

I have lived most of my married life with a fear of letting Sally know some of my own feelings about our marriage, about her, about myself, and about other women. Every now and then I take courage and tell her a little bit more about who I really am. Each time I am afraid, and on many occasions she has been terribly hurt. My openness has also helped her to be more open to me. But the overall result is that we know each other better and our marriage relationship has improved.

Sometimes it is better that certain items are never shared, but simply laid at the feet of God. He alone can provide forgiveness. For example, if an "honesty session" becomes a time to unload our guilt, then we may be loading up the other person with a great deal of stress. Generally, however, I think that most couples should push the frontier of honesty. By doing that they will find greater healing in their relationship, especially during the midlife crisis.

Honesty doesn't mean you tell all the details of your sexual affair, but honesty should push you each to talk about your insecurities and childhood fears. Honesty should also lead you to appreciate the strengths that drew you to each other in marriage. Most people are afraid of honesty—when in truth honesty will bring healing and closeness. The focus of honesty should always be our own errors, weaknesses, failure, and needs—not the mate's. As each one confesses and shares, a new bond of depth will develop which will carry the couple through future stresses.

Sadly, the man in midlife hopes a love affair will somehow help him in the struggle to remain young. He thinks that having a close, caring, alive relationship with a woman will revitalize his whole stale personality—and for a time it does. But the world can't be stopped, nor can he will himself to be younger. Whether he likes it or not, "the sun calmly continues to rise. And we are all, in love or not, a day older. . . ."[5]

> Create in me a new, clean heart, O God, filled with clean thoughts and right desires. Don't toss me aside, banished forever from your presence. Don't take your Holy Spirit from me. Restore to me again the joy of your salvation, and make me willing to obey you.
>
> Psalm 51:10-12

## For Further Reading

*Healing Life's Hidden Addictions* by Archibald Hart (Ann Arbor, MI: Servant Publications, 1990).

*Moving on After He Moves Out* by Jim and Sally Conway (Downers Grove, IL: InterVarsity Press, 1995).

*Torn Asunder* by Dave Carder (Chicago, IL: Moody Press, 1992).

"Virtuality and Its Discontents" by Sherry Turkle in *The American Prospect*, Winter 1996. This is a great article that confronts the falseness of computer relationships.

*When Men Think Private Thoughts* by Gordon MacDonald (Nashville, TN: Thomas Nelson Publishers, 1996).

*When a Mate Wants Out* by Jim and Sally Conway (Grand Rapids, MI: Zondervan Publishing, 1992).

# 12

# A New God

SO FAR, NOTHING HAS HELPED our man escape this intense grinding emotional oppression that has captured him like a giant bogeyman in the night. Depression and alcohol only intensified his problem. A new body, new clothes, new lifestyle, new job, new wife, and even his affair proved to be a mixed bag, providing temporary relief but no lasting solutions.

Now he may try one more solution. If he has been a religious man, he may very well declare that the God of his youth and young adulthood is dead, or at least has been ineffective to meet the needs of his life. Or he may decide to be liberated from any god. On the other hand, he may have been a nonreligious person. He may now conclude the reason for the emptiness and tragedy of his life has been that he has excluded God. Now he may declare God to be alive, and determine to follow Him with all of his life.

In recent years there have appeared a succession of articles talking about ministers dropping out. These articles pointed out the impossibility of the average minister to meet all the needs of all his church, as well as his personal needs. The midlife minister experiences many of the same traumas of men in other professions and businesses. Being a minister does not guarantee he will miss the dreaded midlife plague. Many pastors who are victims of midlife crisis are unable to share their crisis with their people and still feel accepted by them. They think their people expect them to be more than human.

## Fence Hopping

For example, two of my friends, both of whom were ministers, dropped out during their midlife era. One of them still has a very vital relationship with God. The other one, however, struggled with his relationship and at one point said, "I want to follow a new god—or no god."

What a strange fence-hopping process can take place at midlife! Men who are identified as "spiritual" may jump over the fence and become followers of a new god or no god, while men who have followed no god suddenly become God-conscious. However, a midlife crisis is bigger than simply deciding to be religious or not be religious. Without doubt, a vital personal relationship with God will give strength for solving human problems. But simply being a religious person, even a "born-again Christian," does not exempt the midlife man from problems.

Sometimes wives are caught in this trap. They think, "If only I could get my husband to start going to church, then all of his problems will be solved." Certainly, he will have a stronger base from which to solve problems, but he will still have problems. If a person becomes a Christian in order not to face his problems, he probably will be disillusioned. He may later turn his back on God, saying God failed him. It was not God who failed, but the man hiding behind a religious experience who was unwilling to work with God toward the solution of his midlife problems.

## Maybe a New God

This new god for some midlife men is called indulgence. It is the god of pleasure, luxury, gusto, comfort, ease, sensuality—the god of hedonism. The reasoning goes something like this: "I've worked hard all of my life. I obeyed my parents—I ate my brussels sprouts. I did what I was supposed to do in school. I went to church like a good little boy, went to college, got a good job, got married and settled down as society expected. I started a family, bought a house in the suburbs, and even got a second car. I took out life insurance and started retirement funds. I became respectable in the community, was a member of PTA, the Jaycees, and the local church board. I worked hard at my job. Now I'm vice-president in charge of sales in a four-state area.

"I've paid for braces, guitar lessons, and gymnastics lessons. I bought four different stages of bicycles and got new computers every few years. I've footed the bills for all kinds of trips and vacations. And I'm carrying a big load to make sure my kids get a good college education.

"I'm tired of doing all this!! It's time I get some pleasure out of life. It's time for me to indulge myself. I'm going to follow a new lifestyle that does not include the god of sacrifice. I'm going to start using my money for my pleasure, my leisure, to get my freedom! I'm going to get me the kind of intimacy, sex, and pleasure that I want.

God has talked to me all my life about serving other people, giving to other people, supporting other people. Now it's time for *me* to be served!"

We have a little joke in our family: when a person who feels overworked and full of self-pity says, "I've worked my fingers to the bone, and what do I get for it?", the rest of the family joins in cheerfully and yells, "Bony fingers!" Some men see a deep conflict between a God of self-sacrifice and their personal needs. Some midlife men only know God in a narrow way. They think God could never laugh or have fun. Therefore, they conclude they need a new god of indulgence and pleasure. This attempted solution of a new god is really a rebellion—sometimes passive rebellion, but often open anger and rejection.

## Maybe No God

Our midlife man has heard about God ever since he was a child. God was a miraculous person who always did only good things for him. God was sort of a combination Santa Claus, Easter Bunny, and Tooth Fairy wrapped into one. God was only there to help him when he had problems, to give him the answers for tests, to help him win baseball games, to forgive him when he needed forgiveness. But now, God is letting him down. Why are all these troubles and frustrations coming to his life? God must be dead—or He is so inept he can't provide positive solutions for midlife.

This man has a distorted view of God and His purposes. When God doesn't do what he expects, he declares that God is not alive. This problem has been prevalent throughout history. After Jesus Christ was crucified and came back to life, He walked unrecognized along the road with two of His disciples on their way to Emmaus. They said, "We had thought he was the glorious Messiah and that he had come to rescue Israel" (Luke 24:21). These two disciples were disappointed because Jesus had not performed the way they had anticipated. Later in the story, Jesus revealed Himself. In their new understanding of Jesus Christ, they again became His followers, and their whole perspective was changed.

Some men are caught in the same kind of situation. Their distorted view of God, and what it means to serve God, has led them to be disappointed. Ultimately they decide that God is not worthy of their allegiance.

Many of us have been taught from our previous church experiences that if we act good, such as by going to church, then God will reward us with blessings. We reason, "The more a man serves God and sacrifices for Him, the more good he will receive." But God wants a relationship—not religious activities. Years ago, in the Old Testament, God repeatedly told the people He wanted more than their outward worship of sacrifices. He wanted a heart relationship. (See 1 Sam. 15:22 and Ps. 51:16-17.)

### The Process Is the Message

The man in midlife is caught in the American dream, even in his religious life; God is a person to be manipulated to our own ultimate satisfaction. The end product is the important thing—the method of getting there is relatively unimportant. To God, however, the process of moving through life is as important as the end result.

So Jesus encouraged us to trust our day-by-day affairs to God, to live life one day at a time, and to trust both the past and our future to God. Romans 8:28 tells us that "all that happens to us is working for our good." That means God doesn't avoid pain to accomplish our growth. He uses all of life, including midlife pain, to help us develop our character.

At this stage in the midlife crisis, when a man wants to indulge himself and establish his own autonomy, he will probably continue to say there is no God, or he will follow a new pleasure god of his own making.

If he decides to follow no god, his big loss is communication with God. A midlife man is in the greatest turmoil of his life. What he needs most is someone to understand and support him—yet not demean him. Sadly, the midlife man will decide to solve his problems by isolating himself from others—including God.

Men learn early not to share their problems with other people. Somehow it's not macho and shows weakness. They think by midlife they're supposed to have it all together. Our hero is caught in the middle. Even his solutions don't seem to work. So he isolates himself from familiar surroundings, from those who can help and care for him—such as God.

### How to Connect with God

However, suppose you have decided not to throw God away. You've decided to seriously connect with God—or reconnect in a deeper way. Following is a pattern I've shared with many men who are ready to get serious with God. I've deliberately tried to take out all of the "churchy" or religious words.

Your spiritual link with God is an admission that you are surrendering control of your life with its successes and hurts to Him. You are admitting you do not have the ability to change your own life. I've found it helpful to think of this linking with God in two separate ways: the initial contact and the sustained contact.

1. *The Initial Contact:* First, find a quiet place alone, allow your body to slow down and your mind to become restful. For me it's helpful to imagine that I'm sitting on an empty beach, looking out at the ocean and the endless horizon. I'm conscious of the waves continuing their march to the shore, but I deliberately block out all the city life and my own business. I let my mind become quiet. Some people find it helpful to think of sitting in front of a fire or looking into a moonless sky. Whatever it is, first let yourself become quiet.

Now in this quietness, visualize the friendly face of God. Then speak directly to Him, "God, I am powerless. I've tried unsuccessfully for years to overcome my past. I need Your help.

"I'm sorry for keeping You out of my life. I'm sorry I didn't even think about You as being able to help me with this situation.

"Please forgive me. Come into my life. Be God in me, instead of just God to the world in general. Please increase my sensitivity to spiritual things. I do intend to follow the spiritual directions and insights that You give me. I'm open for You to lead me and heal me."

Use your own words. Enlarge on my suggestions in any way you want.

Next, you may want to dump out some of your frustrations, or talk about the inadequacies of your life and your inability to cope. It's extremely important that you tell God whatever comes to your mind. This is not the time to pretend or play tough guy. This is the time to let it all hang out. Be honest! God can handle whatever you want to say.

After you've spent some time talking to God, return to just being quiet and visualizing God's face. Keep your mind in that same open state and allow God to care for you, to love you, to warm you.

Finally, you've invited the Creator of the universe into your problems and into your life. Let God surround your life with His presence as you sit quietly.

Experiences with God vary from person to person. Some men feel an instant sense of relief, even euphoria. For others it is a matter-of-fact conversation. Whatever your experience, remember you're not competing with the experience of some other guy—you're communicating directly and privately with God.

2. *Sustained Contact:* Linking with God is not a one-time experience. It should be repeated each day. In your daily conversations with God, follow the same format of quieting yourself before Him and visualizing His face.

Then thank God for the privilege of this spiritual link. Thank Him for whatever peace you are experiencing—for insights that are coming. Thank Him for your increased sensitivity to spiritual things, even though sometimes you have pain when you're confronted with areas that need change.

Sustaining your contact with God will help you to live in the "here and now." It will help you to link your childhood with your adult life so that all the parts of your life will be healed.

Talk to God about the small group you're in, books you're reading, insights you're getting from other people, and insights you're getting as you spend time quietly meditating with Him each day.

Remember, you are not looking for perfection as you sustain your link with God. You are looking for His presence and peace as you continue to go through your healing and growing process. You are looking for truth about yourself—yes, some things need to change, but you are not all bad. The healing process can only go forward as you know the truth. Jesus said, "You will know the truth and the truth will set you free" (John 8:32).

God is more concerned about your emotional health than you are. His plan is to give you a deep sense of peace and the strength to face your painful past and your current challenges.

Keep in focus the two sides of your contact with God. One part is your talking honestly to God—that's called prayer. But prayer is only one side of the conversation.

The second side is quietly listening—that is called meditation. Reading the Bible gives you a natural way to listen to God as He points out key ideas for you to think about. Let me suggest a little assignment. Start reading a chapter a day from a modern translation of the Bible, such as the versions I'm using in this book—*The Living Bible* or *New Living Translation*. Now start reading with the Gospel of John. (Look in the front of the book for the page number.) Use your daily reading as part of the process of sustaining your contact with God.

Another practice that will help you grow in your connection with God is to be part of a small group of men who also are deepening their connection to God. A good place to start is with a Promise Keepers small group. You can get information about Promise Keepers by looking on the World Wide Web or by calling local churches in your area for a phone contact. *What Makes A Man?* is the major book written under the auspices of the Promise

Keepers, and will give you insight into this movement.

Remember that the old God of the ages is wanting to be a new God for you as you go through your midlife crisis.

> Blessed is the Lord, for he has shown me that his never-failing love protects me like the walls of a fort! I spoke too hastily when I said, "The Lord has deserted me," for you listened to my plea and answered me.
>
> Psalm 31:21-22

## For Further Reading

*What Makes a Man?* by Bill McCartney and others (Colorado Springs: Navpress, 1992).

# PART 4

# Life Is Progressive

# 13

# Adults Keep Developing

WHEN I WAS A TEENAGER, I read several different pamphlets and articles on subjects relevant to teens: dating, sex, career choice, and college. Every summer I went to a youth camp, where specialists helped me understand myself, my parents, the opposite sex, and the whole spiritual and emotional development of my teen years. They told me I was fairly normal, but I was going through the teenage years. They encouraged me by saying the more I understood, the easier the process would be.

Before I was married, I read books on how to how to make my marriage work—and books on sex! I took marriage classes in college and talked to several married people to get my questions answered so that I would make a smooth transition.

When our children came along, Sally and I had Dr. Spock, our pediatrician, plus grandparents and friends. All of them were anxious to give counsel and advice. The transition to parenting was fun, and most of what happened was what I expected.

In graduate school I learned what to expect in my chosen profession, the pastorate. I had three years of graduate study, plus the experience of pastoring churches while a student. All of this was part of the program to prepare me for the transition into my life's work.

## The Information Gap

Then a strange silence dropped over my life, like a great black curtain. No one told me anything about what was coming next. Apparently, everything would just happen naturally. Anyone over twenty-five didn't need to be taught anymore. It was as if there would be no further changes in my life until retirement.

So I launched into my adult life and ministry. I was busy trying to win the world, build churches, help people with troubles, and generally become a smashing success. I was too busy to think about my feelings, or the lack of teachers and leaders for my adult era of life.

At thirty-five, I began to grow restless. I had passed a milestone, and I wasn't ever going to come past there again. At thirty-six, I received an invitation to spend a month in India training national evangelists. I spent several months in preparation for the trip, which would ultimately stretch around the world and take three months.

Upon returning to the United States, I accepted the pastorate of Twin City Bible Church in Urbana, Illinois, and I felt I had passed through a period of disquiet in my life. I eagerly jumped into the responsibilities of preaching, counseling, and administration as I worked with hundreds of students from the University of Illinois.

During my forty-third year, the uneasiness began to resurface. I was now in my sixth year at the church, and I found myself saying that I was only re-living my fifth year. The anxieties, the questions, the pressures I had begun to hear as a faint voice at thirty-five through thirty-seven now became a loud, raging chorus, crying out for answers and solutions. These voices led to the experience I described in chapter three as I came to the point of a near emotional breakdown.

The tragedy was that no one had warned me of any of this. It had been kept a deep, dark secret, like a giant conspiracy. As I've watched the lives of hundreds of other men over the years, I see that many men face this same kind of stress. Yet very few men talked about it—at least no one of my acquaintance. In the late nineties there are still very few books in the Christian community written about the midlife crisis. During my midlife crisis, there were *no* books circulating on the subject in my circle of Christian friends.

It seems to me that a lot of the pressures I've known could have been minimized if I had known about them ahead of time. A lot of the personal guilt, anxiety, and feelings of failure would have been eliminated if I had known that what I was experiencing was a normal process.

## The Resilient Child Fails At Midlife

In recent years, research has emerged about the resilient child—a child who survives the abuse and neglect of a dysfunctional home. These children are survivors who have learned to cope and even thrive in chaotic, abusive homes. They have survived the alcoholic home, or a home with physical, sexual, or emotional abuse—or even the abandonment home, where one or both parents never connected to them emotionally.

Studies have further connected this resilient child with midlife crisis. One study focuses on the man who was emotionally abandoned by the mother—she was present physically, but not emotionally. The boy then tried unsuccessfully to connect with his father, who didn't know how to connect or to talk about any troubles in life.

"The unavailability of the mothers to provide soothing, caring, and holding functions led these boys to attempt a compensatory identification with their fathers. The fathers were hardworking, energetic, active people who were erratically available, and their sons developed in much the same way. However, if there was any recognition from their fathers for these boys, it was for their achievements and not for their pain."[1]

Researchers were surprised that children who had survived so well in childhood now fell flat on their faces at midlife. "[Males] presented at midlife a profound dissatisfaction in their marriages, reduced interest and energy in their work, and a general mood of anhedonia (inability to experience pleasure). Nothing seemed to give them pleasure, their sex lives were disturbed, and in some cases, there was an increase in alcohol consumption. Since these patients bore so much resemblance to invulnerable children, we were intrigued by the fact that they seemed to 'come undone' in midlife."[2]

These men had "success" written all over their lives—they had learned to survive. They were hardworking, intelligent, high-energy, ambitious men. But they were limited in social connections and often isolated from their wives and children. "At midlife they had begun to lose the taste for the success race, or, having won it, they felt that it was no longer enough. The defense of activity had stopped working, and they longed for the unconditional love they had never experienced."[3]

Having a midlife crisis is not a choice a man willfully makes. He doesn't get up on a Thursday morning and say, "Today looks like a good day for a midlife crisis. I think I'll be depressed, hate my work, be abusive to my kids, start an affair, and shake my fist at God!" Some of the driving force for the trauma of midlife may come from his childhood. The home without warmth, affirmation, love, and encouragement—the emotionally polluted home–may now force a man to search for the warmth and love he missed in his home. "Emotional deprivation in childhood is an important risk factor for pathology in midlife."[4]

The deceptive part of this problem is that success and denial may well mask the potential volcanic eruption seething just below the surface. It would have helped if I could have been warned that because I came from a dysfunctional home, I was likely to have a more difficult midlife transition and possibly a crisis.

### Please, Spare Me!

A few years ago Sally and I talked with a young seminary student preparing for full-time ministry. As I shared with him some of the developmental life changes he could expect, including midlife crisis, he said, "Boy, I hope that never happens to me!" I asked him if he went through any transition during his teenage years. He laughed and said, "Wow, did I." I told him he could expect to go through a similar transition in his late twenties, at midlife, and near retirement. Again he acted surprised, saying he thought that after he had made it through his teen years everything would settle down for the rest of life.

It is extremely important that men in midlife under-stand this era as a normal developmental process. And it is also important that wives and friends understand the crisis. Midlife is simply one of the stages that takes place after a person has entered the supposedly tranquil adult life.

## Stages of Adult Development

An increasing number of people have begun to recog-nize the developmental stages of adult life. Before this, experts had given most of their time to defining stages of each end of adult life—the teen years and retirement.

Sociologist Charlotte Buhler from Vienna led the way in the 1930s. Then Erik Erikson continued to study adult development in the fifties and sixties. Dr. Levinson of Yale University became the most noted authority in the seventies. Books, journal articles, and long-term research is continuing at an expanding pace. Adult development and learning is no longer groundbreaking research, but a part of many sociology and psychology courses.

Sally and I came to divide the adult era as follows:

1. "Pulling up Roots"—18 to 22
2. "The Trying Twenties"—22 to 28
3. "Passage to the Thirties"—28 to 32
4. "Rooting and Extending"—32 to 39
5. "Deadline Decade"—35 to 45
6. "Resignation"—after 45

In each of these developmental eras we have impor-tant emotional work to accomplish. During the late teens and early twenties, a man will experience his *first adult unsettled stage* as he moves to establish independence, separates from the parental home, establishes his unique identity, and begins to clearly focus his life goal and dreams.

During his twenties the young man moves into the adult world; usually he gets married and begins a career. This is his *first settling-down stage*. The young man's life dreams begin to come true. A major task of the twenties is to give form to the dreams he had in his teen years and to build a structure around these dreams.

A *second adult unsettled period* comes around age twenty-eight to thirty-two. This is a time for evaluation, a pause that provides an opportunity to take stock of where a man has come from and where he is going. It's a checkup time—is he on target with his life goals?

The difference between this evaluation process and his midlife evaluation is that the thirty year old is only beginning his career. He does not have a lot of commitments. He has ample resources, time, and energy to make major redirections. It is, however, a dangerous period of time, and people around him can get hurt. If a man concludes he is going in a wrong direction, he may make some rather abrupt changes—divorce, or a drastic job change.

The thirties are generally marked by a *second settling-down stage*, similar to the process that went on during the midtwenties. The thirties are generally years of enthusiasm and excitement. Life becomes less provisional as he makes deeper commitments, takes on more adult responsibilities, invests more of himself in family and personal interests, and pursues long-range career goals.

During this second settling-down stage, a man continues to build his nest while pursuing with great ambition the dreams and goals of his life. During this highly active period, he has little time for reflection or to ask crucial questions, such as, "Why am I doing all of this?"

During the later part of this second settling period there will be a strong urge toward nonconformity. He will seek to become his own man—establishing his mark in the world. Sometimes the people who have been the most instrumental in helping him move up the ladder of success will be cast off so he can develop his own unique personality. In short, he will throw off his mentors.

The man's *third adult unsettled stage* comes around age forty. This is even more intense than the one in adolescence or the one at thirty. This is the midlife crisis. It may come any time from thirty-five to fifty-five; generally, however, it appears in a man's early forties. In midlife a man asks many of the questions he asked when he was a teen and again when he was in his late twenties. "Who am I? What shall I do with my life? Who should be my friends?" Now, however, the questions are being asked looking back as well as forward. "What have I been doing? Is what I have been doing valuable? Do I want to continue being who I am or doing what I am doing?"

Following his midlife developmental era, a man moves into a *third settling-down stage*, which starts in the late forties and continues to retirement. The man who successfully navigates his midlife crisis will experience an increase in productivity, a decrease in competitiveness, a greater desire to be helpful to people, to enjoy leisure, and be comfortable with himself and his stage of life. His marriage will generally become more meaningful and satisfying to both partners. There will be an easy transition to becoming a grandparent and trainer of a new generation.

The fourth unsettled stage will come around retirement as the man again asks the same major life questions. Now the questions are asked more with a backward look: "What did I do with my career years?" and "Did I do a good job raising my kids?" He still has future questions: "What will I do in retirement?" and "How can we improve our marriage?"

Yet more questions will be asked and transitions made during another *unsettled stage* if his wife dies before he does. "Who am I without her?" "Do I have a place of continued influence?" "What will my mark be on the world?"

Again, all the same questions will be asked in the *last adult unsettled stage* just before his own death. He will also ask questions such as "Who have I been?" and "Did I do a good job?" These questions are summation questions, and he may need help to forgive himself if life wasn't lived as he thought it should have been.

Notice that the same general questions are asked all along through life. The questions relate to:

- self-identity
- relationships with people
- contribution to the world through work
- connection with God

It's also interesting to note that several people in the same extended family may be asking similar questions, but from different age perspectives. The great-grandfather at age ninety wonders how well he lived his life—and he at least attempts to heal his relationships.

The retiring grandfather at sixty-five wonders what will be his significance, and who will be his friends in retirement.

The midlife man in his early forties wonders if he will ever make a mark in the world—or be happy. Maybe he should make a radical change of job or marriage.

The teen wonders who he is and what he should do with his life. He also wonders if he should go to college. And should he marry?

However, of all the stages and transitions a man goes through in adulthood, the midlife crisis is the most dangerous and painful—for him, his family, and the community. The teen can get angry, run away, do drugs, or suddenly get married, and his actions don't cause many community waves. The grandfather can flirt with a young woman, and everyone excuses him as being in his second childhood.

But when the man in midlife crisis has an affair, becomes a beach bum, or quits attending church, then the whole community is affected because midlife people are supposed to be responsible people—they run the world.

The good news is the midlife crisis demon will lose its terror as we understand that this is a normal developmental stage. Then our understanding gives the midlife man hope.

> He calms the storm and stills the waves. What a blessing is that stillness, as he brings them safely into harbor!
>
> Psalm 107:29-30

### For Further Reading

*Adult Children of Legal or Emotional Divorce* by Jim Conway (Downers Grove, IL: InterVarsity Press, 1990).

*Women in Midlife Crisis* by Jim and Sally Conway (Wheaton, IL: Tyndale House Publishers, 1983, 1998).

# 14

# This Crisis Came to Pass

THE QUESTION I HAVE REPEATEDLY asked myself is, "How much longer do I have to go through this? Six months? One year?" Perhaps a question more to the point is, "Can I speed up the process?"

While I was experiencing my midlife pressures, I read Elisabeth Kubler-Ross's book *On Death and Dying*. Suddenly I saw that midlife crisis can be compared closely to the emotional trauma a person experiences as he faces death. There are definite stages within a midlife crisis. I had noticed this pattern with other men, and as I began to experience my own midlife crisis, I saw the pattern more clearly.

At first, comparing the midlife crisis to death made me feel morbid. However, the more I thought about what I had observed in my life and in the lives of other men, the more I came to see that this is exactly what the man in midlife is wrestling with—death. A man is facing the death of his youthful physical prowess, death of the ambitions of his twenties, death of his hopes for great achievement and advancement, death of some of his sexual fantasies, death of the visions for fame and fortune, and death of some expectations he had for his children.

For the first time he is also facing the reality of his own physical death. As a young man, he knew people died—but not to him. Now death has become a reality. In fact, some of his college friends have already died.

Kubler-Ross outlines five emotional stages through which a person passes in preparation for death:

    1. Denial—"It's not me—it's not true!"

    2. Anger—"Why me?"

    3. Bargaining—"Can't we postpone this?"

    4. Depression—"All is lost."

    5. Acceptance—"I'm ready."[1]

With only minor modification, these stages can be adapted to the man at midlife crisis. They may be very short periods of time or they may extend for years. Some may overlap or run concurrently. From my observation, to help a man make it through midlife crisis successfully, he needs to move progressively through these stages and effectively deal with each one. However, don't be discouraged by falling back. Each new midlife event may trigger a new round of questioning and processing.

### Stage One—Denial

"It's not really true that I'm getting older," a man keeps telling himself. For a number of years I was able to get by with that favorite line, "I'm only twenty-eight." I did look younger than my age, and I've always enjoyed young people. My favorite age group is college age through early thirties. I tend to think young. But thinking young does not give a man a young body. I really was in my midforties when I had my midlife crisis.

In some ways denial can be a helpful process, because

it can start the transition toward reality. The more a man denies aging, the more his brain prepares him to ultimately accept it. He is middle-aged. It has happened to him as certainly as the terminally ill person is going to die. There is no retreat.

Even if a man tries a new body, new clothes, new lifestyle, a new job, a new wife, has an affair or tries a new god, there is no way to turn the clock back and make him young again. During the first stages of the crisis, however, a man will vehemently deny that he is getting any older and laughingly say, "I'm just getting better."

## Stage Two—Anger

A man eventually begins to realize that no matter how much he protests, he is moving into midlife. He no longer is young. True, he is not an old man, but he is not a young one, either.

At this point, he becomes angry. "It's unfair that strength should be wasted on the young. It's unfair that they should have the physical bodies when I've got all the experience. It's unfair that the important young adult period of life is so very short. It's unfair that I have worked so hard, thinking I was going to arrive at satisfaction, only to come up empty. It's unfair I live in a culture that emphasizes youth, and degrades midlife people. It's unfair that God has made men as He has."

Fate seems to have played a ghoulish trick on him. This strong, good-looking, athletic young man with ideas, energy, and ambition now finds himself with a sagging body and low energy, living with dreams and visions like broken seashells along the shore. Humpty Dumpty says, "Why shouldn't I be angry? I've fallen off the wall. My life is broken, and I'll never be able to be put together again."

During this anger stage, no amount of consolation seems to be helpful. Everyone and everything becomes a target for the venom of the midlife man. It is nearly impossible to cheer him at this stage.

We can, however, help the person move along to the next stage by letting him verbalize his anger. We can use phrases that reflect the situation as he sees it. We don't condemn him or suggest a solution. Rather, we leave questions hanging in the air to encourage discussion. "I imagine you feel very angry that your body is aging." Or, "I guess you feel angry that Mike got the promotion over you." Or, "What do you feel when young women no longer look at you with sexy smiles—and only see you as a midlife father?"

The stage of anger is also a very difficult time for a man's wife and family. They are likely to assume his anger is their fault. Even though he may lash out at them, he is really angry at some unknown force. The man in midlife crisis uses people and circumstances near him as convenient scapegoats for punishment.

### Stage Three—Replay

The third stage in a midlife crisis can be called "One More Time." His anger has begun to subside—but now he fantasizes. "Wow! Just to handle the football one more time. To take the snap from center, to take a three-step drop, to lift the ball high into the air, to see the tight end streaking toward the goal, to feel my arm sweeping through the air. To see the ball land perfectly in his out-stretched arms as he steps across the goal line for the winning touchdown. Just one more game! One more time!"

"One more success in business. A success so big that everyone around me notices how great I really am—how important and absolutely indispensable I am. One more big success before I step off into the oblivion of midlife and old age."

"One more time—with one more woman. The newness, the excitement of a new touch, a new face. One more sexual experience before my virility fades away like a wilted celery stalk left over from Sunday dinner."

The "one more" fantasy is played out in all the areas of the man's life. He wants one more time with his children when they were only children. He wants another shot at the young married life. One more time with the boys on an all-night bender. One more time camping out. One more time for a mountain expedition. One more crack at writing a book. One more opportunity to make a scientific discovery, or to invent something that will forever establish his inventive genius. The list is endless.

The replay stage is really a modification of the denial stage. There is an acceptance, "Yes, I am in midlife," but there is still the last grasping attempt to turn back the pages of time. A friend of mine married a younger woman and recently had a new son—by choice. This boy, who has three brothers who are much older, is the pride and joy of my friend's life. He makes his father feel like a young man again, living in that era of a father with a young child—"one more time."

This stage becomes very difficult if the man has a great number of unfulfilled dreams. If he feels he has not really experienced what he wants in life, there will be a great urgency to regress—back to the good old days. The "one more time" stage may become rather lengthy as a man works through the things he missed in his young adult or teen years. This stage will cause great disruption, especially if a man drastically changes his lifestyle or decides to abandon his family to catch up on some things he missed earlier.

During this stage, a man doesn't want help, and that makes it difficult for anyone who might want to work with him. A good counselor will try to keep the marriage together, yet the anxiety of feeling pressured to stay may produce additional stress in the man's life. Sometimes it's helpful if a man can specifically identify what he must experience "one more time." Then he may be able to substitute something that will be almost as satisfying—and yet not destructive.

For example, one very conservative man who felt used by his family wanted to abandon them, take off on a motorcycle, and go wherever he wanted. I suggested that some of his desire for freedom, adventure, and risk could be met in ways that would be less destructive to his family. Perhaps he could try a series of short adventures—backpacking, canoeing, weekend motorcycle trips, running rapids in a rubber raft, learning to scuba dive, climbing mountains. These activities became acceptable substitutes that met this man's needs and at the same time gave his family stability.

The "one more time" stage is most difficult if a man is saying, "One more time—with one more new woman." Naturally the wife views this as rejection. When I speak on this subject at a conference, women will frequently look at me in startled amazement as I suggest to them that their husbands do not want to leave them or lose them. Men in crisis think a new sexual experience will restore their confidence in themselves. These men imagine they have missed something.

If the wife can keep calm during this very painful stage, there is a great likelihood the couple will stay together. If, however, the wife pushes and demands a choice, the husband will probably side with the "one more time" option, and the marriage will dissolve.

### Stage Four—Depression

Each stage seems to have within it the seeds of the next. For example, the first stage of denial helps the man move toward anger. Then his anger at life sets him up to crave replays. The replay stage is not an end in itself, but moves the man toward depression. Sadly, it doesn't matter if he has a successful or unsuccessful "one more time" stage, the result is the same—he is one day older.

Likely he will become depressed because the "one more time" often doesn't help. Not only is he getting older, but there is no way of stopping all the changes. Even his delaying maneuvers have not slowed the grim process of the sun rising and setting on him day after day.

Now depression takes on a deep intensity. Before his depression came, he realized his body was changing and he was getting older. He recognized he was losing his stamina, quickness, strength, and sexual prowess. Now he is even more depressed. He realizes he is moving at an ever increasing pace toward the termination of his life. He begins to imagine pains in his body he never felt before. Death no longer is something that happens to other people—he could be next.

### Stage Five—Withdrawal

Depression may precede withdrawal, or the two may run concurrently. The man in the withdrawal stage asks, "What is my life worth, anyway?" And he concludes, "Nothing!" So he decides to drop out of life.

The withdrawal stage may take two different directions. He may become the passive hermit—"I don't want to talk to anyone, I don't want to see anyone—just leave me alone." I've watched this stage in a number of Christian men. Some of these men have been extremely active, setting the direction and tempo for their whole congregations. However, as they enter midlife and begin to ask what it's all worth, they begin to cut themselves off from life. They gracefully and tactfully decline responsibility and drop off boards and committees. They quietly move to the back pews of the church, and in a few months they are out the back door.

Withdrawal will affect a man's contact with friends. There never is any time to get together—"It's just not going to work out. But don't worry, we'll do it someday." Withdrawal also makes sharp inroads into family relationships. The husband and wife hardly talk. Contact with the children is minimal. In short, contact with life itself is very limited.

Withdrawal may be very active. A man may decide to withdraw into his work. He doesn't need anyone—he just buries himself in endless business that crowds out all chance for feelings, questions, or reflections.

As in each of the other stages, withdrawal has positive as well as negative aspects. The stages of depression and withdrawal can bring healing by giving a man time to be alone, to allow his frayed emotions to rebuild, and even to allow his body to gain strength.

One man's withdrawal took the form of taking off for a month with the family motor home. He was able to go where he wanted, stay where he pleased, be outdoors, and enjoy nature. He got time to fish, lie out in the sun, and allow his head to clear. He took along music, a few books, and even took the early edition of this book. This withdrawal period was extremely important for him, because it prepared him for the final stage of acceptance.

The withdrawal stage may last a month or a year. Frequently a man moves back and forth between the stages as he moves nearer to acceptance. He may fall back into depression or may drop back as far as anger. But lapses into earlier stages will become less frequent and shorter. As he faces his issues in each stage, he will grow slowly and surely toward a mature acceptance of who he is and where he fits into life.

## Stage Six—Acceptance

The movement into the acceptance stage is almost unnoticed at first—especially to the man himself. It's like the movement of a wave to the shore. As you look out at the ocean, it's almost impossible to pick out an individual wave. But as it moves closer to the shore, it begins to take form and rises higher and higher. Then the wave curls over, and a whitecap begins to form. The foam shows underneath the curl, and the water from the shore begins to recede as the wave grows in size. As the wave crashes on the shore, you sense its power and majesty. You wonder where the wave was all the time when it was only a part of the ocean. So it is with the man who is beginning to accept himself. At first he doesn't see the change, but increasingly there is an exhilaration—he is moving out of his midlife crisis to a new and productive era.

He begins to see life differently. Only weeks before he had been saying, as the pessimist says about the pie, "Oh, isn't it terrible, half of the pie is gone!" Now, strangely, the midlife man begins to view his years optimistically: "Wow! Isn't this great—half of my life is left!"

Now he is aware of his assets and his value. He no longer is a worn-out, middle-aged man. Now he is an experienced, able person! He is able to teach and develop the coming generation. He has wisdom and influence. His family and friends no longer are evil people pushing him into old age—they are pleasant companions who love and care for him.

He looks forward to more leisure time, making the creative contribution he has always wanted to. He has a better understanding of his physical body—his real capabilities. Without anger he looks forward to adjusting his activities to fit his real body. Our midlife hero has now moved into what Erikson calls the "generative" period of his life. He has become more mellow. He is entering the *third settling-down stage*. This is the longest stage, and it will be the most satisfying. He will be a very significant, productive, giving man. He has learned to maintain his own individuality, identity, and privacy.

### What If?

The question repeatedly asked of me is, "What if he doesn't make it through these stages? What if he only goes as far as anger, or depression, or withdrawal?" The answer to that question is tragically simple. If a man does not progress through the stages, but for one reason or another stops along the way, then he will probably experience a prolonged period of trauma. He will likely experience recurring cycles of midlife crisis during the next fifteen to twenty years.

As he comes to retirement, he will then be struggling with two stressful developmental stages at the same time—midlife and retirement. At that point he will verbally kick himself—"Why didn't I think about making changes back in midlife, instead of blindly doing the same dumb things for the last twenty years?"

If he fails to resolve his midlife crisis, then his *third settling-down stage* following his midlife crisis, which should have been marked by a great deal of peace, will instead be marked by unsettledness and continual anguish. He is similar to the person who never quite makes it through the adolescent transition into young adulthood. That person forever tries to be a teenager. The man who doesn't make it successfully through his midlife crisis will forever try to be a young adult.

A few men whom I have counseled have deeply concerned me, because I was afraid they would not make it completely through all of the stages. Thus far, however, I have only seen a few who have not made it all the way. In later years these men have become angry that they did not use the midlife crisis time to improve their lives. But the good news is that successful men who make it all the way are more focused, highly motivated, and have a long season of peace and productivity.

> You have seen me tossing and turning through the night. You have collected all my tears and preserved them in your bottle! You have recorded every one in your book. The very day I call for help, the tide of battle turns. My enemies flee! This one thing I know: God is for me!
>
> Psalm 56:8-9

# PART 5
# The Wife's Crises

# 15

# Bewildered at Thirty-Five

BY NOW WOMEN READERS ARE beginning to cry out, "Hey, what about me? I've got problems, too." Yes, that's true. The woman at midlife is also struggling with pressures. If she's going to help her husband—she must have help.

One of the hardest things for me was to watch my wife choke back tears, trying to be strong and carry the responsibility of the family while trying to be optimistic, happy, and a support to me. Part of me said, "It's not fair for her to carry this load." But the other part of me said, "I'm sorry, but I can't do anything about it."

It is extremely difficult to live with a man who is going through a midlife crisis. Some days he acts like an adolescent, with great outbursts of anger, deep depression, or withdrawal. He is a whirlwind of instability. He doesn't know who he is, where he is going, or what he is doing. His total value system is confused.

Just before his midlife crisis, however, this man clearly knew where he was going. He was strongly oriented toward achievement, and seemed to spend all of his energies in clear-cut directions. Now he is like a sailboat caught in a deep fog offshore without a compass and without wind to move him even if he wanted to go.

These personality changes can be very devastating for a wife, especially if she has looked to him for leadership in the family. He may want to be thought of as the leader, yet he is unable to function as the leader. He wants her to help him with his insecurity, his doubts, and weaknesses. He wants her to understand who he is and what is happening. Yet he wants to be thought of as the strong, secure, competent leader.

Women whose husbands are in midlife crisis repeatedly tell me, "It's not fair! I have to continue with the day-to-day responsibilities of my job, caring for the children and the household, answering questions of friends and relatives—always trying to keep things as stable as possible. Yet he can do whatever he wants. He can be depressed, sulky, or totally refuse responsibility. He can get in his car and take off for a day or two. But I'm left with all of the pressures and I have to pretend that things are all right. I'm supposed to be patient and loving—yet I have no one to talk to!"

Because midlife crisis in men generally occurs in their early forties, it means that the average age of the wives is likely to be late thirties or early forties. At this age a wife is extremely threatened by her husband's crisis. One wife who was nearly forty told me, "I can't stand this any longer. He complains about our marriage, says it never was any good and that he never should have married me. He says I'm not attractive to him and I don't stimulate him sexually." Her body convulsed with sobs and tears ran down her red, anguished face. "He says I don't understand him and I never have." She had been broken and crushed under the terrible, distorted indictment laid on her by her husband.

How does a woman stand that kind of pressure? How can she take it when she is told, straight to her face, that nothing she has ever done is worthwhile? And how can she stand the pressure when her husband, in the middle of his crisis, tries to be young just "one more time" and starts an affair with a younger woman? I have repeatedly marveled at the strength of women whose husbands try to put a guilt trip on them.

The midlife woman needs someone to talk to. She can't talk to her husband for fear of driving him away, but she must talk to someone. Most women, however, are too ashamed to talk because they believe the indictment from their husbands. They believe *they* have failed—and, to some degree, they have.

None of us is perfect. No marriage partner always does everything right. But the indictment from the husband during his crisis is an exaggeration filled with anger and confusion. He is lashing out, and his wife is conveniently available. He knows he can dump on her, and she won't fire him as a boss would, nor will she walk off as a friend might. She'll hang in there and see him through it. Why? Because she loves him.

An interesting phenomenon takes place in the lives of women during their forties. They tend to become stronger emotionally. It may have something to do with their husband's crisis, but I think it has more to do with their own crisis that usually takes place in the late thirties.

A major event in a woman's life takes place somewhere between thirty-five and forty, and is basically an emotional crisis of "Who am I? Do I like what I'm doing? Is what I'm doing important?" A second major event, menopause, takes place around forty-eight to fifty-three.

## The Late-Thirties Anxiety

Let's assume that by her late thirties a woman has been married about fifteen years. She likely will feel hit with a strong need to reevaluate her life. About this time her last child goes off to school for all day. It is not the period of the *empty* nest, it is the period of the quiet nest. Yes, there are still children in the home, when they're not at school. She still has a role as a mother. But if she has chosen to be a full-time homemaker, there are long periods during the day when the house is quiet—almost deafeningly so. There is time to think about life.

If she has been working part-time, she may resent that she's only working to supplement the budget. "When will I get time for my career? Why can't I go back to school to finish my degree? Why am I only working to make everyone else's life run smoothly?"

Quite often she will begin to feel that life is passing her by. Her husband is making wild strides at work, moving toward success. Her children are in school and launching toward their own careers. She begins to feel left out, unimportant, and insignificant. Has being a mother with a part-time job really amounted to anything? What doesshe do now with the rest of her life?

Women lash out with feelings such as:
• "Just leave me alone."
• "Why can't anyone do anything right?"
• "You'd think after eighteen years he wouldn't have to know where I am every minute—day or night."
• "I'm sick and tired of always acting the way other people want me to act."

• "Situations seem to get out of hand so easily. Before I know it I'm saying to myself, 'So what? What difference is anything I do ever going to make?'"

• "It's time I had a little fun—you're dead a long, long time."

At this point the woman may decide to go back to school, get another job, look up college friends, or even have another child. There are some genetic risks involved in bearing children at midlife, but the risks of having a child during midlife have been somewhat overstated. And a woman in her own midlife crisis may decide to play her own game of "one more time."

### Inner Feelings at Midlife

How do you describe what it feels like when you are in midlife crisis? A midwestern Christian woman who is forty-four and a frequent speaker at women's clubs described her own midlife crisis in one word: lonely. "You feel as if no one understands, and if they do understand, they don't care. You are in it by yourself."

Another woman, age thirty-four, commented, "For the first time in my life, I am admitting to myself and to everyone around me who I really am and what I really want to be. First, I always did what my parents wanted me to do, then I did what my husband wanted. My parents think I'm acting strange now, but for the first time in my life, I am really acting like myself." This woman had just left her husband and three young children and started working full-time in her profession to fulfill an earlier young-adult dream.

A thirty-eight-year-old East Coast woman declared, "I feel as if I am drowning. Pressures are coming at me from all sides—caring for my children, making my husband successful, meeting responsibilities at church, PTA, and my part-time job. And now my dad has just had a heart attack. I'm caring for everybody. But who am I? And who cares for me?"

## She's Getting Older

About the time all the children are in school full-time, she feels a deep sense of aging. Until now she has thought of herself as a young married woman. But with the children off to school, she begins to see herself as midlife. Magazine articles and newspapers don't help. Almost everything huckstered on television uses a young, attractive female to push the product.

It was such a good, warm feeling when her children used to call her Mommy. Now they call her Mom, and she senses her youth has slipped away. How soon will it be before she is called by that dreaded term "mother-in-law"?

The physical aging process and its devastation are heard in the bitter words of an extremely beautiful actress at age thirty-nine. "At thirty-seven or thirty-eight, a woman is at the peak of her beauty. After that your hair, your skin, your teeth, your eyes, they all deteriorate. Everybody knows that's true. A woman of thirty-nine's already lost everything worth having."[1]

The woman experiencing this emotional stress is undergoing many of the same pressures of a man in midlife crisis. She feels a great emptiness and uselessness in life. One husband, speaking of his wife, said, "Her big problem is that she's sure there's not going to be a tomorrow—and nobody can convince her otherwise."

## The Affair of a Wife

"All of a sudden, you know, I've noticed that the streets are full of men, the way they haven't been since I went boy-crazy in high school. For years I must've been going by them with my eyes closed, but now I see them all right. I hardly see anything else."[2]

This reawakened sexual drive happens when the husband is preoccupied with his career—which may appear to his wife as a rejection of her. Along with feeling she is growing older, her purpose as a mother is also beginning to slip. In addition she may never have gotten to develop her career. Many of the reasons for her existence and evidences of her self-worth are toppling like a house of cards.

If she tries to keep her career going, plus be a mom, plus encourage her insecure midlife husband, plus do all the housework, plus face her wrinkles every time she looks in the mirror—it may be too much. "Why can't someone just love me for me—instead of what I do for them?"

Often a woman's midlife affair is a way to affirm her own sense of self-worth and attractiveness. She wants to prove to herself that some man still wants her, and that her body is still sexy—that she is worthwhile.

It's easy when we hear about an affair to say to ourselves, "That would never happen to me." It's also easy for Christians to say, "It would never happen to me because I'm a Christian." Over the years I have counseled scores of couples where one or both have been involved in an affair. Christians wrestle not only with the problems that caused the affair, but also with the guilt. I've asked women what caused them to get involved with another man. Some of these women were leaders in their church. Their response was simply, "I don't know. I just felt something was missing in my life. It just happened."

As I compare the motivation of women and men involved in affairs, they are similar. It's not so much a basic sexual need as it is a need for understanding and intimacy. Both men and women who feel insecure, who lack intimacy, and who feel unappreciated are extremely vulnerable to the potential of an affair.

## A New Look

A woman will probably try a new appearance as she wrestles with her midlife crisis. She'll become increasingly aware of her figure and diet. She buys new clothes to show off her figure and her weight loss, and she may try a new hairstyle and hair color for those first telltale streaks of gray.

During her mid- to late thirties, a woman will probably throw herself more fully into the work world. This can be a very frightening experience. She may be forced to use skills not used for a number of years. As she looks for a full-time position in the field of her interest, she may find it awkward to explain to a twenty-eight-year-old male personnel officer that she only worked a series of part-time jobs while she raised her family. She may be confronted with subtle age discrimination at work, which could intensify her emotional stress.

But it is from this crucible of the late thirties' midlife crisis that we see a stronger, more self-assured woman emerging. It is her strength (discussed in the next chapter), developed through the testing fires of her own experience, that will enable her to help her husband through his midlife crisis.

It is unfortunate that most men are not aware their wives are going through a midlife crisis. Men are too pre-occupied with their own achievements to share the agony of the wife in her late thirties.

> This I declare, that he alone is my refuge, my place of safety; he is my God, and I am trusting him. For he rescues you from every trap, and protects you from the fatal plague. He will shield you with his wings! They will shelter you. His faithful promises are your armor.
> Psalm 91:2-4

## For Further Reading

*Women in Midlife Crisis* by Jim and Sally Conway (Wheaton, IL: Tyndale House Publishers, Inc., 1983, 1998).

# 16

# Barren at Fifty

SOMETIME BETWEEN FORTY-EIGHT and fifty-three most women experience a second major midlife stress time called menopause. Both physical and emotional changes are involved in menopause, although the emotional stress often begins before the actual physical changes start.

A hundred years ago menopause came basically at the end of a woman's life, but with the increased age span (the average woman is now expected to live into her eighties), the change of life comes slightly past the halfway mark. She has many years of productivity and opportunity ahead of her. How she copes with her physical and emotional difficulties during menopause will be important.

Help with physical aspects of the transition, such as the cessation of menstruation, hot flashes, insomnia, and dryness of mucous membranes of the vagina, is available from gynecologists. Books such as *Menopause* by Sally Conway, *Menopause and Midlife* by Robert Wells and Marry Wells, and *What Wives Wish Their Husbands Knew About Women* by Dr. James Dobson have good information and some helpful suggestions.

The physical changes that take place are real, but the psychological fears a woman may experience can be far more damaging to her life. Her physical symptoms pass, but if she has not dealt with the emotional fears, these may continue the rest of her life.

## The Fear of Being Barren

It is strange that many women do not actually want to have any more children, but when they lose the capacity to do so, they feel they have lost a part of themselves. If a woman gets most of her identity from her role as a mother, she will probably experience a great deal of dread as the physical change of life comes upon her. If, on the other hand, a woman views bearing children and being a mother as only part of her life, then she will probably not be shaken.

Childbearing is generally limited to the twenties and early thirties. There has been a trend among professional women and highly-educated boomers to wait into their mid- to late thirties to start families. But by the late thirties ,most women have decided they do not want to have any more children and they direct their energies toward raising the ones they have.

When she hits her forties, her children generally are adolescents or in college—these are launching years. The focus of her fifties, sixties, and seventies will be grandchildren and great-grandchildren. The time of actually bearing children is a very limited segment of life. A hundred years ago the childbearing era was a bigger percentage of a woman's life, including most of the adult years. Today, however, it may be less than 10 percent of a woman's life. As a woman sees herself as more than a birth mother, she will not struggle as much with the loss of her capacity to bear children.

## The Fear of Losing Her Husband

If a woman has been highly body-oriented and has felt that her ability to bear children was what kept her husband committed to her, then she may feel that menopause will take away her power. If she felt she won her husband and held him by the sexiness of her physical body, then she may fear that her husband will reject her in favor of a woman who is still "complete."

## The Fear of Becoming Sexless

Some women, and men, mistakenly feel that menopause causes a woman to lose her sexual interest and ability. The opposite is most often true. As the woman comes through her own midlife crisis in her late thirties, she has an increased sexual awareness and drive that intensifies in the forties and fifties. In some ways, menopause actually assists the expansion of sexual interest. There are no more monthly cycles, no more fear of pregnancy, and no more bothersome contraceptives—for the first time in her life, she can be "instantly available" for sexual intercourse with her husband. This freedom often enhances the physical relationship.

Old wives' tales suggesting a woman becomes sexless as she reaches menopause are just not true. As women of all ages have become freer sexually, they have begun to experience a greater amount of sexual satisfaction. This new freedom and sexual satisfaction in women is not due to their ability to bear children. Capacity for orgasm has nothing to do with reproduction. So there is no reason for any diminished sexual desire after a woman has lost her capacity to bear children. Most women become more orgasmic when the fear of pregnancy is completely removed.

## The Empty Nest

The late-thirties stress time was the "quiet nest" period. Children were off at school, parents at work, and the home was strangely silent during the day. With the late forties comes the "empty nest"—children moving from the home into single life or marriage.

The empty nest is difficult because of the sharp contrast in noise. When our three daughters were in junior and senior high, there were always extra teens around, loud music, extra people at dinner, and both telephone lines constantly in use—not to mention the oil spots on the driveway from the junk cars the guys were driving. When all of the girls went off to college, the volume and the rate of activity sharply decreased.

A woman is extremely busy and often frustrated with the conflicts and the moods of her adolescent children. Yet when the empty nest comes, the sharp contrast of silence will cause her to wish for the good old days when she felt needed.

Around age fifty it's important for a woman to put her childrearing stage into total perspective. The tragedy of not letting go of children is an unconscious rejection of the second half of married life. Many women think of married life as always having children around. In reality, a woman will probably have more years alone with her husband than she had with him when children were in the house.

The empty nest causes many a woman to feel under-employed, because she has only been working part-time or working in jobs that didn't fit her gifts and dreams. She may still have her part-time job, plus homemaking tasks and responsibilities in the community and the church, but she may not be doing things that utilize her full capacities and abilities. A couple should make sure their future plans include full utilization of all the gifts, strengths, and abilities of both of them. If the woman is underchallenged, doing only the routine and mundane, she will have a shrinking self-image, less marital satisfaction, and difficulty moving through her menopausal era.

### Empty Marriage

Some of the marriage conflicts at this age appear because of long-standing problems that have never been resolved. The wife was too busy with her part-time job, raising children and caring for the needs of the family to be concerned about marriage stress.

For twenty-five years the husband and wife may have done little or nothing to maintain the couple relationship. They went from the courting days before marriage directly into the childbearing and rearing years, almost totally neglecting their own companionship. Now they sit across the table, wondering whether a marriage relationship is possible. "Can we really be companions? Do we know enough about each other even to live together?" Tragically, some couples at this stage decide there is not enough to work with, and they divorce.

During the wife's late-forties crisis, the couple should realize that marriage instability is very normal. Out of the shakiness of their relationship can come a new relationship that is deeper, more mature, and richer than either of them has experienced. During this stress time the couple will realize they possess a great number of assets between them—psychologically, financially, and in their combined history.[1]

## The Battle of the Mind

In both of the woman's midlife stress periods, the big battle is the battle of the mind—her evaluation of herself, her strengths, and her ability to contribute to her family and to the community.

Throughout her adult life, a large part of a woman's identity has been anchored to her relationships with other people—her husband, children, parents, and friends. If she derives most of her self-esteem from these sources, she will experience greater trauma through the two stress periods in her life. Her husband will be going through his own midlife crisis and will not be the stable person she has counted on. Her children will be establishing their own identities and will need to break away from the close mother-child relationship. Her parents need more care and, in some sense, the woman in midlife now becomes the responsible adult overseeing her parents in their later years. And sometimes friends don't understand her rapidly changing desires and emotions.

The woman's sense of self-worth must come from within rather than only from significant others. She should see her value as something larger than a manager of a household. At age fifty-seven Eleanor Roosevelt wrote, "Somewhere along the line of development we discover what we really are, and then we make our real decision for which we are responsible. Make that decision primarily for yourself because you can never really live anyone else's life, not even your own child's. The influence you exert is through your own life and what you become yourself."[2]

A career, hobbies, volunteer service at church or a hospital can provide a broader base for her sense of self-worth. Yet the sense of worth must come from within the woman—and not simply because she keeps busy with activities. She must say, "I am worthwhile, I am valuable—not because of what I do, but because I am God's creation, because I am me."

Another aspect of a woman's life that will help her improve her self-image is her own physical appearance. Whether we like it or not, society values a good physical appearance. We have been brainwashed to believe that fat is old and fat is irresponsible. Fat, therefore, contributes to a low self-image in many midlife women. A woman's self-image can be greatly improved as she begins to work on her appearance, including diet, exercise, and proper rest.

Regular exercise has an added benefit because it can help her to manage stress. Physical exercise burns off anxiety, helps a person sleep better, and leads to greater productivity in waking hours.

## The Touch of God

There is a depth of a woman's personality that cannot be touched by external changes or activities, or what other human beings think. Only God can meet her deepest needs. She may not be satisfied by what she does. She may not even be satisfied with the way her life is evolving.

Yes, it *is* important that other people encourage her to utilize her gifts and abilities. But there may be an emptiness in all of those activities and affirmations if they don't touch the very deepest levels of her self-worth. Part of Judith Viorst's poem "Self-Improvement Program" expresses the potential emptiness and the need to make activities really nourish the woman. After a recitation of her many new advances in everything from needlepoint to guitar to advanced Chinese cooking to Primal Scream Therapy, she concludes:

> And I'm working all day and
>     I'm working all night
> To be good-looking, healthy, and wise.
> And adored.
> And contented.
> And brave.
> And well-read.
> And a marvelous hostess,
> Fantastic in bed,
> And bilingual,
> Athletic,
> Artistic . . .
> Won't someone please stop me?[3]

A deep personal relationship with God can provide nourishment for the personality and build our self-image so we can move through midlife stress with an internal confidence, rather than trying to manufacture confidence through busyness.

In the Bible, the apostle Paul talks about the kind of confidence God wants to place within the depths of our personality:

> If God is on our side, who can ever be against us? . . . Who dares accuse us whom God has cho-

sen for his own? Will God? No! He is the one who has forgiven us and given us right standing with himself. Who then will condemn us? Will Christ? No! For he is the one who died for us. . . . For I am convinced that nothing can ever separate us from his love. . . . Our fears for today, our worries about tomorrow—nothing will ever be able to separate us from the love of God demonstrated by our Lord Jesus Christ when he died for us.

Romans 8:31, 33-34, 38-39

This deep confidence in God comes from a personal relationship with Him. You can experience this confidence by inviting God into your life. He will forgive your sins. Mentally exchange your life and its weaknesses for Christ's life and His strength. Receive His righteousness and strength for yourself. Christ takes our guilt onto Himself, and we then belong to God.

This confidence also comes from a conviction that God deeply cares for us and is moving for good in all the events of our lives. The Bible says, "And we know that all that happens to us is working for our good if we love God and are fitting into his plans" (Rom. 8:28).

Another concept that will produce strong self-esteem and spiritual confidence is the understanding that God is also helping us to grow. We have a future. God is not finished with us. We are still under construction. There are amazing things yet to be accomplished in our lives. "For because of our faith, he has brought us into this place of highest privilege where we now stand, and we confidently and joyfully look forward to actually becoming all that God has had in mind for us to be" (Rom. 5:2).

Yes, we are in a place of high privilege now, but more than that, something good is going to happen in the future. We don't yet fully know what we are going to become, nor the great things God is going to do through us. We do know they will happen because of the supernatural activity of God working in our lives and in the events around us.

This deep confidence in God is produced as we spend more time personally with God, more time thinking about what He has said in the Bible and reflecting on those ideas with God in prayer. We will become like the ideas we take into our personality. That's why the Scriptures encourage us to "fix [our] thoughts on what is true and good and right . . . and the God of peace will be with [us]" (Phil. 4:8-9).

The successful midlife woman can draw on God's strength to give her that inner sense of peace and poise she will need to carry her through midlife stress. A quality relationship with God will enrich her personality for her own enjoyment—and for the blessing of other people.

> Lord, with all my heart I thank you. I will sing your praises. . . . When I pray, you answer me, and encourage me by giving me the strength I need.
>
> Psalm 138:1, 3

# PART 6

# Unavoidable Concerns

# 17

# The Marriage Knot

THE SOONER A MAN IN midlife begins to work on his problems, the sooner he will move through this traumatic time. The two major areas he must work through to make the transition successfully are his work and his marriage.

## New Marriage Lifestyle

Marriage today is different from what it was in the early 1900s. Couples then had more children, who were living in the home a longer part of the married life. In addition the life span was shorter, and people in their forties were old. In the 1950s the average marriage age for women was twenty-two and men twenty-four. In 1994 the average age for marriage had climbed to 24.5 for women and 26.7 for men.

Actually there are two marriage age patterns in the nineties. Some couples follow the earlier age pattern and are married in their early twenties, with all of the children born by the late twenties. A recent age pattern has emerged of marriage in the early thirties with childbearing taking place during the thirties. The late marriage couples tend to delay marriage while the women attend graduate school or get their careers started.

Because families have fewer children, some marriages today may begin to experience the empty nest when the parents are in their late forties. Our life expectancy has increased dramatically—both parents may expect to live into or beyond their seventies. Couples now have half of their marriage without children in the home. Yet some late marriage couples may have grade-school children in the home while the wife is going through menopause.

As recently as a hundred years ago, we measured a woman by her ability to bear children, to care for the garden, and to manage the household. We measured a husband by his physical strength and his ability to provide. Love, companionship, intimacy, if they came, were extras—but not the primary goals in marriage.

Today society expects marriage to be marked by love, intimacy, companionship, and mutual happiness. It also expects couples to live in this state of bliss for a longer period of time than any other culture has ever experienced. Some people believe that our expectations are too high and cause marriage breakups. "American marriage has been especially impossible. They set out to mix in one stew what older societies had discovered to be unmixable: romantic attachment, sexual adventure, love, domesticity."[1]

Now watch the changing scenario as a man and a woman come to their forties. Their romantic dreams of endless bliss have evaporated, the novelty of sex and their fascination with it have vanished, and the activities of getting a home in the suburbs, raising a family, and getting their children launched are generally accomplished. They find themselves at midlife with a deep need for a solid marriage—but they have done practically nothing for twenty years to improve the quality of their marriage. Instead, they have long-standing problems that may cause their marriage to break—excess baggage from earlier years, the myth that marriage will bring happiness, the hope of changing each other, and the belief that neither of them has changed.

## No Counsel Before Marriage

In addition to the problems I've listed, most couples made their choice of a marriage mate with very little counsel and help. In many older cultures of the world, the parents and the community have a great deal to say about the mate decision. In our culture we allow adolescents—who do not yet fully understand themselves or their own needs, who have had absolutely no experience in choosing a mate, and who are likely to be insecure, vacillating, and immature—to make a choice that is supposed to last for more than fifty years. Premarital counseling is still thought of as unnecessary by some couples. If any counseling is done, it is normally by a minister with little training in marriage counseling who spends a few hours arranging the format of the wedding service.

In premarital counseling, I often ask the engaged couple to list several needs they feel must be met to make their marriage a happy, growing relationship. Most couples have never thought to list their own needs—or those of their future mate. They have not considered if they are compatible. Most couples seem to conclude that because they enjoy touching each other, staring into each other's eyes, and eating out, they will have no problems with marriage.

## Dating Is Deceptive

The courtship process is basically dishonest. We try to present our best side. We repeatedly work at keeping the other person from knowing our faults, and thus we begin a tragic lifelong pattern of sweeping things under the carpet. From this unconscious dishonest act grows a relationship without intimacy.

With all of these built-in disadvantages, it is no wonder marriages at midlife have great stress, and many people think marriage in general is obsolete and bankrupt. In spite of all the problems, however, there has never been a time in our history when marriage has been more popular. The styles of marriages are changing, but marriage itself is more popular than in the past, in spite of the high divorce rate.

People have a deep need to share their lives with one person who will know them as a companion and confidant. They look for someone who will give them a relaxed psychological and spiritual security to develop and become all that they can be. They look for warmth, closeness, cuddling, and legitimate safe sex.

## What Makes a Marriage Happy?

A number of factors influence marital happiness. Generally speaking, more education tends to lead toward more marital happiness. This correlation may be true because people with more education tend to delay marriage, gaining more life experience and maturity first. People mature rapidly during the college years. If the marriage choice can be delayed, then people tend to make a better choice of partner.

People who place high emotional expectations on

their marriage tend to be less happy in marriage. Those who stress romantic love and personal uniqueness, who are extremely sensitive, and who have a great deal of drive tend to be less contented in marriage than couples who have lower or more traditional expectations for marriage.

Couples tend to evaluate their marriage's happiness differently as the marriage progresses. Most people are very satisfied with their marriages during the first few months, but are very dissatisfied twenty years later. Couples also report an increase in marital happiness after they have passed through the midlife crisis and the children have left the home.[2]

Children do influence marital happiness. In the early years of marriage, children tend to build an emotional bond between the couple. But during the children's adolescent years, they tend to reduce their parents' emotional happiness because of the increased tension they bring into the household. After the couple has passed midlife crisis and has an empty nest, marital happiness improves. With the absence of children, the couple relates more intimately.

### Reaction—Fear Or Hope

Couples react differently to the previous information. Some conclude there is no hope for their marriage because of a poor mate selection or wrong expectations or the presence of teenagers in the home. Other couples see the information with hope, realizing that they are not the only ones experiencing marital stress. Together, they decide to work on their problems and make their marriage more successful.

We expect more of marriage than in the past. It has become more emotionally complex. But at the same time, remember that God has been involved in marriage since its beginning. He is the one who built the human personality. He is able to fit us together so our differences don't chafe, but become a means of making the union stronger.

The Bible says, "And the Lord God said, 'It isn't good for man to be alone; I will make a companion for him, a helper suited to his needs' " (Gen. 2:18). God didn't make Eve a servant girl. In other Old Testament references the same word for "helper" is used to refer to a person greater than the one being helped—such as God our helper. God made a companion, someone to share the man's life. Macho-type men need to realize that this verse could easily mean that the woman is superior. At least there is no concept of "bossiness" or "servitude" intended here.

God was fully aware of the complexity of the human personality. These personality differences did not come as a shock to God. He designed us to be unique individuals. He also said people would never be fulfilled by being alone. He intended that unique individuals should blend together in a complementary relationship.

## Typical Problems

When couples seek our counseling help after several years of marriage, they usually report an overall unhappiness and discouragement with marriage—and they want out. They say they don't love each other, there is little sexual relationship, and/or one or the other has been involved in an affair. They also may report physical or emotional abuse, feel ignored, or claim that the spouse is not carrying a fair share in the marriage.

Often couples will stay together because of social, financial, or religious reasons, or because they have children at home. They commit to a grin-and-bear-it approach. Their actions say, "Okay, I've made a bad marriage, but I'll stick with it at least until the children are gone."

It's difficult to put all marriage problems into a few easily digested concepts, but many marriage problems do fit patterns and fall into general groupings.

1. *Preoccupation with the process of living.* When a man and woman first date, they spend a great deal of time talking to each other and seeking to win and please each other. After they marry, they feel this "connecting" time is a luxury. They don't work on the relationship, but each goes about separate preoccupations—with careers, raising the kids, paying on the mortgage, and accumulating things. The routine of life robs them of true companionship.

2. *Lack of communication and intimacy.* It isn't that husbands and wives don't talk. They talk about many topics—children, bills, social responsibilities, repainting the house, or caring for the garden. But they don't talk *to* each other—about how they *feel* toward each other and how their goals and aspirations are changing. They aren't sharing a growing understanding of the other person—what makes them happy or causes them to be uneasy.

But our problem isn't new. In 1943 David L. Cohn wrote a book entitled *Love in America.* "It is the rare husband and wife," he wrote then, "who pull up the chairs and spend an hour talking for their own pleasure about non-utilitarian things. Their intellectual and spiritual lives remain personal and separate, with the result that it involves no spiritual communion and no completion of minds. This is a large factor in the loneliness of people."[3]

People need to have intimate relationships with other people. They need to have at least one person with whom to be open, to share their real joys and anxieties. Most people expect marriage to provide that kind of intimacy. When they don't find it in marriage, they feel they have made a mistake. They begin looking for some other person who may be able to provide intimacy.

As communication and intimacy begin to disappear in marriage, each person becomes more aware of the other's failings. Any intimate communication that does take place tends to center on criticism and blame fixing. Negative communication tends to spiral the marriage relationship downward toward disaster.[4]

In his play *The Bald Soprano*, Eugene Ionesco depicts the same sad state of relationship I commonly see in marriage counseling. In one scene a man and woman happen to meet and engage in polite conversation. As they talk, they discover they both came down to New York that morning on the ten o'clock train and they both have the same apartment house address on Fifth Avenue. To their surprise, they discover they both have a daughter seven years old. To their final astonishment, they discover they are husband and wife! They live together, share the same bed and the same kitchen table, but intimacy has fled from their relationship, leaving them strangers.

3. Unmet personal needs. The problem of not having needs met has its roots back in courtship days when the couple didn't understand themselves and didn't ask if this relationship would meet their needs. Now they go to a counselor, reporting marital unhappiness and a deep dissatisfaction with each other. They say their sex life has

stopped, and they just don't love each other any more.

People reporting dissatisfaction or saying that they have fallen out of love are really reporting that their needs are no longer being met. The tragedy is one or both partners are unable to verbalize that their needs are not being met—they simply say, "I don't love you anymore."

A typical example is a husband and wife from another city who came to see me. The husband said he no longer loved his wife, but felt obligated to remain married to her because of his spiritual conviction. They were both unhappy with a series of affairs in which he had been involved.

We soon discovered a very domineering wife who subtly controlled her husband's life and, at the same time, resented his extreme passivity. As a young man, because of his own insecurity, he had unconsciously chosen this woman who would make all the decisions. She had unconsciously chosen a man whom she could dominate. As they moved into midlife, he resented her dominance, but was too weak to tell her he now had different needs. His affairs were with women who were less dominant and who allowed him to be more of an equal.

This couple began to work on their marriage from the point of view of need fulfillment. They shared who they really were and tried to meet the other's needs. Strangely enough, they fell in love again.

Marriages can be healed. It will not be the same old marriage. Both persons will need to grow and change and allow God to build a new marriage that fits them now.[5]

Because we are continually changing, it is ordinary to expect that our needs will also change. Meeting needs is part of the glue that holds a marriage together. Only as we understand each other's needs are we able to communicate, resolve conflict, enjoy sex, plan a compatible future, and be able to relax, laugh, and have fun.

4. *A lack of personal growth.* Old baggage from adolescence or childhood may be present. Personal inadequacies can be covered up with busyness for many early years of marriage. But if there is no growth, they will likely resurface at midlife. A man may have married to escape problems—he was lonely, came from a bad home, or felt inadequate and inferior. He hoped marriage would cure these problems. Unfortunately, a marriage is two people who each bring problems to the union. We do not escape emotional problems by getting married. If we were unhappy before marriage, we will likely be unhappy after we are married. The unhappiness may not be visible while we are busy pursuing a career or raising children, but unhappiness will certainly reappear.

Boredom with marriage is a common complaint. Boredom is often directly related to the lack of growth. The word *"bore"* means to "tire with emptiness or tedium." The human personality enjoys a certain degree of sameness, habit, and routine. These provide security. However, the human personality also needs variation, novelty, and change.

If both people in the marriage are growing, there should never be a time when they know all there is to know about each other. Their relationship will remain fresh, and there won't be the likelihood of boredom. Some individuals complain they have lost their identity—they no longer feel individual and unique. One man said, "I actually had a zero identity apart from her. I instinctively did it 'her way' because I was part of her and she was part of me."

Occasionally one of the partners will not allow the other one to grow because the first one feels insecure. One wife during midlife felt she needed to return to school and become more involved in community activities as a leader. The growth and aggressiveness of the wife caused her husband to feel very insecure. He selfishly forced her into a role of caring only for the household, the children, and his needs. The pressure from the husband caused greater marital friction, and ultimately they divorced.

Each person needs to grow and encourage the growth of the other. Each needs to work at communication and meeting the other's needs, as well as resolving old childhood problems and ultimately having realistic expectations of each other. Then their marriage will become a source of strength rather than a drag.

> But Lord, you are my shield, my glory, and my only hope. You alone can lift my head, now bowed in shame.
>
> Psalm 3:3

## For further reading

*Passages of Marriage* by Frank and Mary Alice Minirth (Nashville, TN: Thomas Nelson Publishers, 1991).

*When a Mate Wants Out* by Jim and Sally Conway (Grand Rapids, MI: Zondervan Publishing House, 1992).

# 18

# In Love Again

THE AUTHORS OF THE BOOK *The Dance-Away Lover* say there are three cycles in most marriages: falling in love, falling out of love, and falling back in love. They say that the last cycle is the most difficult, but it is the most rewarding.[1]

Falling in love again will not be like the adolescent experience. The man in midlife will need to work at it. This new relationship will have deeper dimensions and more lasting qualities than the first time around. However, it will require a deeper commitment to each other and a willingness by both to work through problems.

## Time

The first requirement of marriage renewal is time. Time is difficult to find in the busy midlife years. Careers are usually the most demanding at this era in life, adolescent children need additional time, and the community is calling on the couple for their leadership and involvement. Privacy is almost an impossibility.

If renewal of a marriage is to come about, there must be time for a couple to be alone to rekindle the dying fire. It's not enough to say, "Too bad, the fire is going out." You need time to rebuild the fire. New pieces of wood must be added, old coals need to be stirred, and probably you will need to get down on your hands and knees and blow on the embers. But finally, a small flame leaps up through the new wood, and you can begin to enjoy the warmth and fascination of the fire.

Lack of time becomes an excuse a couple uses not to work on renewing their marital fire. Men say the pressure of business is too demanding to have time to work on the marriage. But a simple weekend away at a motel or at a marriage conference, reading a book together, or talking to each other in a restaurant late at night are some workable rekindling activities. All of these take time, and often the couple won't stop running in order to find it.

The real reason behind not being able to find time may be that the couple does not want to rekindle the fire. We always seem to find time for what we want to do. Unfortunately, one partner may have given up hope, thinking that the marriage is beyond the point of being salvaged—or that the spouse will never meet the other's needs.

A marriage counselor can often help to reestablish hope so that both partners are willing to give time for renewal. Sometimes talking to another couple or sharing marriage stresses in a small group can also bring about hope. Les and Leslie Parrott, writing in *Partnership*, say, "It's interesting how mentoring ignites new optimism in the mentor couple. Whenever you transcend the borders of your own marriage to give something to somebody else, it cultivates the sense of being soul mates."[2]

## Commitment

A second essential ingredient for renewal is commitment. If it's really to happen, both people must *want* the marriage to be renewed. It's common for one partner to come for help, but the other partner, unfortunately, not to be interested. Sometimes it's helpful to work with the spouse who is willing to change. Then as that person begins to meet the needs of the partner, these changes give hope to the unwilling partner and bring an agreement to work on renewal.

It is true that if both partners do not work on the marriage, it probably will not be renewed. One of the partners may say, "My husband [or wife] will never come to see you for help."

"All right," I respond, "let's work with you and bring about your spiritual and emotional growth, so that you become an effective mate. I'm hoping your growth will cause a change in your spouse's attitude. If it doesn't, you've not lost a thing. You will be a happier person because of your growth. If your marriage does fall apart, you'll be better able to cope with the breakup and relate to people in the future."

Commitment means working with the here and now, not the past or the future. The here and now means the real person to whom you are married. Some people, unfortunately, try to make their mate into the ideal person, or they try to turn time backward to an earlier day. All of these attempts are unrealistic and guaranteed to fail. Commitment means a willingness to understand the other person's unique personality, a desire to see the spouse's needs and understand what will help the spouse enjoy life more completely. The commitment must be to work with this particular person, at this age in life, in the society in which we live.

Commitment means we are willing to fight with each other—willing to express who we are, how we feel, what upsets us. We also commit ourselves to allow the other person to express who he or she is. Too often, people withdraw when conflict comes. I tend to react this way. I stick my head in the sand, hoping the storm will blow over. This doesn't really resolve problems—it only delays them.

Couples who fight together fairly are the couples who generally stay together and have stronger marriages. There is great benefit as we pass through the conflict barrier and experience the tranquillity on the other side.

> On the other side of this conflict lies the relief, security, and comfort of being stark-naked to at least one person in life before whom we can take off our masks, shed our psychological fig leaf, and not have to pretend anymore. Such a relationship with a marriage partner can enable me to move more easily with others because someone knows my faults and still accepts me and cares for me, as well as frees me to realize my greater potential because I am not hung up on feeling guilty or stupid.[3]

### Forgiveness

A third essential ingredient in marriage renewal is forgiveness. But forgiveness is only one side of the coin—the other side is confession. The New Testament has many accounts of people who are sinning and alienated from God. There are large and repeated discussions on how people should relate to each other, and extensive teachings on forgiveness and confession. Yet most married couples feel they have failed if they need to confess *anything* or forgive *anything*. Forgiveness and confession are not abnormal experiences. We should expect that every day there will be *something* we need to confess— and *something* we need to forgive.

It is more common in marriage to fix blame instead of confessing our faults. Blame fixing is a way of trying to guarantee our rights, to make sure we are not mistreated—and also to make sure the other person is properly punished. Blame fixing also tends to focus the attention on the other person's faults rather than our own.

Blame fixing is an escape—we pass off our failures as the responsibility of the other person. This is exactly what Adam did with God in the Garden of Eden. He said, in essence, "Yes, I've sinned, but I would not have sinned if it hadn't been for the woman you gave me." Adam blamed both the woman and God. This was supposed to get him off the hook by diverting attention.

However, when a couple commit themselves to forgiveness and confession, their concentration moves totally away from fixing blame. The Bible says, "Admit your faults to one another and pray for each other so that you may be healed" (Jas. 5:16). Confession should be a routine part of our life together.

Scripture also speaks pointedly about forgiveness. "Stop being mean, bad-tempered and angry. Quarreling, harsh words, and dislike of others should have no place in your lives. Instead, be kind to each other, tenderhearted, forgiving one another, just as God has forgiven you because you belong to Christ" (Eph. 4:31-32).

Forgiveness does not mean delayed retaliation! When we forgive someone, we commit ourselves never to bring up the offense again. We commit ourselves never to use the problem as a club on the other person.

One wife told me she was having an affair. She wanted out, and she wanted help with the causes so this would never happen again. She made the break completely and began to work on her own marriage. As part of this process, she told her husband about the affair and asked his forgiveness. She also told him that she was lonely and needed his time and love.

The husband was uncomfortable as we talked about how he could help his wife and strengthen their marriage. His feeling was that she got involved in the affair by her own choice, and he was totally without fault.

I told him that he had two choices. One choice was divorce, and he certainly had legal and scriptural grounds for that. The other choice was to forgive her and work on the marriage. No other option would really work.

He said he would forgive her, and for the first few weeks he did work at building the marriage. Before a month had gone by, however, it was evident that he had not really forgiven, but held her past sin over her head. He used her failure as a club to force her to do what he wanted. His unwillingness to really forgive drove them apart, and they finally divorced.

The basis of our forgiving is not that the other person is worthy; nor do we forgive because we are such marvelous people. We forgive because God has forgiven us. We are *obligated* to forgive each other. In fact, as we repeat the Lord's Prayer, we are saying to God, "Forgive me to the same degree that I am willing to forgive someone else."

In the Old Testament book of Job we learn the results of forgiveness. Job's three friends had been criticizing him unjustly. As the story moves along, we realize that all of Job's friends were dead wrong. The Bible doesn't say these men came forward and apologized to Job, but Job forgave them, and we see the result of his forgiveness. "Then, when Job prayed for his friends, the Lord restored his wealth and happiness!" (Job 42:10).

There is a release as we forgive. As we let go of anger and hostility, we experience tranquillity and happiness. The purpose of forgiving others is not only to let the other person off the hook so he can begin to heal, it is also to drain off our anger and hostility so we can experience emotional freedom.

You may say, "I know I should forgive, but why can't I?" You may not be able to forgive because you have been hurt very deeply. Forgiveness really demands that you draw on the strength of God. If you have been deeply hurt, you need to let God heal that hurt so you can have the capacity to forgive.

We may have trouble forgiving because we feel that if we do, the person will go out and do the same dumb thing again. We feel the other person should be punished—and our lack of forgiveness is part of that punishment. We will, however, be able to forgive by yielding the whole punishing process to the justice of God and trusting Him to do what is right.

Marriage renewal will never happen without regular and continued confession and forgiveness by both partners. But God can help us to be open to giving and receiving forgiveness.

## Acceptance

A fourth requirement for marriage renewal is that we accept each other. The Bible says, "Be humble and gentle. Be patient with each other, making allowance for each other's faults because of your love" (Eph. 4:2). This doesn't mean we grit our teeth and simply endure the other person's strange thoughts and ways of behaving. Rather we completely accept the other as is—"This is the reality of my mate today."

Scripture clearly teaches that each person is unique and that this uniqueness is going to be abrasive. We must be humble, gentle, and patient with each other. If there is going to be healing in a marriage relationship, we must accept the other person as unique. This uniqueness, and even the other person's abrasiveness, will have a positive effect on our lives. We are smoothed out by each other like two rough stones in a gem tumbling machine. As we continue to bump and tumble into each other, the polishing compounds and grit of life cause the hidden qualities of beauty to be seen.

Recently a woman shared with me that she longed for her husband to carry some leadership in their home. She had nagged him for years, and he had stubbornly resisted. They had achieved an effective stalemate. Finally, the wife came to the point where she trusted the matter into God's hands—and she told her husband about her decision. She really did back off, allowing him to develop—not from her nagging, but from the quiet prodding of the Holy Spirit.

Several weeks later he called her from his office and said that he had been reading his Bible and wanted to share a verse of Scripture with her that had been meaningful to him. The wife was astounded with joy. The drastic change had come about when she was willing to accept her husband where he was and free him so that he could grow at God's pace. Acceptance had freed up the husband and "mellowed out" the wife.

## Support

A fifth dimension of marriage renewal is learning to support one another—to carry each other's load. In Galatians there are specific instructions, "If a Christian is overcome by some sin, you who are godly should gently and humbly help him back onto the right path, remembering that next time it might be one of you who is in the wrong. Share each other's troubles and problems, and so obey our Lord's command" (Gal. 6:1-2).

Part of the responsibility of being a true mate is to express your needs as well as help to carry your partner's load. But we may be too embarrassed to ask for help, or to let anyone know we have needs. Then we miss the opportunity of being helped. And we may wrongfully accuse our mate of not caring, when the real problem was we didn't communicate our need. Men especially are unwilling to admit they have needs. Sometimes they feel they will be less of a man if they ask for help.

Jesus, with all of His strength, repeatedly allowed us to see His human side. He allowed people to minister to Him. He allowed His disciples to do ministries He easily could have done Himself. He set a pattern by sharing His ministry and His burdens with His disciples.

There is an old story about a farm couple who learned how to signal each other when they needed some encouragement. If the man needed some TLC (tender, loving care), he would walk into the kitchen and toss his hat on the table. This was a signal to his wife that she needed to encourage and strengthen him. If the husband came from the field and saw his wife wearing her apron backwards, this was a sign that he needed to bear some of her burdens.

You guessed it! One day he walked in from the field and threw his hat on the table—and she had her apron on backwards. But as a couple practices encouragement and support—even when they both need help at the same time—they can, in the midst of their need, put their arms around each other and cry together, each receiving strength from the other.

Sometimes a mate will see the other in need and take advantage of that opportunity to get the upper hand in a power struggle. By deliberately withholding help, a person may temporarily feel superior, and the weak person is further weakened. The stronger mate is cutting off the legs of the weaker mate. It's as if the strong mate is standing next to the wounded mate and saying, "See how tall I am." It's a sick and brutal process, yet it goes on repeatedly in many homes. The Bible says very simply, "If anyone thinks he is too great to stoop to this [helping another], he is fooling himself. He is really a nobody" (Gal. 6:3).

## Love

The last important ingredient for marriage renewal is that partners must learn to love each other. Love is not "feeling sexy," but helping each other to become all you can be. True love is sacrifice for the other person's benefit.

Ephesians gives us a broader definition of love than simply having our needs fulfilled. "Live a life filled with love for others, following the example of Christ, who loved you and gave himself as a sacrifice to take away your sins" (Eph. 5:2 NLT). Jesus Christ loved us and was willing to die for us. That kind of sacrificial love is the quality of caring that is to exist between a husband and wife if there is really to be marriage renewal.

To love other people with the intensity with which God loves us means we must know them. We must know who they are and understand their needs and aspirations. We must love them so they will sense they are being loved.

A contractor, referred by another counselee, came to my office. He was in a panic because his wife had walked out right after he had given her a birthday present. He had come home in the middle of the day to their new house with all the latest gadgets, thick wall-to-wall carpeting, and the latest furniture. He greeted his wife with "Happy Birthday!" and handed her a set of keys. When she looked confused, he told her the keys were to the new Cadillac Coupe de Ville he had bought for her birthday. She looked out the front window to see the car, then threw the keys into the thick carpet, stomped upstairs, packed her suitcase, and walked out. He couldn't understand what had happened.

After a few weeks, she was willing to come with her husband for counseling. When she was sure I was not her husband's ally, she turned on her husband in a rage I'm sure he had never seen before. She started with her verbal hammer and nails and nailed his hide to the wall in a caustic assault. "You have bought me all kinds of gadgets all our married life! They were always things you thought I wanted! You've never really known me as a person. I wouldn't care if we lived in an old house and had a beat-up old car, as long as you spent time with me.

But you are so busy trying to impress everybody with the things you buy for me that you don't have any time to spend with me. All I want is to spend time with you!"

It is impossible to love someone unless you know that person's needs. This husband certainly was expressing love to his wife from his point of view—but he did not understand his wife's needs. He really loved himself, not her. His love was like the love of a child who gives his father a toy truck at Christmas. The child wants what he gives. He has no understanding of the parent's needs. God's love is so different because He understands our needs and loves us at the point of *our* need.

After we understand the needs of the other person, we must be willing to give energy from our lives to meet our mate's needs. If we understand the other person's needs and don't meet those needs, we don't love. The apostle James tells the story of a man who told his friend he needed food. The friend gave him only a verbal spiritual blessing and sent him away. James criticized that action; even though nice words were spoken, the need of the man was not met. The verbal expression of caring was useless. The friend's love was not directed to the first man's hunger (Jas. 2:14-17).

### Practical Steps Toward Renewal

There are some practical steps a man can take toward rebuilding his marriage. First, consciously think of looking through your wife's eyes. What does she see when she looks at you? What do your actions show? What does she want as her goals and purpose in life? What stresses and anxieties does she feel? As you begin to look through her eyes, you'll gain a new perspective, and your marriage will take on different dimensions.

Second, a man should begin a deliberate program of building the emotional self-image of his wife. At least once a day think of some specific compliment. At first, the congratulations and expressions of praise to your wife will probably center around the things she does. But as the weeks go along, the process of encouraging her should move toward praising her for qualities within her personality. "Thank you for being the kind of person who understands me. Thank you for being patient. I'm really grateful you're a praying woman. Thank you for the great qualities you've instilled in our children. I'm proud of you because you have a caring heart for lots of people." Praising her personality will cause more rapid growth than praising her activities. Emphasize who she is rather than what she does. After a few weeks, we hope, building up your wife will become a habit.

Next, a man might agree to carry out a specific contract with his wife. This process is often helpful to get both parties moving toward meeting each other's needs. It is also a tangible way to measure success.

For example, one husband complained that his wife was not interested in sex. She complained that he was not interested in doing anything around the house. They worked out a simple contractual agreement—the husband did some of the jobs his wife had been wanting done, and in return, she was more responsive sexually. As a result, they each felt their marriage relationship was more meaningful. She saw his concern for keeping things repaired as a part of his love for her, so it was easier to be sexually warm to him. Her sexual responsiveness made him feel like caring for her in tangible ways. Warning: don't just do a loving act to manipulate your mate. See the act as just that—an act of sacrificial love.

Finally, a man and his wife should sit down with the calendar and plan specific times when they will have special fun activities. Plan a variety of events, some taking a whole weekend, others only a few minutes. For example, you might plan to do a major event once every two months—a weekend away at a motel, camping out, a special trip. In between you should plan dates—a movie, dinner, biking, a walk around the block, a cup of coffee after supper, or listening to the same song on the CD player. Or you might plan a project or hobby to do together. The point is, you should not say, "Someday we're going to do that." Sit down with a calendar and begin to outline *when* you are going to do those things.

I firmly believe in the power of God and the absolute possibility of marriage renewal. I also know that marriage renewal does not usually come about by a simple one-two-three formula. There must be a deep commitment on the part of each person to follow the positive directives God has clearly established in Scripture.

> Blessings on all who reverence and trust the Lord—on all who obey him! Their reward shall be prosperity and happiness. Your wife shall be contented in your home. And look at all those children! There they sit around the dinner table as vigorous and healthy as young olive trees. That is God's reward to those who reverence and trust him.
>
> Psalm 128:1-4

## For Further Reading

*Adult Children of Legal or Emotional Divorce* by Jim Conway (Downers Grove, IL: InterVarsity Press, 1990).

Becoming Soul Mates  by Les and Leslie Parrott (Grand Rapids, MI: Zondervan Publishing House, 1995). A book to help a couple maintain or restore intimacy.

*Love's Tug of War*  by David and Jan Congo (Grand Rapids, MI: Fleming H. Revell, 1997).

*Marriage in the Whirlwind*  by Bill and Pam Farrel (Downers Grove, IL: InterVarsity Press, 1996).

*Moving On After He Moves Out* by Jim and Sally Conway (Downers Grove, IL: InterVarsity Press, 1995).

*Traits of a Lasting Marriage*  by Jim and Sally Conway (Downers Grove, IL: InterVarsity Press, 1991).

*Winning Your Wife Back* by Gary Smalley (Branson, MO: Today's Family, 1996). The book is a play-by-play approach structured to winning a football game.

# 19

# A Sexy Marriage

DURING A MIDLIFE CRISIS, A man's sexual capacity might be his single greatest concern. Often he is afraid he is losing his sexual ability. The drama goes something like this: a man is overextended at work. He is running out of energy. Younger men seem eager to take his place. He is on innumerable boards and committees for the community and the church. His family has giant financial needs, and there never seems to be enough money to go around.

With that as a background, he crawls into bed at night. His wife, who has just gone through her own midlife reassessment, is experiencing a new sexual awakening. Instead of being passive, she begins aggressive sexual moves on him. To his amazement, he finds he is extremely slow in responding. Part way through intercourse he may lose his erection, and at that moment, he suddenly believes life is over. He no longer is a man. It's exactly as he had heard—midlife means the end of sex.

As he rolls over and drops off into a fitful sleep, he wonders if the problem is really his or if his wife has lost her ability to stimulate him. For a moment, there is a glimmer of hope. Maybe he is still capable of sex. "That's it! It's all my wife's fault!" Unfortunately he knows very little about male sexual functioning. He does not realize that the problem is not with his wife, but with him. The solutions he will try, sad to say, will probably further deflate his self-image.

People in midlife today are different from a few generations ago. If a midlife couple fifty years ago engaged in sex frequently (two or three times a week), they were considered oversexed. If they talked about it, they certainly were perverted.

Today, however, with extended life and improved health, sexual relationships in midlife can be the best of any era. The midlife woman has a great deal of sexual freedom, and has a stronger sex drive than many college-age women. At the same time, her husband has learned about caring, so intercourse can be a deep expression of their relationship rather than simply animal sex (well, let's keep a little animal sex). Also, because he is now a mature man, he is better able to control an ejaculation, and both of the partners will experience a greater ecstasy in sex than many younger couples experience.

There are, however, problems with the midlife sexual relationship. An effective and meaningful sexual liaison in midlife is only possible if the rest of the marriage is going smoothly. If the couple is struggling in several other areas, their sex life will indicate that. Sexual relationships become a sort of barometer, indicating how well other areas of life are functioning.

There was a time when most of the sexual complaints came from men. They complained that their wives were frigid, unresponsive, disinterested in sex. Now an increasing number of wives complain that their husbands are not meeting their sexual needs. The sexual revolution has made it acceptable for a woman to respond the way God made her. Previously, a woman felt she had to suppress her feeling of excitement during sex. She also had to suppress her assertiveness. A "good girl" never thought about sex, let alone initiated it. Now a new door of sexual experience has been opened for women.

## A Problem for Men

This new freedom for women, however, places a greater burden on men. Previously, men thought it was their wife's fault when they didn't have sex. Now men are surprised to find that women are extremely interested in sex and can experience orgasm after orgasm in one sexual encounter, perhaps far outdoing their husbands. A man may also be startled to learn that the ability of his wife to enjoy sex and to respond enthusiastically is basically his responsibility. Many men are not prepared to assume this kind of sexual leadership. They are intimidated by the desires and ability of their wife.

The explosive growth of strong men's movements such as Promise Keepers may be one of the most positive results of this greater freedom for women—and of the emotional intimidation men have felt. Thousands of men searching for answers have gathered to truly become men of God, to understand their wives, and to take strong stands of commitment. As a man understands his wife and what makes a good marriage, there can come a new day of openness and sexual joy for both of them.[1]

The Bible has never been silent on the subject of sex and has never treated sex as dirty. Sex has always been a gift of God. The Bible is very open, far more open than many evangelical churches.

The sexual revolution, however, not only opened the door for sexual communication, but it also moved increasingly toward distortions. Good sexual relationships might be compared to rowing a boat. Both oars must be used at the same time and matched in strength. In our society we have overemphasized the physical aspect of sex—the animal dimension—and we have ignored the qualities of love, commitment, warmth, and fidelity. As a result, a sexual partner is often thought of as an "it."

Yes, sex is physical. But the physical part alone, like a person using only one oar of the boat, will cause the boat to go around in circles, never achieving a goal or a direction. The other oar is the emotional aspect—understanding and caring for the other person. Great sex needs a depth relationship requiring time, commitment, forgiveness, acceptance, support, and love. This caring oar of sex gives meaning to the physical dimension. Sex is not simply an isolated physical act enjoyed off and on during a week. It is a continued demonstration of care, expressed by words, togetherness, and prayer as well as through intercourse.

### Is There Sex After Forty?

Sometimes the problem with a man at midlife is that he has leftover attitudes from youth that convince him that sex is over by age forty. Studies of college students show the distorted view of sex activity that is held by many young adults.[2]

A study reported in *Psychology Today* revealed that 646 Illinois State University students felt their parents "had intercourse once a month or less, never had intercourse before they were married, [and] never had oral genital sex."

The students had great trouble accepting the reality of their parents' sex life. "Ninety percent of students who felt their parents were happily married and still in love believed they maintained this happy state without the help of sex, or at least not much of it."

Some students reacted very negatively, apparently not wanting to even think about their parents' sex life: " 'This questionnaire stinks.' 'Whoever thinks about their parents' sexual relations, except perverts?' 'What stupid person made up these questions?' "[3]

Men in midlife tend to carry the same convictions as the college students regarding sex after forty. They believe sex is over by midlife, so when they first experience some sexual slowness, they react with trauma and believe they are now too old for sex.

## Sexual Expectations

The problem of a midlife man is that his sexual expectations are not based on reality. For example, a man who was a pole-vaulter in college and cleared 16' 2" does not expect at age forty-five to match that performance. Yet, when he thinks of his sex life, he anticipates his sexual recycling speed will be the same as when he was a young adult.

The male in his late teens is at the very peak of his sexual capacity. He achieves an erection very rapidly and can experience a number of ejaculations with only a few minutes' recovery time. From the early twenties there is a very slow loss of recovery speed throughout the rest of his life. A man in good health in his seventies, however, still should have no problem having sexual intercourse, although it will take more time to achieve an erection and more time until ejaculation.

It is a mistake for a man in his forties to expect the same kind of sexual capacity as the adolescent or young adult. However, a man at forty, while his sexual pace is somewhat slower, is by far a more effective lover. He understands more completely the needs of his wife, and his slower pace until ejaculation makes the sexual relationship more fulfilling. This slowness is not negative for women—they have always wanted more cuddling and foreplay.

Some midlife men have been trapped by office or locker room escapades. They feel they must prove they are "macho." Many women, however, are not looking for a sexual performance like that of the adolescent boy, but of the mature man who understands love, warmth, and caring.

## Sexual Problems

The loss of sexual ability is most often due to fear rather than physical reality. Some men have become fathers very late in life. "A South African called Henry Potts and a Pole named Kasper Raynold became fathers at the age of 105. It's said that a Frenchman, Pierre Deformel, fathered children in three centuries, the birth dates being 1699, 1738, and 1801."[4]

Sometimes a man worries that he may lose his capacity if he has a heart attack. Drs. Ernest Friedman and Herman Hellerstein of Case Western Reserve University state that "the pulse rate [during sexual intercourse] does not rise more than it does during many other routine activities, and the period of maximum acceleration usually lasts only about fifteen seconds"; they conclude that "over 80 percent of men (and presumably women) who have had coronaries can fulfill the demands of sexual activity without evidence of significant strain."[5]

An increasing number of men in midlife are showing up in the doctor's office, complaining they are impotent. Yet most impotence is really emotional. Quite often the man who claims to be impotent will have sexual intercourse while he is on vacation, or may be sexually aroused by a porno movie, or has no problem performing with a mistress. Fear, fatigue, and marital problems are the basis of many, if not most, of midlife sexual problems.

The correction of sexual problems must be seen from more than a physical point of view, as shown by a number of studies and experiments using hormone therapy. Years ago a study was run in which fifty men complaining of impotence were given hormone tablets, and another fifty complaining of impotence were given sugar pills. Seventy-eight percent on the hormone tablets improved their sexual capacity after a month, and 40 percent on the sugar pills improved.[6]

Masters and Johnson list six general conditions that cause midlife or older males to lose sexual responsiveness:

1. Monotony of a repetitious relationship
2. Preoccupation with career or economic pursuits
3. Mental or physical fatigue
4. Overindulgence in food or drink
5. Physical and mental infirmities of a man or his spouse
6. Fear of failure in the sex act[7]

As shown from several studies, when there is a loss of sexual capacity in midlife, it usually has little to do with medical causes but is related to a low self-image, fatigue, being overextended at work, or too much alcohol. For example, about 75 to 80 percent of a man's self-image is related to his job. If a man is going through stress at work so that his self-image is being diminished, he likely will have sexual problems. Stanley Frank reports what happened to men sexually when the stock market crashed in 1929: "Six months later, it was routine to hear women say that they had had no sexual relations with their husbands since Black Thursday, the day the bottom fell out of the market."[8]

Technology is another destroyer of the sex drive because it forces us to live at an exhausting pace. "Life is moving at warp speed. On average, we make decisions on over 8,000 informational inputs per day! The pager vibrates. You have to decide if and when to respond. The answering machine records a message. Do you screen the call or pick it up? Faxes, E-mail, the cell phone—more decisions. Your mind is exhausted because you've decided so much. Many are little decisions—but there are so many!"[9]

Without a doubt, there is a slight slowing down of the sexual response of the man in midlife. This slowing down is not negative, but should make his sexual relationship with his wife richer and more pleasurable. Fear that he will lose his sexual capacity may, however, cause him to lose it. But as a man learns to relax, he will find he has become the "best lover" he has ever been.

Not all sexual problems at midlife are from emotional stress, however. A number of studies show that a hormonal imbalance can develop at midlife, similar to some of the hormonal changes of women. This hormonal imbalance strongly affects the man's emotional life. Male hormonal imbalances can cause morning fatigue, depression, nervousness, difficulty sleeping, and sometimes affect the heartbeat, as well as sexual potency. He seems to lose stability, becomes easily irritated at work, and may have wildly vacillating moods.

## Improving His Sex Life

It's a mistake for a man to think the answer to his sexual problems lies in some new techniques. The basic way to improve sexual relationships is to practice love with sex. The real issue isn't making love—it's feeling loved. Or as Frank puts it, "A man is never more alone than when he is locked in a loveless sexual embrace."[10]

If a man is going to improve his sex life, he must shift his attention away from himself and begin to concentrate on his wife and her needs. As the emphasis shifts from performance to caring, the relationship will improve in quality and performance.

Sexual therapists Masters and Johnson, when helping a couple reestablish their sexual relationship, try to build the emotional relationship before the couple gets involved in the physical relationship. The couple agrees *not* to have sexual intercourse until it is eagerly sought by both of them. The concentration is shifted to building the relationship through sharing common interests, talking, and touching. The emphasis is always on the relationship—not on sexual intercourse. These therapists have found when the pressure for sexual performance is shifted toward the relationship, sexual interest returns.

A man's religious convictions may have to change to

improve his sex life. Many Christians still believe the original sin in the Garden of Eden was Adam and Eve having sex. That's ridiculous! The original sin was disobeying God by eating a piece of fruit from a forbidden tree.

Before the act of disobedience, God instructed Adam and Eve to "multiply and fill the earth and subdue it" (Gen. 1: 28). Somehow many people believe God was stunned when He came into the garden one evening and discovered that Adam and Eve had had intercourse. Sex is not a surprise to God—He planned it. He intended a sexual relationship.

One of the purposes of sex is to have children. *Procreation* is not the only purpose, however. The Bible clearly teaches that sex is also *recreational*. Scripture says the woman's body is to be enjoyed all the time by her husband. "Let your wife be a fountain of blessing for you. Rejoice in the wife of your youth. Let her breasts satisfy you always. May you always be captivated by her love" (Prov. 5:18-19 NLT). Sex is not only for bringing children into the world. A man is to be intoxicated with his wife's love.

The Song of Solomon is a celebration of love. The man talks about his beloved's eyes, hair, teeth. He speaks of her lips, mouth, neck, and also the beauty of her breasts. He declares, "You are so beautiful, my beloved, so perfect in every part" (Song of Sol. 4:7 NLT). Some people have tried to make this an allegory of God's love for us. Certainly it can be used to show that, but the primary purpose is to show the physical love relationship between a husband and his wife.

The New Testament gives instructions about a husband and wife's sexual relationship: "So do not deprive each other of sexual relations. The only exception to this rule would be the agreement of both husband and wife to refrain from sexual intimacy for a limited time, so they can give themselves more completely to prayer. Afterward, they should come together again so that Satan won't be able to tempt them because of their lack of self-control" (1 Cor. 7:5 NLT).

The Bible clearly teaches that sex has a recreational aspect. Couples should refrain from sex as they mutually agree to spend time in prayer. After prayer, they are to engage in sex again. I can hear some guys saying, "Let's say amen more often."

The Bible not only teaches that sex is for procreation and recreation, this passage also points out that sex is *relational*. The husband and the wife agree on when to have sex and when not to. They both make decisions about sex. It is *not* male-dominated; both the husband and wife, who mutually love and respect each other, are to sensitively communicate their needs to each other.

When couples seek help with sexual problems, we generally start by looking at their emotional relationship. Eighty to 90 percent of sexual problems can be cured by reducing tension and improving communication. After we have worked through the emotional differences, some simple teaching and hints often help the sexual relationship to improve. There are a number of good books and tapes available at Christian bookstores that can help a man in midlife with his sexual life.

## We're Different

A common element that many couples don't understand is the different excitement levels of the male and female. Most men are aroused very rapidly and reach the point of ejaculation quickly. Then they roll over and go to sleep. The husband's excitement rate can be compared to a gas stove—quickly on and quickly off—while the wife is more like an electric stove—slowly on and slowly off.

When a husband and wife don't understand their excitement differences, they begin to think the other is taking advantage of them. The wife feels the husband only wants to satisfy himself and doesn't care about her—she feels used. The husband, on the other hand, feels his wife is frigid and unresponsive. If the husband understands this difference and slows down his excitement rate, together they can reach a peak of excitement at the same moment. If a couple will spend more time in foreplay, arousing each other before intercourse, they are more likely to arrive at a climax at the same time.

Remember, men, your wife is slow in coming down from her sexual high. If you roll over and go to sleep, she is more likely to feel used. The "coming down" time is a good time to talk, to say how much you appreciate each other. Thank your wife—not only for sex, but for the little things she does for you. The "coming down" time is a great time to make plans for what you want to do as a couple, things you'd like to achieve. Some men feel that the "coming down" time is a waste; they'd rather go to sleep. But if the wife continues to fondle her husband and he continues to touch and caress his wife, the "coming down" time can be a rich period for building the marital relationship.

### What Turns You On?

A couple needs to tell each other specifically what

gives them the most pleasure—how they like to be touched, what position they like best—in short, what gives them the greatest sexual satisfaction. Many couples have never shared what causes them sexual pleasure. Sometimes they are too embarrassed, or they are afraid their partner will feel bad if they bring this up. Most sexual relationships could be improved if the couple would share these simple facts.

## Variety Is the Spice of Sex

A couple told me in a counseling session about their growing disillusionment with sex. It had lost its sparkle and excitement. Before they were married, they could hardly keep their hands off each other, but now it was "just plain Dullsville." I encouraged them to think back to their courtship days to the things that aroused them. I challenged them to break out of the mold of having sexual intercourse late at night just before they went to sleep. That time is probably most typical, but from an energy point of view, it is the worst choice.

Why not go for a drive in the country and have sex there? How about sex over the lunch hour? Why not on the living room floor, or in front of the fireplace? What's wrong with sex in a canoe, on the picnic table, or in the shower? Ask each other what could enhance your sex life.

One doctor tells of an older couple who had tapered off to having intercourse about every four weeks. Then the wife became ill and they had no relations for about six months. When she tried to resume intercourse, the husband could not get an erection. So the wife bought a book on sex. She learned that if a wife fondled her husband's penis it helped him have an erection. You might think this is common knowledge, but she had been taught that playing with sex organs was not something a decent woman did. She bravely tried it anyway and it worked.

In fact she found their lovemaking far better than thirty years ago, and her husband was a changed man, cheerful, optimistic, and vigorous. The wife then remarked, "Maybe I shouldn't admit it, but I enjoy our relations more than I used to. I'm even thinking of trying some of the other things I read about in that book."[11]

Sexual intercourse is a renewable resource to be enjoyed repeatedly, and each time it can be new, full, and complete. One time it may take on a very serious tone with deep, interpersonal sharing. Another time it might be just plain fun. Dr. David Reuben, author of *Everything You Always Wanted to Know About Sex But Were Afraid to Ask*, says with tongue in cheek, "one act of intercourse is equal to half an hour of jogging, and 'once around the bed' is the exercise equivalent of running four times around the park."[12]

It's time people realize that sex is God's idea. He intends it to be a pleasurable experience, enjoyed frequently by a husband and wife. When a man and a woman accept the biblical basis for sex, work on their emotional relationship, and learn all they can about each other, then they will have a fun sexual relationship and overcome one of the major problems of a midlife crisis.

> Thank you for making me so wonderfully complex!
> It is amazing to think about. Your workmanship is marvelous—and how well I know it.
>
> Psalm 139:14

# 20

# Work That's Fun

THE SECOND MAJOR CONCERN a man must face, if he is to successfully make it through his midlife crisis, is his work. Marriage and sex will be the most significant areas emotionally, but the problem of work will probably consume more of his time. He can't avoid facing the work crisis at midlife. Dropping out by taking an early retirement is not a long-range solution. It only delays the inevitable question, "What kind of contribution do I want to make to society that will enable me to earn a living?"

When a man starts out on the ladder of success, he seems to find only upward progress through his twenties, thirties, and into the forties. As he succeeds, his job expands in scope. It's an inverted pyramid. The job starts out small, but as he rises toward success, his responsibilities move both upward and outward.

## Less Snap in the Rubber Band

As the job responsibility expands, he feels a greater pressure to succeed personally, as well as help the company succeed. By the time he reaches his mid-forties, he is probably overextended. At the same time, his physical energies are beginning to level off.

Typically we add 10 percent more to our total life workload each year. If he had thirty tasks at age twenty-five, he might have as many as 250 responsibilities at age forty-five. But now he doesn't have the twenty-five- year-old body that can handle the stress of 250 tasks.

As soon as the man begins to recognize that he cannot continuously expand in his job because of his limited energy, he often begins to feel insecure. His self-image may be damaged, and he may feel trapped—trapped because he cannot slow down due to financial pressures, trapped because the people in the company want him to keep advancing, and trapped because there are younger competitors wanting his job. If he shows weakness, he may be replaced.

Or he may be in a situation where he is approaching forty. After making steady progress for almost two decades, suddenly he finds himself on a career plateau. Should he take a chance in a job with a new company? Or should he trim his ambitions and coast to retirement? Wow, that's a long way to coast in a boring job!

The forties for many men are career panic years—"Is this as far as I'm going to advance? Do I really like this company? Should I start my own business? Why are those 'young turkeys' in the company doing so well?"

Sometimes he thinks, "If I looked younger, I'd be more valuable to the company!" So he goes for the hair restoration, facelift, liposuction, and caps on his teeth. "Men are also getting 30 percent of nose jobs, and 17 percent of facelifts."[1]

"Men are now responsible for nearly one in four cosmetic surgeries. Whatever type of cosmetic shortcoming a man has, it is likely to be a liability in his career. The world of business is prejudiced against the ugly. Conversely, an individual's path to the top will require less effort if he is attractive. Too many employers believe that old faces mean old ideas. Hence, in a period of wholesale layoffs, men would be foolish not to avail [themselves] of cosmetics or cosmetic surgery that would make them look livelier."[2]

## Unstable Ground

Another change comes to a man in his midforties. He is now expected to shift from being a competitor to being a trainer. Up to this point, he has been working himself up in the company, trying always to do something better than others so he can be recognized and promoted. He advanced by competition from stockroom boy to loading dock, to foreman, finally to vice president in charge of shipping. Now the company asks him to change his direction and begin to train younger men under him, to work with the stock boy, the foreman, and to pick out key men in the company and train them for advancement.

It is never said aloud, but the vice president knows what he really is being asked to do—train someone to take his job. This requires a totally different mindset. He no longer is in competition with men beneath him. Now he is to equip them to eventually take his position. This shift of direction may trigger a deep and pervading reality of the man's own mortality and ultimate death. Suddenly he passes over a line. He begins to feel that not only machines, but men—especially midlife men—become obsolete.

## Changing Attitudes Toward Work

A man must resist the temptation to run, get away, retreat into self-pity, or react in anger or cynicism. He has to go back to basics: What is work all about? Why do we work in the first place? *Leben und arbeiten* ("to love and to work"), said Freud, is the need of every man. If he hasn't found fulfillment here, he hasn't reached maturity.

"Work supplies an answer to some of the deepest and most basic of all human drives: the need to produce something, the need to create something, the need to gratify curiosity, the need to be useful, the need to be needed. Wise men have always known this. 'Blessed is he who has found his work,' wrote Thomas Carlyle."[3]

There is a basic, built-in need for men to work. Work is not a violation of man, it is an important ingredient to fulfill a man. Some people believe work was part of the curse God placed on man because of sin. But work was present before the Fall: "And God blessed them and told them, 'Multiply and fill the earth and subdue it; you are masters of the fish and birds and all the animals' " (Gen. 1:28). The Bible continues, "The Lord God placed the man in the Garden of Eden as its gardener, to tend and care for it" (Gen. 2:15).

From the beginning, God gave man the opportunity of work. Before the Fall, man was given management, as well as the physical activity of tending the garden. We see two dimensions of work here—the laborer and the manager. Work is part of God's plan to enrich the life of man.

God is to be involved in man's work as well as in every other dimension of life. More than that, as he gives his life to God, God will form interests and desires within his personality that should then be expressed through work. "For God is at work within you, helping you want to obey him, and then helping you do what he wants" (Phil. 2:13). God also gives a man the capacity to carry out those desires. It is completely appropriate to ask God's direction in our work life. It is absolutely right for a man to look within himself and ask, "What are my interests?" Finding the right job is matching our God-given interests and abilities with various occupational opportunities.

Over the years I have noticed a number of men caught in unhappy work situations. When I was in college, my father told me no one really enjoyed work. It was something everyone had to do to live. At that time he was in the heating and air-conditioning business.

When he got into his midsixties, he felt God wanted him to start a retirement village in Florida. My father worked as many hours as in the old business, but at the village he was doing what seemed to have a greater purpose. His God-given desires and abilities were meshed so that out of a pastureland in central Florida has sprung up a retirement village—an expression of a man who found that work, even though tiring, can be very exhilarating.

## The Workaholic

There are three major ways a man reacts to his work crisis at midlife:

•He may push harder than ever to demonstrate that he is valuable.

•He may feel discouraged, exploited, sick of the rat race, and decide to completely drop out.

•He may change jobs, perhaps entering a very different occupation, and find more fulfillment in his work than he has ever known.

The present generation of midlife men was raised on

the work ethic. Some men resent the fact that their fathers worked so much. But most men still measure worth by work. The problem is if the measure of worth is *only* work, then he will be frustrated at the peak of midlife when he no longer has the energy for the ever increasing responsibilities in his job.

If a man chooses to work harder, he will find a dead-end road. The man who becomes a workaholic to prove himself is only delaying the inevitable. Sooner or later he must face himself and make some realistic evaluations of his capacities and strengths. His physical body will not allow him to work at an ever expanding pace.

I tend to be one of those workaholics. In recent years I have found it necessary to say to myself, "Your energy and strength are limited. Now choose to spend energy in the way you can be most productive." The problem with my job is I enjoy doing so many different things. I now must choose to do the ones which will be the most helpful to the larger community and the most satisfying to me.

### The Dream Has Gone Dry

The second direction a man may take is to give up, to become disillusioned with his job—"What's it all worth, anyway? I've broken my back for this company all these years, and now they're just going to push me out."

A sign of giving up is that a man's productivity at work drops. As a man becomes less productive, he is passively resisting his job. He is quietly waving a red flag. In a sense, he is saying, "Please fire me or move me to another job. I don't like what I'm doing, but I don't have the courage to get out without someone pushing me." Instead of dropping out or being less productive, a man needs to face the reasons for his job dissatisfaction and then change—get more training, take a paid or unpaid vacation, or look for a new job.

## He Hates His Job

Another common way of expressing dissatisfaction with a job is anger. A man may become extremely cynical about work itself, or about his job in particular. He will probably also be difficult to live with at work. He will be short-tempered and critical, walking around with a chip on his shoulder. Young associates may receive his greatest mistreatment, especially if he sees them as competitors for his job. His anger may also verge on insubordination with his bosses if he feels the business is not succeeding, or if he feels he is wasting his life working for this company.

Thumbing impatiently through an airline magazine while waiting for a plane to take off, I was captured by a powerful article. Jan Halper, writing in *American Way*, spoke with 4,126 men in preparation for his book, *Quiet Desperation: The Truth About Successful Men*. These were all highly successful men, yet hear the statistics:

• Forty-eight percent of all middle managers said their lives seemed "empty and meaningless."

• Nearly 60 percent of the high achievers felt they had sacrificed their identities and wasted years of their lives pursuing material rewards.

• Sixty-eight percent of the senior executives said they had neglected their family lives in pursuit of professional goals. Half of those executives said if they could start over again, they would spend less time working and more time with their wives and children.

• There were, however, 23 percent who seemed happy with themselves and their circumstances. Their secret was having fun at work, valuing personal growth, cherishing family and friends. Status, fame, and money weren't on the list of motivators.[4]

There are many reasons why a man doesn't like his job, but most of these reasons come down to a value mismatch—a man's interests, values, goals, and abilities do not match his job. The closer a person can come to matching his entire personality and lifestyle with a job, the greater degree of satisfaction he can expect.

Often at midlife people suggest to men that they slow down, take it easy. Sometimes the man in midlife decides this is the solution for his job frustrations. Often the problem is not fatigue, it is a *mismatch* of the man with his job.

Why can a man work nine hours at the office and come home absolutely drained and worn out with emotional frustration, then over the weekend take a bunch of Boy Scouts through the trauma of camping out and come back exhausted—but not emotionally fatigued? Escaping from work is not the answer. The answer is a better alignment of the man with his job.

If a man is following a normal growth pattern, we should assume that he will outgrow a series of jobs. Emotional gaps will develop as the man grows personally while his job stays the same. It's okay, and even normal, to outgrow your job.

One summer in Cleveland during my college years, I worked in a machine shop. I ran several different machines, but I quickly learned that none of them demanded all of me. A highly trained gorilla could have carried out my tasks. My job was to punch a button to start the machine, dump a pan of bolts in one end of the machine, wait for a pan to fill up at the other end—then remove it. To keep from going insane, I wrote letters and memorized large sections of the Bible. Get a different job, or make this one really work for you!

## Hopeful, Yet Afraid

The same pressures that cause a man to become a workaholic, or to be disillusioned and want to drop out, can also be the springboard toward an exciting new work alignment. Consider an intensive evaluation of yourself, then make the career changes to fit your personality and abilities.

Many midlife men will not go through this process because they are afraid to find out about themselves. Truth may bring a man greater unhappiness with his job. Now his quiet uneasiness becomes a deep frustration that may force him to quit. Then what? Many men can't live with that kind of uncertainty at midlife.

It's a common hope that somehow this frustration with work will simply disappear. One man put it this way. "I'm fifty-four years old. Fifteen years ago, if they had told me, 'Listen, we can't give you a raise,' I might have said, 'Take this job and shove it,' and I would have left. But now—where could I go? Who is hiring old men like me?"[5]

Another man said,

I am fifty-two years old now, and I became a vice president when I was forty-four. That was considered quite young at the time. I felt very successful and secure. Two weeks ago a twenty-seven-year-old kid became a vice president of the firm! He's sharp and bright and "with it." The top executives are aware of how rapidly the world is changing. I agree, but I get a hollow feeling of terror in the pit of my stomach; if vice presidents are made at twenty-seven, when am I going to be obsolete?[6]

Arthur Miller's play *Death of a Salesman* is a classic yet tragic commentary on our society's ability to throw away people. It is the truth of this play that causes many men in midlife not only to live with an uneasiness about losing their jobs, but to live in *stark terror*.

Willy Loman is a shoe salesman in his sixties. He is a broken, worn-out man who has traded his life energy to benefit the company. He asks for an easier job, but instead is fired. Willy's response is, "I put thirty-four years into this firm, Howard, and now I can't pay my insurance. You can't eat the orange and throw the peel away—a man is not a piece of fruit."[7]

A wife may not fully grasp the intensity of the terror her husband feels regarding work. He has always come across as strong and secure. To her, he has always seemed to know where he was going. Unfortunately, his job is an expression of his worth. If he loses his job, he has lost his worth.

When a man in midlife crisis asks, "What will I do if I lose my job?" his wife thinks it's simple—"Get another job." But a man without a job is a man without an identity. He feels he has nothing to offer a new employer. Unhappiness with his work or the fear of losing his job can cause physical and emotional effects such as ulcers, high blood pressure, colitis, impotence, or an emotional breakdown.

## He Loses His Job

The only thing more devastating to a man than being dissatisfied with his job or being afraid of losing it—is actually losing it. When a man loses his job he also loses his salary and his benefits—hospitalization, retirement accounts, paid vacations, sick leave, and company perks such as a car or recreational facilities. He may also lose his expense account or other fringe benefits.

There is, however, a greater loss than either the salary or additional benefits—his self-identity. He feels like a "zero." It's difficult to meet people because most conversation centers around, "What you do?" as an identification of who you are. A man then retreats into a black hole of fear and isolation.

When I graduated from seminary, I experienced eight months of joblessness before being called to a church. There were a number of opportunities, but I did not feel that any of them were where God wanted me to be. Later I was three months between churches. During both of these periods in my life, there was a tremendous loss of self-esteem. I felt as if no one really wanted me or my services. I was convinced that God didn't care for me. I didn't want to be with people. I was even embarrassed to talk about the situation with my children. In short, I felt extremely wretched.

During both of these times I was employed full-time, but not at a job that used my gifts, abilities, and my calling from God. During these times Sally repeatedly encouraged me, "You are still a pastor, even though you are not actively ministering in a church."

## Job Discrimination

In 1967 Congress passed an act prohibiting age dis-crimination. This legal action was groundbreaking. But age discrimination is still practiced and seems to be growing. An article in *Money* entitled "Too Damn Old" says, "Age discrimination is pervasive and appears to be getting worse." More than 16 percent of workers ages fifty-five to sixty-four lost their jobs because of layoffs or downsizings between 1991 and 1993. That's up from 11 percent from the years between 1981 to 1983. By compar-ison, the portions of workers ages twenty to twenty-four who lost jobs fell from 19 percent in 1981 to 1983 to less than 16 percent in 1991 to 1993.[8]

## Keeping Yourself Employable

It's a waste of time and psychological energy to fight a three- to five-year court battle trying to prove that you are the victim of age bias. Stop being a victim! Keep your-self employable. *Money* magazine suggests steps to take to ensure your career future:

• Don't tie your career to any single job or company. "Develop a portfolio of skills and experience that will qualify you for either a different position with your cur-rent employer or for a move to another company. For example," says Greenberg, "a manufacturing specialist who understands how the company markets its products is more valuable than one who simply knows how it makes them."

• Take advantage of training. "The greater the number of skills you have, the less vulnerable you are to layoffs or extended periods of joblessness," says management consultant Frank Landy.

• Fight the stereotype. "Show your employer at every opportunity that you're physically and mentally fit and eager for new challenges."

• Keep networking. "Older workers have at least one advantage over younger job seekers: they know more people. And don't forget to network within your current company as well. Though your division may be in jeopardy, some other part of the company could be hiring."

• Don't let fears of age bias hold you back. "'You can't be defensive or apologetic about your age. Sure, age bias is real. But, older workers have talent and expertise to offer.' And fortunately, some companies still value that."[9]

Better yet, think of being self-employed. There are lots of new small business opportunities. With a computer, fax/copier machine, an 800 phone number, and a well-designed letterhead, you can look like a "big business" even if your office is in your den at home.

## Changing Careers

Gone are the days for most men when they can choose a career in their adolescent years and follow that job completely through their lives. Fourth, fifth, and sixth careers are not at all abnormal these days because of rapid technological changes and the knowledge explosion. A man is not failing if he changes careers; instead he will be more successful if he moves to a career or job that more adequately fits him. It is unfortunate for a man to stay in a job or career that no longer challenges him or matches his life. But change is not enough. It must be a change that puts a man's work in line with his gifts, abilities, and values in life.

The book *New Life Begins at Forty* by Peterson highlights fascinating career changes men and women have made at midlife. For example, Charles Darrow at age forty-five lost his job as a stove salesman and then invented the game Monopoly, which earned him more than a million dollars. Wallace Johnson was broke at age forty, decided to go into business, borrowed money to build a house, and later became one of the cofounders of Holiday Inn.

Walter Knott was in his forties when he decided to start selling boysenberries. This venture later became the famous Knott's Berry Farm. Jack Nagle of Streator, Illinois, owned a dry-cleaning business. He and his wife wanted more free time, so they sold that business and bought a seasonal drive-in restaurant. They were able to work hard for six months and have six months of vacation. Peterson records incident after incident of people who evaluated their lives, interests, and abilities, then changed their jobs to fit that new interest and lifestyle.[10]

A career change may not mean moving to a totally different job or even to a different company. It may be a horizontal move that does not increase responsibility or workload, but fits the man's personality more completely. Sometimes the horizontal movement will mean accepting a similar job with another company.

### How to Change Jobs

Resist the temptation to take *any* job. You may be unemployed now, but don't become wrongly employed. A man came to my office a couple of years ago wanting advice about a job. At that time he was earning in the $60,000 range. He had a job offer starting at $120,000, with promises of a salary raise to $150,000 in a couple years. I asked him why he was attracted to the job. His first answer was the money.

When I asked what other reasons he had for liking the job, the answers came more slowly and seemed forced. Then I asked him to list the reasons he did not like the job. Those responses flowed freely. Soon he began to realize that job would not solve his problem, even if it had a great salary. As a result, he did not take the job, but went into business for himself.

Perhaps the best book available today about career change is *What Color Is Your Parachute?* by Richard N. Bolles. This book is updated every year. It is a tough, no-fooling-around book that deals with the problem of unemployment and underemployment. It's a self-study involving a great deal of time. Bolles points out that a man in midlife may have anywhere from twenty thousand to sixty thousand hours of working time ahead, which can produce hundreds of thousands to millions of dollars.

Bolles makes no apology for the extensive time involvement a man will take in the process of finding the right career and the right job. It is worth spending two weeks or two months or whatever it takes to plan well—so that what you do is something you enjoy, you do well, and fits with your life goals.

Bolles's purpose is not only to help people find another job, but to help them find the right job that matches their God-given abilities. He offers three keys:

Key No. 1: You must decide exactly what you want to do.

Key No. 2: You must decide exactly where you want to do it.

Key No. 3: You must research the organizations of greatest interest to you, and then approach the one individual in each organization who has the power to hire you for the job that you have decided you want.[11]

This self-help book leads people through an evaluation of goals, an inventory of skills, the establishment of time lines, and the development of job self-confidence.

## Career Counseling May Help

Bolles emphatically warns the job hunter not to depend on employment agencies to find a job. Big corporations receive as many as 250,000 resumes a year, and the Federal Trade Commission has reported the success rate of private employment agencies at about 5 percent.

Finding a job or moving into a new career will finally come down to first, knowing yourself—your lifestyle, values, strengths, and abilities; and second, doing research to discover where you'd like to live and the kind of company you'd like to work for. The third step is to make yourself invaluable to that company and available to the one person who can hire you. Bolles coaches the reader in each of these areas.

## Work Self-Image

The battle for a great job is won or lost in a man's mind—the way he thinks of himself. He must realize he is worthwhile and crucial. People in midlife are in command. The whole of society hinges on the ability of midlife people to continue contributing.

A job-seeking midlife man has distinct employment advantages over other age groups. For example, nondisabling job injuries generally are highest among twenty to twenty-nine year olds, and decline for each age group to their lowest levels for workers in the seventy to seventy-four category. Older workers also have lower absentee rates than younger ones, despite the generally better health of the young.

Studies over the years have shown that older workers in the steel mills and various light industry plants were generally as productive as younger men, while those in retailing, clerical, and managerial work were actually more productive than their younger coworkers.[12]

It is encouraging to know that men in midlife have the lowest unemployment rate. Figures from the Bureau of Labor Statistics show that, rather than being discarded by society, people in midlife seem to be more eagerly sought.

1995 Unemployment Percentage Rates[13]

Total Unemployment Rate

| Age | Total | Male |
|---|---|---|
| 20-24 | 9.1 | 9.2 |
| 25-44 | 4.8 | 4.7 |
| 45-64 | 3.4 | 3.5 |

One scholar evaluated the lives of 738 creative people, then categorized their output in each age of their lives by percentage. His studies found the overall productivity of creative people was not in their early adulthood, but during midlife.[14]

### His Wife Can Help

If a man has a good relationship with his wife, and she is willing to stand by him, he will have the courage to consider a job that might be a better fit. Women were asked the question, "If your husband told you he hated his work and wanted to quit, go back to school, or get a job with less pay—how would you feel?"

Common responses were, "I guess I'd be scared at

first—I would worry, but I would never say, 'No.' I'd be willing to change our way of living. After the first shock, I think part of me would be relieved and glad." Quite often the process of considering a career change will draw a husband and wife closer together—the two of them against the world.

A wife can help her man not to be driven by panic or fear. She can help him focus on positive steps toward a career change or advancement, such as eating right, exercise, weight loss, skill development, and a deep trust in his friends and God.

## Take Hope! God Is At Work

God can improve a man's work self-image as He quietly works deep within the man's personality. If a man believes that God is his friend and wants the best for him, then he'll be able to trust God during this uncertain process of work adjustment. Trusting God doesn't imply that the man is passive or inactive. He still does his research for a new job under a divine umbrella of protection. But God will control his thoughts and open doors of opportunity that really fit his life.

Many sections in the Bible have personally encouraged me about my future. The Psalms are my favorite. An example is Psalm 37:23-26. It doesn't promise I won't have struggles, but it does promise that my struggles won't destroy me and God won't forsake me—not because I am so good, but because He loves me. Further, it promises that God will bless me so I can be a blessing to other people. The blessing and impact of God in my life will not end with my life, but will continue on in the lives of my children.

Sometimes people say to me, "I know God loves me. I know He wants the best for me. I can see He is giving me special gifts and abilities. But how do I know an employer will want me?" Proverbs 21:1 says, "Just as water is turned into irrigation ditches, so the Lord directs the king's thoughts. He turns them wherever he wants to." God is at work in your life! He also is at work in the lives of other people who will be involved in your employment process. God is going to fit all the pieces of the puzzle together for the full utilization and development of your life.

Trusting God should arouse the midlife man's expectation and fuel the search to find the place God has for him. "Our nation wasn't built by men and women who got off the boat in New York, Boston, or Baltimore and waited for someone to employ them. If they couldn't find work in harbor cities they went hunting for opportunities where they could find them. They learned a new language. They acquired new knowledge and understanding. And they demonstrated a willingness to master new skills and go where the jobs were. This pioneer philosophy should guide mature job seekers today."[15]

During a job search, if a man frankly faces his job situation, his own personality, his interests, and his God-given abilities, he will begin to find a resolution to another crucial concern of his midlife crisis. Each time the midlife man resolves another major issue in his life, he will notice that other areas will also improve. It isn't important to tackle all of the areas at once, but it is important to face the major concerns of midlife and resolve them—one by one.

I stand silently before the Lord, waiting for him to rescue me. For salvation comes from him alone. Yes, he alone is my Rock, my rescuer, defense and fortress. Why then should I be tense with fear when troubles come?

Psalm 62:1-2

# 21

# Aging with Finesse

THERE IS NO WAY OF sidestepping the aging process. A man in his forties *is* getting older. There aren't any creams or special injections or fountains of youth that will stop the process. While it is true that his mental and physical processes are aging, it is more important how "old" he thinks he is. Some men are very old at thirty-five because they have lost their reason for living. They feel they have nothing more to contribute to life. Other men are extremely productive at sixty-five because they believe they have a contribution to make.

The trick to aging is to be both realistic and optimistic. Will a man give up as he sees the first gray hair and wrinkles, or will he structure his energies in ways that cause him to continue to be valuable? If a man has always felt that "old is bad," then when midlife hits, he will have a mental image of a shriveled, helpless old man, rocking endlessly on the porch of a local nursing home. This vision is not based on reality but on his own self-image and fears.

## Facts about Mental Aging

Studies show a story different from that of a worthless man. "In one study, for instance, a group of college freshmen were tested with the Army Alpha intelligence test, and forty-two years later those who were still alive were given the same test—and showed an increase in scores. . . . Psychologist K. Warner Schaie of the University of Southern California completed a major longitudinal study which showed that distinct increases take place in various dimensions of intelligence during middle age."[1]

Creativity that requires the absorption of wisdom tends to come after the young adult years. There is no basis in fact to say that the aging process causes a person to lose overall creativity.

The common saying is that you can't teach an old dog new tricks. The truth is, the older dog may be too smart or too independent to learn your tricks. The question is, can midlife people learn new tricks? Yes, the studies show they can, but they might not learn them as quickly. The greater problem is that midlife adults are not as easily convinced that they *need* to learn new tricks. It isn't the ability they've lost, but the desire.

People at midlife commonly complain about their forgetfulness, although studies show there is little long-term memory loss. What bothers most people is the business of misplacing things—setting something down and not remembering five minutes later where they put it. I jokingly say, "I need my glasses to see where I've left my glasses."

Forgetfulness, however, seems to have nothing to do with a man's brain cells. It is more likely related to what he thinks he can do. It has been estimated that as few as 10 percent of our brain cells disappear over our entire lifetime. It is only the *fear* that you are too old to learn new tricks that limits you, not any shortage of brain capacity.[2]

## Physical Aging

A man in midlife will notice physical aging more than mental aging. He is confronted daily by his mirror when he shaves; he sees the receding hairline, graying temples, and deepening facial wrinkles. Then he looks where his chest used to be. "Oh dear God, where did it go?" Then he looks at his waist and breathes a sigh of relief—it has slipped south ten inches. But that bulge is so disgusting! It's a good thing God created belts to stop the fat slide, or we might all walk around with fat feet!

If a man's self-worth is tied to his physical abilities, he is likely to experience a great deal of self-image loss. Athletes, who focus on their physical prowess, can become old in their early thirties. On the other hand, a teacher or a salesman who does not draw his worth from physical performance may not be old until he is in his seventies or eighties. The overall health of a midlife man does not sharply decline, but the types of physical problems he has will change.

What are the aging processes for a man in midlife? The recuperative powers at midlife are reduced. "At twenty, you can stay out until 3:00 a.m. and still be in the office at 9:00 a.m. without the boss or you knowing the difference; but in middle age, if you are out after midnight, it may take a day or two to regain normal efficiency. The skin wound that heals on a twenty year old in seven days heals for a forty year old in fourteen days."[3]

People in midlife are less likely to have allergies, and

statistically they have fewer accidents. On the other hand, there is an increase in diabetes between fifty and sixty. Arthritis usually begins after forty. There is an increased likelihood for heart attacks and prostate problems for midlife men. Yet studies have found only about 3 percent of all men at midlife are wholly incapable of carrying out their major activities because of some chronic physical condition. Although he loses physical strength, this should be more than compensated for by his increased experience.

A man's appearance may be the most noticeable indicator of his age. His hairline recedes and his hair begins to turn gray. His skin loses its elasticity. Wrinkles become more obvious. His muscles become flabbier, and he moves with less grace as his joints become stiffer.

Weight is also a problem. There is a shift of weight from the arms and legs to the torso. The percentage of fat in his total makeup increases. "One study shows [fat] to change from 9.8 percent of body weight in young men to 21 percent in men of forty-nine."[4]

## He's Going To Live Longer

The life expectancy of men has increased through the ages. For example, men were said to live an average of eighteen years in the Bronze Age and twenty years on average in ancient Greece. Men averaged thirty-one in the Middle Ages, thirty-seven by the eighteenth century, and by 1900 in the United States the average was fifty years. Today life expectancy is in the seventies. Since a man will age more physically than mentally, the midlife man must shift his energies toward developing his mental capacities rather than relying on physical strength.

Midlife can be a great adventure or a torment of the soul, depending on the man's view. It can be a great adventure filled with opportunity, or only a dismal descent into the abyss of old age. The name of the game is "loss." Whether we really win or lose depends upon how well we can handle loss—loss of job advancement, loss of youthful appearance, loss of control over our children's destiny, loss of support and encouragement from aging parents, loss of our ability to delay the aging process, loss of vitality. The poet Yeats so beautifully expressed it, "Now we find out what we're made of."

A man's aging problem does not catch God by surprise. God is not primarily youth oriented! He loves people at every age, and He cares for us so our lives continue to be productive and contented. Psalm 23 begins, "Because the Lord is my Shepherd, I have everything I need!" The psalm concludes with a deep confidence in God's goodness for all of life and His plan for us to be with Him after death. "Your goodness and unfailing kindness shall be with me all of my life, and afterwards I will live with you forever in your home" (Ps. 23:6).

As a man accepts his own aging process as normal, sees his wife, friends, and God as allies, and shifts his energies toward his mental capacities, he will reduce the nagging pressure of a midlife crisis.

> But the godly shall flourish like palm trees, and grow tall as the cedars of Lebanon. For they are transplanted into the Lord's own garden, and are under his personal care. Even in old age they will still produce fruit and be vital and green.
>
> Psalm 92:12-14

# 22

# Children in Transition

WHEN OUR OLDEST DAUGHTER WAS in her last semester of college, it felt to me as though she had been there only six months. In contrast, my college years were so very life changing, it seemed as if I had been in college about a third of my life. I kept asking myself, "Is she mature enough to graduate?" But what I really was asking was, "Where did the years go?"

Many men during midlife ask similar questions. "Where did all the time go since they were born? It seems only yesterday I was taking videos of my baby—now it's her college graduation?" It's easy to feel guilty, because we've spent so much time on our careers—and so little time on our children.

Some midlife men feel they have failed with their kids. They give up, writing the kids off as a business man writes off a bad debt. But your children can help you make it through your midlife crisis. It is worth the effort to stay connected, or get reconnected, for your own mental health.

A study of midlife men and which factors will help them have a successful midlife transition showed that closeness with their own children was one of the strongest factors. This study reported, "In addition, contrary to other research, the father-child relationship was found to be highly related to well-being at midlife for the men in this study. This study would suggest that, at least among well-educated, professional men, the intimate nature of the father-child relationship is very important to men's adjustment to changes associated with the midlife transition."[1]

Earl Henslin, a California psychologist, has written a powerful book entitled *Man to Man, Helping Fathers Relate to Sons and Sons Relate to Fathers*. Earl believes that men have a strong desire to relate to the generations on both sides, but they have not learned how. Most men carry a deep "father wound" (from a lack of connection to their fathers). This painful wound isolates men from each other and from their children. Dr. Henslin's book and weekend men's retreats have been powerful forces to heal the brokenness in men and enable them to connect to their fathers as well as to their children.[2]

By midlife, a shift has happened in our thinking process. We feel a strange conflict of emotions. Only yesterday we had been eagerly looking forward to greater and higher achievement. Now we're beginning to look back. Our adolescent children are the ones looking forward with great anticipation to the future. For them it means independence and their own lifestyle. For us there is a growing melancholic reflection of days forever gone—and perhaps guilt for delayed or wasted opportunity.

Sadly, it isn't that fathers want to spend more time with their children now, but they want to move the clock back and relive those years when the children were younger. They can't seem to cross that chasm—the lost years of communication. Men keep waiting for their teens to make the first move, but it's the dad's place to be a "man" and make the connection.

Very few men realize that if they would apologize to their teens or young adults, many bridges could be quickly rebuilt and wonderful relationships started. Most teens and young adults are eagerly waiting for Dad to reach out and to say, "I'm sorry! I put my time into getting material stuff instead of connecting with you."

## Understanding Gives Hope

If a man is going to resolve the tension with his adolescent or young-adult children, he must learn what they face and how they think, and come to love and respect them. The more we understand our young adults and the more they understand us, the greater the potential for love. The only thing we can do about the past is savor the good moments—and ask forgiveness for our failures.

It is easy for a man to become emotionally separated from his children. He keeps thinking of children in terms of what they were when he was a child—before cable TV, before the Internet, before the new sexual morality. But young people today know that more than half the world goes to bed hungry every night. They see real wars taking place on television. The parents of most of their friends have divorced. They are exposed to more choices in school. Drugs are everywhere. They are led to believe that everybody is involved in sex and alcohol, and everyone cheats at everything. They believe politicians and religious leaders are deceptive. Young people are not looking for more toys and gadgets—they want "real" people who are vulnerable and trustworthy.

If a man is not aware of what is happening in his children's heads, he is likely to have trouble communicating. If he can't communicate, he will not only feel he is failing—he will fail. This will be a crushing blow at midlife. He will add that to the list of his other failures: he's aging, he's not doing well at work, his marriage is in trouble, and now he can't communicate with his own children. "Why did I ever have children anyway?"

Communication with his children, however, will help a man understand them, and give his children the opportunity to crystallize their thinking in a healthy, accepting environment. But watch for the danger signs. If you see in your children a lack of enthusiasm, lack of normal interest in life or people, moodiness, a tendency to be withdrawn and solitary, these are bad signs. Our drug-soaked culture is an easy escape for an uneasy child. Your children may need professional help—but most of all they need a dad. Also remember, a child who is always good, who never gets into trouble, who never talks back, is not a normal child. All these signs indicate that a child needs a deep relationship with a mature adult—an opportunity to let it all hang out with an understanding adult friend who has been there—like Dad!

Perhaps the most helpful thing a father can do is to sit down and listen. We spent a great deal of time with our three daughters at bedtime when they were young. This was casual time when the girls talked about everything. Sometimes this process required three hours an evening, but it was worth it. Even later when the girls were in college, there was a casual sharing at bedtime when they were home. We talked about where they were emotionally and spiritually, as well as the problems they wrestled with. Bedtime seems to be a good time for sharing confidences.

## Stress with Young Adults

It's strange as you think about the young adult and the midlife father. The son is emerging from childhood into young adulthood, and the father is emerging from young adulthood into midlife. Each one is asking life-issue questions such as, Who am I?  What should I do with my life?, and, With whom should I relate?

They have a love/resentment relationship. The son resents the father's control and lack of understanding. The father resents the son's opportunities—he wishes he could go back and replay some of his life.

He is proud of his son, yet jealous of his strength, youth, and the newness of life before him. He is also proud of his daughter, glad for her brains and beauty. At the same time he may be very jealous that his daughter is willing to give her affection to another man who, of course, is not at all worthy of her.

Sometimes children become judges of their parents. These young adults are extremely idealistic. They go on a hunger fast in order to save food for the world. They get angry about energy usage and are willing to make drastic lifestyle changes to save the environment. They see direct routes to solutions of problems and feel impatient when their parents get distracted by so-called realism.

They expect perfection in relationships and yet have a low tolerance for working things out. This idealism of youth demands a lot from a midlife dad. The young adult wants ultimate answers now, and Dad can only offer worn-out solutions that may seem too tired and too middle-aged.

Sometimes young adults become very unforgiving and caustic in their judgments. This tends to widen the gap. Bergler records the words of a man who was struggling with his young-adult son. "I remember a line from *A Woman of No Importance*: 'Children begin by loving their parents; after a time they judge them; rarely, if ever, do they forgive them.' And remembering this line makes me furious with [my children] all over again."[3]

The problems of young adults quite often reawaken unresolved problems from a man's own youth. He may be frightened, thinking that somehow he has passed on to his children his unresolved problems or habits. Talking with his young adult will very likely help both Dad and young adult to work through their anxieties.

## Children Become People

Children are not playthings, like sports cars, tennis rackets, or sailboats—they are persons. They are not our possessions. It is a man's responsibility from the moment of their birth to move his children toward maturity and independence—to enable them to function at every age in life with confidence and effectiveness.

From the moment of birth there should be a gradual transfer of authority to the child, so that by the time the child reaches maturity, he will be trained to take responsibility and authority for his own life.

For an adolescent to complete the transition into young adulthood, there must come a major change in the father, as well as in the child. They each must be able to look at the other as adults, and their relationship should move increasingly toward an adult peer relationship instead of "superior parent and inferior adolescent." Become your young adult's coach instead of his boss.

Fathers will not only have to give up their direct authority, but also their anonymity. It's easy for parents to hide behind the role of a parent and never let the children see them as people. It's wrong for the parent always to be ministering down to the child and never allow the child to minister back to the parent. It's an incomplete view for the child to always see Dad as perfect and never get to know him as a real person with both successes and failures.

The stress of my midlife crisis helped me to relate in realness with our daughters. It was a natural opportunity for them to see me as a very imperfect person with great needs. They graciously ministered to both Sally and me at the point of our needs.

Some of the stress between a man and his adolescent children will be reduced if the marriage relationship is secure and positive. A solid marriage tends to reduce frustration and uneasiness in a child's life, and it gives the child the ability to cope with pressures more effectively. This is another example of the teeter-totter effect— as a man works to stabilize one area of his life, other areas will also be helped. Stronger marriages equal more success with young adults.

With tears in his eyes a father said to me, "My children don't need me anymore." His children were married, and they did need him. He thought because they didn't need his food and shelter anymore that they didn't need him. But they needed him to point the way, to give counsel and wisdom, to help them navigate emotional and spiritual stresses throughout their lives. But he needed to shift roles from being the director of their lives to being the counseling friend and coach. He did! And he found a continuing place of strategic importance in his children's lives as they moved from being adolescents to young adults.

The instruction to fathers in the Bible is important to notice. The emphasis is not on meeting a child's physical and material needs so much as on being a wise counselor and guide, pointing the way. "And now a word to you [fathers]. Don't keep on scolding and nagging your children, making them angry and resentful. Rather, bring them up with the loving discipline the Lord himself approves, with suggestions and godly advice" (Eph. 6:4).

I've learned a simple plan from a book by Ross Campbell entitled *How to Really Love Your Children*. He suggests that a parent do the following three things:

•Touch your child—hand on shoulder, or arm over their shoulder.

•Look directly into their face.

•Speak words of affirmation—"I think you're great. I love you. You are becoming a great person. I'm proud of you."[4]

The combination of all three acts has a powerful effect to build the self-esteem of your child or young adult and lessen tension between the two of you.

### Becoming an In-Law

As young adults move toward marriage, the midlife man must adjust to another new role—support without interference. Suddenly you've become the dreaded "in-law." You barely tolerated your in-laws when you were married, and now you feel as if you might also be ignored. But the newlyweds need to establish their own family unit. They need to develop their own family lifestyle. The combination of their two backgrounds must now form a new unique unit. Parents must restrain themselves from giving helpful advice, even though they so desperately want this new marriage to work out perfectly.

Money is usually a problem for a new family. How can parents help financially without strings? One family put several thousand dollars of their savings into a revolving fund for their married children. Any one of the three young families could borrow what they needed, without interest, to be paid back as soon as possible.

No daughter-in-law or son-in-law will ever be quite good enough. This is a common prejudice of parents. But it's important to realize that your son or daughter chose this person. Your son or daughter wants very much to have their parents' approval of this husband or wife. If the parents see a son-in-law or daughter-in-law as a rival and try to compete for the affection of their children, they will not only antagonize the new mate, but probably will lose the love of their own child as well.

All three of our daughters are married, so we have firsthand experience with sons-in-law. Our approach over many years was to develop close, vulnerable relationships with the girls, to talk freely with them about the important values in marriage and about important qualities to look for in a potential mate. Ever since our girls were born, we have asked God to mold our daughters' lives—and the lives of their potential mates. We prayed that each of them might have the joy of experiencing a totally satisfying marriage relationship with the man of God's choice.

We are deeply grateful that God has brought a great man to each of our three daughters. They are wonderful, godly, growing men who are helping our daughters become all that God has planned for them. These sons-in-law are also effective fathers coaching their own children.

Perhaps the most significant things a man can do to lessen any potential stress with his children is to accept them, understand them, and be a friend whom they can trust. They need a dad who is not going to put them down—in short, a dad who can love them in the same way Jesus Christ loves us, as He understands our needs and willingly gives Himself for us.

> O God, you have helped me from my earliest child-hood—and I have constantly testified to others of the wonderful things you do. And now that I am old and gray, don't forsake me. Give me time to tell this new generation (and their children too) about all your mighty miracles.
>
> Psalm 71:17-18

### For Further Reading

*How to Really Love Your Teenager* by Ross Campbell (Colorado Springs, CO: ChariotVictor Publishing, 1993).

# 23

# Parenting the Parents

IN MIDLIFE A MAN IS likely to have a great deal of anxiety about his responsibility for his aging parents. They have always been the strong generation ahead of him, but now his role is changing. They increasingly need his care. As they need more of his care, it also occurs to him that shortly he will become the oldest generation and in need of care. As he resolves his issues with his aging parents, as well as other issues, his midlife crisis will become a quieter positive transition.

Our American society has treated old people with various indignities. On the one hand, we isolate older people into retirement homes or nursing homes. We let them know we don't want them or need them. At the same time, in the name of medical progress, we prolong their lives beyond the point at which life has meaning.

"On certain South Sea islands, feeble male 'senior citizens' were forced to inch their way to the tops of tar coconut palms. The trees were then shaken vigorously by the tribe's young bucks on the ground below. The old boys who managed to hang on were allowed to stay in this world a while longer."[1] In 1850 only 2.5 percent of our population were over sixty-five. In 1900 the figure was 4 percent, and in 1974, 10.3 percent of the population were over sixty-five. In 1995 that number had grown to 12.8 percent.[2]

## A Time to Care

Older people have become the prey of unscrupulous salespeople for insurance policies, mutual funds, burial plots, vitamin pills as sex stimulators, fraudulent travel excursions, and faulty hearing aids. The list is almost endless. Sometimes older people are cheated because they are isolated from the rest of society, cut off from information and people who could give them wise counsel.

Perhaps one of the biggest indignities an older man faces is when he loses his driver's license. He has had a love affair with his car ever since his teen years. The car has meant masculinity, power, prestige, and authority. Now in his old age the car becomes his master and intimidates him. The highways become frightening. The older man not only gives up driving, but there is a loss of self-worth as he lets his driver's license expire, never to be renewed.

The question to be faced by a man in midlife is, what does it mean to honor his parents? Is he to obey them in everything? The Bible says, "Honor your father and mother, as the Lord your God commanded you. Then you will live a long, full life in the land the Lord your God will give you" (Deut. 5:16 NLT).

But Scripture also clearly teaches that there is a transition from childhood to manhood. When a man establishes his own home, he is to leave his parents and form a new emotional unit with his wife.

The concept of "honor," however, continues as a responsibility all of a man's life. The midlife man must realize that it is possible for an adult not to do what his parents want him to do—and still honor and appreciate them. He can still be grateful for who they are and what they have contributed to his life. Obedience is an act children do for their parents for a limited number of years; honor is an attitude that continues all through life.

## Uneasy with His Parents?

Repeatedly, I hear couples in their midyears talking about how their parents still treat them as children. In my case, I think of myself as being fairly mature. To a younger generation I'm somewhat of an authority. To my contemporaries I am thought of as a successful speaker and writer. To people needing help at midlife, I am viewed as a helping person with insight. To my relatives, however, I'm still Jimmy.

And for most people in midlife, that really hurts. They most want to be respected by their parents. But unfortunately, many times these people who are so important to the man in midlife still think of him as "little Jimmy."

The relationship between older parents and midlife children is also complicated because, during the childhood and adolescent years, the parents were the custodians of law and order. The person in midlife still carries mixed feelings toward his parents, a sense of carry-over fear from earlier life.

We had friends come to see us from out-of-state. Before they came they called and warned us not to talk to their parents, who lived in our area. They said, "If our parents know we are stopping to see you, they'll be angry and feel slighted." It's strange that this high-level executive was still being terrorized by his childhood fear of his parents.

Social class climbing may also cause a breach between the midlife "child" and the older parent. Most parents want something better for their children, but they don't realize what will happen in the process. For example, a father who did not go to college will urge his son to go to college and perhaps to graduate school. The son may then take a job as a professor in a college or a researcher in industry, or he may become a medical doctor. A social separation between this son and his parents subtly comes about. Not only has the son spent more years in school, but he has moved upward in social class definitions.

Years ago Cavan pointed out this problem: "In the upward climb, it is not sufficient that the climber should affiliate himself with the class level above him, assimilating their culture, he must also break his identification with the class level left behind him, most often represented by his parents."[3]

The midlife "child" who, because of education and job position, has moved to a different social class may have very little in common with his older parents—who were really the promoters of a better way of life for him. Tragically, when they get together, they talk about areas that essentially mean nothing to either of them, usually the childhood years that are now irrelevant.

### Where Will Our Parents Live?

Perhaps the biggest problem people in midlife and their older parents face is where the parents will live.

Should they move to a retirement community, live in their own home, or move in with their married children? This question can cause everyone in the family—brothers, sisters, and parents—to be angry and disappointed with each other.

One reason this problem is difficult to answer is there are so many possible solutions. Sometimes living in the child's home is the happiest solution for everyone. However, some older parents feel more secure in their own home with familiar surroundings, but they need help with housekeeping and yard care. Other times the retirement community is the ideal solution, or they may need a special-care facility. It must be a common decision owned by every person involved.

Tragically the most frequent pattern is "Let's not talk about it." If we talk about it, someone will feel hurt, or the parents will feel they are losing control. The midlife children often feel guilty if they say the arrangements the parents want are not feasible. So everyone simply keeps smiling and pretending that no one is getting older.

Closely related to the problem of living arrangements is financial support. Again, everyone should be involved in discussions about Medicaid, Social Security, investments, and savings. Then the older parents don't have to be frightened about a lack of money or the inability to care for themselves.

### Parents Continue to Minister

Families are smaller, but life is being extended. Tomorrow's families may well include one or both sets of grandparents, plus a great-grandparent or two. Soon we may have the possibility of four generations living on one property.

One problem with today's young people is that they are rootless, living only "now" with no sense of history or continuity with other generations. Grandparents can give a link to history and past genealogy. The memory of a grandparent may span 150 years of family history.

A grandparent can also contribute spiritually in the extended family. One of the people who most influenced me during my adolescent and young-adult years was my grandmother Mary. In old age she did not quietly retire, feeling sorry for herself. She was an extremely exuberant woman whom I never really saw as old.

Grandma used all kinds of circumstances to teach and care for me. One time as a young boy I was responsible for raking all the leaves in our backyard. I'm sure the task wasn't very great, but from my perspective it was as if I'd been asked to clean up the whole city of Cleveland. My grandmother, who lived across the fence from us, saw me leaning on the rake. She came over, put her arm around me, and said, "I'll help you. We'll get it done."

She was also the one who continually asked me where I was spiritually. She most influenced my decision to receive Christ as Savior and my decision to enter the ministry. Grandma and Grandpa ministered intensively to me, as they did to all the other grandchildren. They had a broad impact as they continued to coach their own children, other grandchildren, and the new mates of the grandchildren. My wife, Sally, adopted "Grandma Mary" as her model of a godly woman.

## The Death of Parents

Dr. Abraham Maslow said, "One learns more from the death of a parent than from all the academic subjects one studies."[4] When a man's parents are still living he is more protected from his own death, because he always thinks they will die first. When his parents are gone, he unconsciously knows he is next in line.

The death of a parent can be a time of profound growth and change—if you allow yourself to experience the sadness and guilt as well as the joy of how deeply you have been influenced by your parents. Often children come closer to a parent at the time of death than ever in life. The death of a parent opens up new insights about dependency, mortality, the meaning of love, and the meaning of family.

## Attitudes Are Important

A wonderful old book, *In-Laws—Pros and Cons*, offers a number of good insights and attitudes necessary for positive relationships between parents and their married children. It's important, Duvall says, that midlife children see their parents as persons with needs. As the midlife child understands his parents' needs and seeks to make these parents feel significant, a relationship of love will develop. If the parents are treated as castaways and unimportant, antagonism and animosity will grow.[5]

Tim Stafford has written an extremely sensitive and instructive book that helps the midlife couple prepare to care for aging parents. In addition to the nuts-and-bolts information about caring for parents, Tim goes on to say, "I felt that I had to probe a harder question, one that the vast literature on aging almost entirely ignores: What is aging for? Is there a point to it, and if so, what? If we insist on believing in dignity for all human beings, dignity for Alzheimer's victims, dignity for the poor, dignity for the dying, how may we understand that dignity as anything more than a theoretical sentiment? I think old age forces such questions on us. So much may be stripped away (though it is not always). What is left? And what is its meaning? And why the stripping in the first place? What is God doing with old people?"[6]

I like the story of the midlife father who sent his adolescent son to the attic to get an old horse blanket. He explained to his son that Grandpa was getting very old and cantankerous, so they were going to send him away. The heavy horse blanket was to keep him warm as he rode away in the buggy.

A few minutes later the son returned with half of the blanket and handed it to his father. Startled, the father asked, "What happened to the blanket?"

The boy replied, "I'm saving the other half for you."

Old people, all people for that matter, need to feel their lives have meaning, that they are contributing to life, that they are loved. A man's positive growing attitudes toward his parents will have a powerful calming effect on his own midlife crisis.

> But our families will continue; generation after generation will be preserved by your protection.
>
> Psalm 102:28

# 24

# Creative Retirement

SOMETIME IN LATE MIDLIFE a man gasps in startled amazement—society is pushing him toward retirement. He may be pressured, enticed, or shoved into an early retirement by his company. They pleasantly suggest he might like to live out his years from fifty-five on doing all the things he always wanted to do. The truth is, some businesses have a planned program of obsolescence. Early retirement is a deeply ingrained concept to cut the bottom line by making room for younger, cheaper people.

The prospect of retirement, even though highly praised, means a loss in self-esteem to most men. Earlier we pointed out that a man's work is often equated with worth. So he must now face the truth that society is going to do it to him—push him into retirement. The statistics are startling. If present trends (longer life expectancy and a lower birthrate) continue, in the year 2025, Americans over sixty-five will outnumber teenagers by more than two to one. "Two-thirds of all the people in the entire history of the world who have lived beyond the age of sixty-five are alive today. Children born in the closing years of this century can expect to spend up to one-third of their lives in retirement!"[1]

Western society seems to be one of the first to force the retirement idea onto people. There is certainly no concept of retirement as we know it in the Bible. The Bible does show that men change as they move along through life; they modify their responsibilities and activities. But there is no biblical concept of sitting on the back porch rocking away several good years of life.

The Bible does speak of retirement which comes after death, "At last the time has come for his martyrs to enter into their full reward. Yes, says the Spirit, they are blest indeed, for now they shall rest from all their toils and trials" (Rev. 14:13).

The Bible also teaches that people need periodic rest, sometimes for extended periods of time. Jesus said every person needs emotional and spiritual rest. He gave His disciples an invitation that should be a pattern for us as well: "Then Jesus suggested, 'Let's get away from the crowds for a while and rest.' For so many people were coming and going that they scarcely had time to eat. So they left by boat for a quieter spot" (Mark 6:31-32). So the Bible does teach the need for periods of physical, emotional, and spiritual rest all along through life—but no rocking chair is envisioned.

### Forced Early Retirement

Most midlife men never even consider the possibility that they may be forced into an early retirement. Midlife men tend to think of themselves as being at the most productive era of their lives. They understand how their company functions, and they have become quite efficient at doing their job. The midlife worker is an extremely valuable person, as we have seen in an earlier chapter.

But business increasingly is driven by the bottom line. Often company executives are not looking at how productive the midlife man is, but rather at what he costs the company. The reasoning goes like this: "Yes, Tom is really doing a great job in that department, but with the salary increases, bonuses, and cost-of-living increments, we can hire a twenty-seven year old fresh out of graduate school with new ideas for half of Tom's salary. Yes, there will be a little learning curve until the young man catches on, but within a year he may be more productive than Tom." So Tom becomes expendable.

Psychological development might also cause Tom to be forced into early retirement. The twenty-seven year old is eager to please, willing to do almost anything. He certainly is a solid company man—but by the time that twenty-seven year old becomes forty, he will change psychologically. He no longer will give blind obedience to the company. He will throw off the mentors in his life. He will want more company leadership, and he may be very outspoken about the things that are wrong with the company. He may even push for new directions within his company, just as Tom has been doing.

The young man, as he becomes a midlife man, may be forced into early retirement just like Tom because he may be rocking the boat politically. Someone in company leadership will suggest they buy him out or encourage an early retirement.

Sally and I have watched this process happen with a number of men in their late forties and early fifties. One executive friend (we'll call him Bill), started with his company as a young man. By the time he had reached his late forties, he was vice president of sales for a large regional company. In his early fifties, the company went through a very difficult time and barely survived an economic downturn.

The company hired a consulting firm to help them correct their problems and to better focus them for the future. The consulting firm reported that our friend Bill was the key person who was holding the company together, and probably the brightest prospect to fill the position of president. The president had been fired during the recent slowdown.

About this time a man in his midforties bought a massive amount of the company stock and became chairman of the board. He wanted younger leadership and so convinced the board to hire a forty-year-old president—in spite of the information from the consulting firm and the company-wide opinion that Bill would be the next president.

Shortly after this abrupt move, the chairman of the board met with Bill and told him they appreciated his commitment and service. The company wanted to reward him by helping him into an early retirement. The chairman outlined the package of perks they were offering Bill as an inducement for his early retirement. But Bill responded that he wanted to continue working for the company. He still had thirteen years until retirement.

The chairman of the board leaned across the table and looked Bill straight in the eye. "Bill," he said, "maybe you've not understood. This offer to help you into retirement is on the table for two weeks—after that we're going to withdraw the offer and fire you."

Bill was so stunned he was speechless. He staggered out of the office and immediately went home. Then he went up to his bedroom, took off his clothes, curled up in his bed, and wept like a baby. His wife was so shocked at what was happening that she admitted him to a hospital. After some days, he was released—but he was a broken man. He had never expected the company he worked for all his life to suddenly throw him out. His self-image was so damaged that he never did get back into major leadership again.

Maybe you're thinking, "That could never happen to me." But look at the truth! It's happening to thousands and thousands of people as business and industry become increasingly depersonalized, as markets narrow, and as competition becomes more fierce.

I believe that as the boomers near retirement, we will see attitudes change and the mandatory retirement age move up. *US News and World Report* shows the growing changes. "According to the U.S. Bureau of Labor Statistics, 1.6 million people work past seventy, and of those, 448,000 are in managerial and professional jobs. Workers fifty-five and over are the fastest growing sector of the labor market, with their ranks expected to increase 44 percent between 1990 and 2005. Consequently, most observers expect mandatory retirement rules for top management to end within a decade."[2]

If a man interacts with his midlife crisis fully, it can be the most profitable experience to make his next twenty-five years extremely effective and prepare him for his own voluntary retirement. The midlife man must come to a peaceful sense of self, maintain an enthusiastic relationship with his mate, adjust his career to fit his life, and work through pressures with his children and parents. Working on these problems is the best preparation to guarantee that all of his years up to retirement will be productive.

If, on the other hand, a man does not face these concerns at midlife, they will fester in the back of his soul, waiting until he has been pushed out of a job or enters his normal retirement. Then all of the festering midlife issues will spill out as from a lanced boil. It will be as if the world collapsed around him. Now he is forced to deal with all of the old midlife issues—in addition to the normal retirement concerns.

In that scenario, he will face retirement in misery. He will punish himself with guilt as he realizes his fears kept him from thinking about the midlife issues. He locked himself into a pattern of doing the same dumb stuff for the last twenty-five years. What a waste!

### Questions For Nonretirement

Barbara Deane has written a very practical and insightful book guiding a person through the process of getting ready early for retirement. I like her positive approach on understanding ourselves and our needs first. She says, "My philosophy is that you can always find a way to finance your true needs, if only you know what they are. (Maybe not all your wants, but hopefully your needs. There is a difference.)"[3]

Midlife is the time to begin asking the questions about lifestyle and activities for later years. If possible, a man should never retire. In order not to, however, he has to plan now so he can make the necessary transitions from his present work into "nonretirement." If a man believes God is going to continually use him and his abilities, he can prepare now to make a series of small adjustments to remain effective. Don't wait! Start asking the questions now!

1. *Where should we live?* A man has been helping his parents decide where they should live. This research and evaluation can provide the basis for his own decisions. Where to live should not only include the area of the country or of the world, but also the cost of living, kind of housing, type of people in that area, medical facilities, and most important—the spiritual climate.

A creative solution that some have tried is to get three or four other friends to move into the area, or even jointly purchase a small apartment building. The apartment may lower the cost of living for each couple and even provide some income.

The retirement village my father started in Sebring, Florida, is a good example of nonretirement. We have jokingly teased my father that people work harder when they move there than if they had stayed in their own houses. It's sort of an unwritten expectation that everyone in the village is going to work—building more apartments, planting trees or grass, painting walls, making roads and driveways, and helping people move in. And since it's a Christian community there are always opportunities for spiritual growth and service. If there is always work to be done, or people to be helped, then we all continue to feel important and useful.

2. *What will be our lifestyle?* Style of living is another question that will influence the size and location of your housing. It will also influence automobile ownership, recreational activities, and travel. If a couple envisions traveling regularly to other countries, owning a new automobile each year, and living in a large estate, they need to prepare now for that expensive style. If the couple, however, plans for more modest experiences, they also need to learn to live inexpensively now before they

get to the time when they must.

3. *How much income will we have?* Money will be a major concern, and careful planning at midlife is critical. After a couple has decided where they want to live and what lifestyle they want to follow, then they need to evaluate savings, investments, pension plans, and Social Security benefits. They should consider how much money these plans will produce. Calculating for continued inflation, what will the couple actually have to live on when the time comes?

Without being too pessimistic, it's important to remember to carefully investigate your dollar resources. For example, many pensions are not transferable from one company to another. A man may lose many years of pension or health benefits if he changes jobs.

Savings are another example of a financial source with false security. A man may feel greatly elated that he is earning 5 or 6 percent on long-term savings. What he fails to take into account is that he is paying income tax on the earnings, plus losing a certain portion to inflation; his savings are continually shrinking in buying power. Money sources must be tied to inflation so when a man needs them, they will buy as much then as they would buy now.

4. *Should we work during retirement?* Working should not be an option, it ought to be part of the long-range nonretirement plan. Working may not be for the purpose of earning money, but a man should continue to contribute to society. Older people were asked, "If you inherited enough money to live comfortably for the rest of your life, would you continue to work?" The overwhelming response was "Yes."[4]

5. *Baby steps toward the future.* Following the evaluation of these areas, the couple should lay out a program of

small steps that will lead to their ultimate goals. Part of this plan may mean using vacations to explore various parts of the country as potential retirement sites. They might need to begin talking with other friends about the possibility of pooling resources for later years. They may shift their investments or seek new investments. More education or job training may be needed to gain new skills for the years of nonretirement. Long-range planning will also include the children and their families so that regular contact and communication can be maintained.

At this point a man must also consider his or his wife's unexpected death. What will his wife do if he dies first (which is likely to happen, according to statistics)? How would this affect the nonretirement years, and what specific steps and directions should his wife follow? This process might be called "Teaching My Wife to Be a Widow During Retirement."

For years I've updated a file in my computer listing our assets and telling where important documents are located. In addition, I've written suggestions of what to do when I die. I've included instructions about my funeral, what to do with bank accounts, the cars, and the house. Then I've laid out a financial plan that provides income yet assumes continued inflation.

I've altered these plans over the years as we've aged. But without a plan, a man simply drifts along toward retirement, and perhaps toward frustrating chaos.

> Jehovah himself is caring for you! He is your defender. He protects you day and night. He keeps you from all evil, and preserves your life. He keeps his eye upon you as you come and go, and always guards you.
> Psalm 121:5-8 NLT

# 25

# Sooner or Later

INTELLECTUALLY, WE ALL KNOW that people die—but before midlife we tend to think of death in terms of *other* people. Suddenly, during midlife some event or thought causes us to realize that death is going to happen to us.

I was at Fuller Seminary working on my doctoral studies when my wife, Sally, called me late one night. Gaston Singh, a close friend, had died of a massive heart attack. The news hit me like a sledgehammer. Gaston was only in his midthirties. Two weeks earlier he and his family had stayed in our home. Sally and I had spent a month ministering in India, Bangladesh, and Burma with Gaston and another close friend. In a few months I was to return to India again to minister with him—but now he was gone! Everything had changed.

In retrospect, Gaston's death and my turning forty-five a few days before were the two incidents that plunged me deep into my midlife crisis.

I had helped many other people through the stress related to death. I knew what the Bible taught: "No man can live forever. All will die. Who can rescue his life from the power of the grave?" (Ps. 89:48). The Bible teaches that everyone is going to die, or be taken directly when Christ returns, and that our time of death is uncertain. "How do you know what is going to happen tomorrow? For the length of your lives is as uncertain as the morning fog—now you see it; soon it is gone" (Jas. 4:14).

Suddenly death became real for me. Freud said, "No one believes in his own death. In the unconscious, everyone is convinced of his immortality."[1] But now I began thinking not in terms of how many years I had lived— but how many I had left.

## How Does a Man See His Own Death?

In midlife, as death takes on real meaning, there seem to be four major ways in which men cope with the truth of their own death.

1. *A man may deny death's reality.* For many men, death is linked with old age. If he is still trying to deny the aging process, he will find it difficult to accept the reality of his death. Paul Tournier, the Swiss Christian psychiatrist, says: "I could not dissociate acceptance of old age from that of death. The two problems are so intimately bound up together that we may say that acceptance of old age is the best preparation for death, but also, conversely, that the acceptance of death is the best preparation for old age."[2]

2. *A man may give up.* Our culture treats death as abnormal. We rush people off to the hospital, sedate them heavily, and isolate them from everyone so no one will have to be exposed to death. A man may be so discouraged by the reality of his ultimate death that he may give up the desire to continue living. A Greek poet in the

seventh century B. C. wrote:

When the springtime of life is past
then verily to die is better than life.
For many are the ills that invade the heart.[3]

3. *A man may be overcome with a fear of death.* "The idea of death, the fear of it, haunts the human animal like nothing else," says Pulitzer Prize winner Ernest Becker.[4] This fear may come because a man is unprepared to face life after death, or to have his life evaluated by a righteous God.

Fear may come because of a lack of information about what happens at death. "Does it hurt to die? Will I still want to live even when I'm dying? How can I be sure where I'm going after I die?" The saying on the back of a T-shirt may sum it up, "A life lived in fear is only half a life."

Don't wait. Work through each of these anxieties. Getting factual information will prepare you for the stage of acceptance. As you settle your standing with God then you will have peace about meeting Him. And don't count on that classic deathbed confession—you may die of a sudden heart attack or be in a coma. (If you need help in this area, reread the section in chapter 12 entitled, "How to Connect with God.")

4. *A man may accept death.* Acceptance can take many forms. Some grant a grudging acceptance, such as W. C. Fields, who had these words chiseled on his tombstone: "I'd rather be in Philadelphia."[5] He was saying, in essence, that he looked at death, didn't like it, and would rather ignore it—but he would have to accept it.

Coming fully to accept one's ultimate death gives a serene stability to life and prepares a person to enjoy the current life more completely. Abraham Maslow shared his feelings after he had a heart attack:

> The confrontation with death—and the reprieve from it—makes everything look so precious, so sacred, so beautiful that I feel more strongly than ever the impulse to love it, to embrace it, and to let myself be overwhelmed by it. My river has never looked so beautiful. Death and its ever present possibility make love, passionate love, more possible. I wonder if we could love passionately, if ecstasy would be possible at all, if we knew we'd never die.[6]

During midlife a man must not only peacefully accept the reality of his own death, he also has to accept the fact that his mate may die before he does. If he can accept this, then he'll find a measure of freedom and joy in the marriage relationship. There is a valuing of hours and days that gives a special, loving intensity that might not be realized if the death of one's mate is feared or denied.

### Words Put to the Test

The ideas you've read so far in this chapter were written nearly twenty years ago. But seven years ago, in the summer of 1990, my hypothetical discussion of death suddenly became very real when my wife, Sally, discovered a large lump in her breast. A biopsy showed that it was malignant. Now real life would test my theology!

Within days she had a "modified radical mastectomy" (removal of the breast and all of the lymph nodes on that side). The detailed lab report showed there were thousands of small tumors in her breast, and more than half of her lymph nodes (sixteen) were malignant.

Sally was put on massive doses of chemotherapy because her tumor was larger than a walnut and so many of her lymph nodes were malignant. She was on chemotherapy for about ten months and spent much of her time in bed or in the La-Z-Boy. She was unable to work or travel to speak at our marriage seminars, or to keep any of our radio or television appearances.

These were difficult, troubling years for both of us. From the beginning we let our friends around the world know about Sally's situation. We asked for prayer, because there were no assurances from doctors. We tried to be as optimistic as possible—but always lurking in the back of our minds was, "Someday the other shoe might drop." We had been told by several doctors that breast cancer can reoccur at any time.

Our relationship took on a whole new alignment as I took over Sally's part of the ministry plus the responsibility of running the house, cooking meals, shopping, doing laundry, and all the other stuff that Sally had always done.

A year and three-quarters into the process, Sally was about 75 percent of her normal self, and we resumed our traveling and seminar work, plus writing books and doing radio and television. All the time we lived with the specter that Sally's breast cancer could return.

Four years and eight months after the first tumor, Sally discovered another lump in the area of the previous surgery. The tumor was the size of a grape—again it was malignant. This time she went through surgery and extensive radiation in addition to chemotherapy. She was so weak that I had to move her from the bed to the car in a wheelchair, and then by wheelchair to her daily radiation treatments at the hospital.

Sally had not recovered from this round of radiation and chemotherapy when we discovered that the cancer had spread to her spine in two different places. The tumor in her lower back was pinching a nerve, so she was unable to walk. She was given more radiation to shrink the tumor and give her just a little more mobility.

But on July 2, 1996 she was unable to walk up any steps. So I set up a bed in our family room. For a few more weeks, with my assistance and the use of a walker, she was able to use the nearby rest room. But this was the beginning of an eleven-month period of nonstop care. I slept on the floor near her bed to care for her during the night. I was grateful for the hospice people who helped me three days a week. They gave Sally baths, helped change her bedding, monitored her medications, were the liaisons with the doctors, and provided moral support for me.

Sally was so weak that many of our family and friends thought she might die at any time. In late July, our whole family came to say good-bye to her—our three married daughters, their husbands, and our ten grandchildren. It was a wonderful time of singing, praying, and sharing about all the great things God had done in Sally's life.

Then like an Old Testament patriarch, Sally gave each of us a blessing. In addition she gave each person a gift to remember the occasion—and her.

A few weeks later, as I was helping her to the bathroom, she collapsed and broke both of her legs. She was hospitalized for a month and required additional humiliating surgery for a colostomy. Gradually I assumed her total care, twenty-four hours a day, as her resident nurse.

I dispensed the massive amounts of drugs, prepared the special foods, hand-fed her, changed her Attends, gave her baths, and did the laundry—up to seven loads a day. But I was also privileged to bring her flowers, tell her I loved her, and assure her that her presence with me was more important than her doing any work.

## How Do You Accept Your Wife's Dying ?

It happens as a very slow process. Even as I dictate these paragraphs, I cry between sentences. I am just four weeks from the day Sally died. I was standing next to her bed in those last hours. Her breathing all through the night had been labored. That morning as I told her I loved her, she was only able to give me a slight smile. I stroked her forehead, talked to her, and prayed out loud. Finally I had the courage to say, "It's okay if you want to leave me now."

Then Sally's breathing began to get more shallow, and her eyes, which had been wide open and staring, slowly began to close. I kept rubbing her forehead and praying. Her breathing was almost imperceptible as her eyes continued to close. Her body just began to relax. I realized she was not breathing, nor was her heart beating.

A close pastor-friend at her graveside service described what took place at that moment. He said, "Sally just got up and walked out of her body."

How do I feel now? Wretched. I feel as if I've been cut in half. It's as if I'm trying to walk on one leg, think with half a brain, see with only one eye, and digest my food with only half of my bowels. Sally was not "only my wife," she was my ministry partner. We spoke side by side at our seminars, wrote our books as joint ventures, and made our radio and television appearances together. She was not "just a wife," she was an integral part of me and all I do. She was the wind in my sails, but more than that, she was the rudder of my ship. No! She was much, much more than all of that!

## So How Am I Going to Get Over This?

At this point I can't answer that question. But I can say that I do believe God loves me—and I don't think Sally's death happened outside His knowledge and His permission. I do believe God has continuing as well as new ministries ahead for me. And I do believe that Sally's writings, and the impact of her life, will continue to affect people.

I also believe that God is using this process to help other people. And I do believe the pain that Sally and I experienced, and which I continue to experience, will be used to build bridges to other people who are experiencing pain in their lives. Every "pain event" in my life has been used by God to make me more tender, vulnerable, and more sensitive to the needs of people. This experience is connecting me to a new deep level of human pain.

Death is not fun, but it is not to be feared. I was standing in the cemetery in Urbana, Illinois as Sally's body was being lowered into the ground. I stood next to her casket on the very ground where my body will someday be placed. There was no sense of fear, only a deep sense of loss.

There was also a commitment to live whatever years are left in such a way that people will be helped—that somehow I'll make a difference in the world.

## Life Events Change Our Perception of Death

An interesting phenomenon takes place as a man experiences his midlife crisis. At the beginning, he is very preoccupied with the possibility of his death. During the crisis, he hopefully moves to a peaceful acceptance of his own mortality. At the end of his midlife crisis, as he enters the third major productive era of life, the preoccupation with death loses its grip on him. As the midlife man is able to face the possibility of his own death, and that of his mate, his new emphasis will be to live life to the fullest and make a difference in society.

Scripture can be extremely important in helping a man face death. The Bible teaches that when we place our personal trust in Christ, God the Holy Spirit comes to live in us. Death is only a transition to a continued experience with the living God. In John 14 and 17, Jesus expressed very clearly that God is planning for each believer to be with Him for eternity.

In addition, 1 Corinthians 15 teaches us about the resurrection, life after death, and being eternally with God. The chapter concludes with these ringing words, "So, my dear brothers, since future victory is sure, be strong and steady, always abounding in the Lord's work, for you know that nothing you do for the Lord is ever wasted as it would be if there were no resurrection" (1 Cor. 15:58).

When I was a boy I worked long, tedious hours gluing every stick of a model airplane in place and carefully covering the frame with paper. I was careful to construct my plane correctly so that it would fly perfectly. There was a special exhilaration as I went to the third-floor attic window and watched my newly made masterpiece soar into the sky. My heart went with it.

## Unavoidable Concerns

Building a model airplane is much the same as a man working his way through the concerns of his midlife crisis. If he says he will work on all of the other problems except his marriage or his job uneasiness, then it's as if he's saying he will build his airplane but won't build any wings. Each part of the plane takes time to build and has its own unique structural problems. Yet each part enables the airplane to fly.

Do it right—you'll fly now, as well as in eternity.

> Death stared me in the face—I was frightened and sad. Then I cried, "Lord, save me!" How kind he is! How good he is! So merciful, this God of ours!
>
> Psalm 116:3-5

# PART 7

# Help Is on the Way

# 26

# We Can Help

THE MAN IN MIDLIFE CRISIS is up to his armpits in quicksand. The more he struggles, the deeper he sinks. He is struggling with a real crisis. He may well have tried several dead-end roads. Hopefully he is working to improve several major areas of his life. But help must also come from the outside, and he must be willing to accept that help.

He may respond with indifference to outside help. He may even use his indifference to impress people with how "bad off" he is. However, his bad attitudes ought to be overlooked and help offered anyway. He doesn't have to ask for help for the help to be effective. Nor does he need to admit he is in a midlife crisis. Just go ahead and help him. It's best if help comes from several different sources, including his employer, the church, his children, friends, and his wife.

## A Man's Employer

An employer can best help the midlife man by realizing that the crisis is just that—a short-term crisis. When he is through the crisis, he will continue to be a productive employee and probably more valuable because he has an increased perspective and deeper desire to serve.

An employer can help by offering a job change within the organization to better meet career aspirations. An employer can offer further education or training so the man's skills improve. New challenges will strengthen the midlife man's self-image, which has been under severe attack during the crisis. The employer might also encourage him to seek counseling from someone on the company payroll, or from community services through the company medical provisions.

The biggest help I received from my employer—the church I served at this time—was their understanding. The board of leadership said, in essence, "We don't really know what you are going through [most of them were much younger than I], but we love you and we want you to tell us how we can help." That open attitude gave me a great deal of encouragement and reduced the pressure of job performance.

## The Church

The midlife crisis is not often talked about in churches, although many members are going through the problems. Our studies have repeatedly shown that about 75 percent of men experience a mild to severe midlife crisis. And these people lead and control much of the power in the church.

The church needs to recognize that all adults go through a developmental process of moving from young adulthood to midlife. Youth workers spend full time with adolescents because we recognize this to be a key time of life. We hire full-time music directors and Christian education directors, and some churches have full-time business administrators. But midlife crisis continues to fester secretly in each midlife individual's heart—each one thinking he is the only strange person experiencing this kind of stress. And he tries to work through it alone without any special church staff person to help.

The church needs to become more vocal on this issue. More family conferences need to be set up, with the midlife problem included. Couples' retreats and Sunday school classes should discuss the crisis. Retreats for men only or women only with this topic as one of the major discussions would be a positive help.

Over the years I have watched scores of people in midlife quietly slip out the back door of churches. Each one felt he was a failure—morally or emotionally and most of all spiritually. He had been taught all of his life that being a Christian would guarantee that no problem would ever defeat him.

But when his midlife crisis hit, he was literally flattened as if in a boxing match. As he lifted his head from the canvas and staggered to his feet, he looked at the church filled with people who seemed to be so successful and arrogantly sure of themselves. He saw people with whom he was afraid to speak, people who would only compound his guilt. He saw a church speaking about forgiveness, love, and acceptance—but he didn't experience any of that. So, disillusioned, he quietly walked away to his dressing room and out into the night—away from the church.

One of the difficult things I've had to carry as a counselor is the secret burdens of people who are hurting. In a large church, there are always several wrestling with the unmentionable areas of a midlife crisis. Sometimes it is almost emotionally overwhelming for me to know what people are experiencing and not be able to share that with anyone.

As the church grows in acceptance, talks more freely about midlife crisis—and even jokes about it—and offers genuine forgiveness to people who've failed, then some of these people will turn back to the church and find it to be a community of strength and support.

A pastor friend called me recently and shared a difficult problem. Two of the officials in his church, a midlife married man and a divorced woman, were secretly having an affair. What should he do? Does he tell the board? Does he put the couple out of the church? What if it all blows open and everyone learns he has kept it a secret?

The church needs to move away from blame fixing and jump in to meet needs. The person in midlife crisis needs a friend, not an accuser. In 1 Corinthians it says the church is to function as a body: "If one part suffers, all parts suffer with it, and if one part is honored, all the parts are glad" (1 Cor. 12:26). A man in midlife needs friends who are willing to accept him and suffer with him.

During the time I went through my midlife crisis, I shared my anxieties with the church. Sometimes I felt in my messages I was *only* talking about my depressing struggles or illustrating my sermons from my conflicts. Yet the more I shared, the more other midlife men and women began to verbalize their own frustrations.

Learning about adult development was a lack in my seminary training. I was not taught how to cope with people in midlife. As a young pastor, I could not minister to people at midlife because I did not understand their problems. As the pastors and leaders become more vocal and help people through midlife crisis, we will see a great deal of mature, caring strength in the church. Midlife people won't want to slip out the back door.

## A Man and His Friends

Friends are likely to get a lot of abuse during a man's midlife crisis, but they are extremely important in helping him through this time. If a friend will hang on and continue to care, the friendship likely will move into a new depth after the crisis is over.

The man in midlife crisis will probably have little time for friends. If he is in the stage of trying to replay his young-adult years, he will not have much in common with the friends near his age. As he moves into the depression and withdrawal stages, he will not want to be bothered with his friends and will give all kinds of excuses: "It's just too much work getting together," or "I really don't enjoy doing that anymore," or "Those people never were my friends anyway."

The quality of friendships will quickly be seen during this time. Surface-type friends will drop away. Other friends who only use him, or whom he uses for political or social status, will probably be lost during this period.

"A close friendship starts when we accept ourselves as we are and then present ourselves to others in a way they will perceive as authentic. The only coin that passes in the kingdom of friendship is authenticity.

"Genuine friendship requires unqualified acceptance. It precludes the demand that you think, feel, or act like me. It resumes the acceptance of the undesirable as well as the desirable. Since there is no danger of rejection, acceptance permits anger as well as affection."[1]

True, caring friends will stay and be vulnerable, honest, and supportive. Friendships, such as David and Jonathan's in the Old Testament, tend to grow under pressure. There is a desire in each one to meet the other's need rather than use the other. David said, when he heard of the death of his friend Jonathan:

How the mighty heroes have fallen in battle!
Jonathan lies dead upon the hills.
How I weep for you, my brother Jonathan!
Oh, how much I loved you!
And your love for me was deep,
deeper than the love of women!
(2 Sam. 1: 25-26 NLT)

During my crisis, a number of people helped me. But it was difficult for me to change roles and let others care for me instead of my caring for them. There were times I felt it was a sign of weakness to let them care for me—but it deepened our friendship.

After my month's leave of absence from the church, I told the board of leadership that what I most appreciated was their friendship. They hung onto me with confidence and hope through prayer and friendship when I didn't seem to be able to hang on for myself. Proverbs 17:17 says, "A true friend is always loyal, and a brother is born to help in time of need."

A man is likely to have a new growing commitment toward the friends who offer genuine support. He will be more sympathetic, more willing to extend himself to others, because of the care he has experienced. From this point on a man's friends are not likely to be people he will exploit, or who will use him. They probably will be people who genuinely relate to him and with whom he can be vulnerable. However, I know men who have refused to grow during the midlife era and are less connected and lonelier than before.

Several men I know are currently going through various stages of their midlife crisis. One is involved in an affair, another is in divorce court, another's wife has left him, and others are wanting to change jobs or run away. Each of these men now faces the greatest question he has ever asked, "Do I have one friend to stand with me?"

Many men want to connect to other men, but have never learned how. They wish they could have relationships as easily as women do—but how? The book *Friendship* coaches a man on how to develop the six skills of friendship.[2]

Where are the Christian men?? It is not important for a man to have many friends during his midlife crisis. One friend can be truly significant. One friend can turn the tide from hopelessness and despair toward restoration and meaning.

### The Midlife Man's Children

If children in the family are to help their father, they first need to have some idea of what he is going through. More than understanding what is happening, they need to commit themselves to helping. This commitment will not only help the man through his crisis, but will also help the adolescent children to mature as they care for their father. We've found, and studies have verified, that children can have a powerful effect in helping a man through his midlife crisis.[3]

It's important that children not withdraw or treat Dad

as though he has typhoid fever. They can help by allowing him to continue as leader in the home. They can remind him of how much they appreciate him and mention specific things to build his self-esteem. Even though he may seem to reject their words, when he is in the depth of his despondency, the building remarks do carry an overall positive effect.

The children can also ask God to move their dad through this crisis. Jesus said, "I also tell you this: If two of you agree down here on earth concerning anything you ask, my Father in heaven will do it for you" (Matt. 18:19 NLT). My wife and daughters often had to claim verses such as this during my midlife crisis when there was little else to lean on.

My three daughters each were extremely sensitive to me during this time of my need. They sought opportunities to care for me. Typical of these expressions of love was a story written by my oldest daughter and given to me as a Christmas gift. It expresses our daughters' appreciation of me as well as their love and support:

> Once there lived a man in a quaint harbor town who repaired ships. He was known by nearly everyone,because he was the most skilled craftsman for miles around. Often he would repair damaged boats for no charge at all. He worked on sailboats of all sizes and types.
>
> When a sailboat would become unseaworthy, it would be brought straight to him. Ships were brought that had been torn by bad weather, had collided with other ships, had been misused, or even boats that were never built properly at first. He would take each one and soon have it ready to sail again.

The man was a great artisan and had been in constant apprenticeship all of his life to the Master Craftsman. The Master Craftsman was a builder of great ships—the most skilled builder ever to have lived. The Master Craftsman taught the man the art of repairing broken ships, and because they were such close friends, the Master Craftsman even taught him how to build his own ships.

The man always seemed to have dozens of damaged ships he was working on at once, and more always waiting. Often the man would work years to rebuild a single ship, working day and night.

Many times he would become discouraged, for he saw only broken ships. He longed to leap aboard a fine new ship and sail toward the Morning Star. He longed to feel the fresh breeze at his face and the salt-foam about his feet.

The man's fame continued to grow and often he was called to other port cities to work. Everything he did flourished. Many other men became apprentices to him and his work increased. Through his work and teaching, more and more ships were repaired each year.

Now, although this man worked most of his life at rebuilding ships, his greatest work was not the remaking of broken sailboats, but it was the building of three beautiful new ships. These were his greatest pride and showed all of his finest arti-san craftsmanship, because into these three ships the man had put his life and love.

Barbara Conway Schneider, Psy.D.

## A Wife Can Help

The one human being who can be the most help to a man during his midlife crisis is his wife. He may get help from his employer, counselors, the church, his children, or friends—but his wife is the most strategic person to help. A study done at Ohio State University shows that the most powerful people to help a man through his midlife transition time are his wife and his children.[4] Many women give up if their husband starts attacking them or if he gets into an affair. But don't quit! You are a powerful connection!

Unfortunately, helping her husband through this crisis will probably be the most difficult task a woman ever has in her life. If at the same time she is wrestling with her own midlife problems, the demands to help her husband may put such a great strain on the marriage that it could fall apart.

*Understanding the Problem:* She should view her husband's midlife crisis as a stage in his developmental process, but not as a kind of flu. A midlife crisis is not a temporary frustration that he'll shake off in a day or two. He's in a three- to five-year developmental process, much the same as a teen becoming a young adult.

She may feel that a nightmare has somehow intruded into their previously peaceful and pleasant lives. If she doesn't understand the overall crisis, she is likely to believe everything her husband says about her—that *his* crisis is *her* fault.

A woman needs to be prepared for the widely vacillating moods her husband will experience. It's like riding a roller coaster—you are sometimes upside down, and the person next to you continually vomits all over you.

You want to get off—and you want to help. But your husband says, "Leave me alone! I never wanted to get on this ride in the first place! It's all your fault!"

A wife should be prepared to be blamed for her husband's depression and their bad marriage—everything! He may say, "I want to be happy, loved, admired, I want sex, and youth. But I can't have any of these because I'm stuck in this stale marriage with you—my elderly, sickly, complaining, nagging wife."

A man is likely to strongly state that he is not aging or causing problems in the marriage, she is responsible and is dragging him down. A wife is going to need a great deal of strength to handle this unrighteous onslaught from her husband as he lists her failures.

In a letter to the editors of *Medical Economics*, a physician's wife wrote that her husband was experiencing all of the symptoms of the male midlife crisis. The editors recommended psychiatric treatment. There followed a flood of letters from men who strongly disagreed with the advice given to the woman. Almost to a man, the male letter writers stated the primary cause was neither his hormones, nor his neuroses, nor his environment— but his wife.

Sometimes during the crisis a wife may need to fill the leadership vacuum—he's not doing anything or making any decisions. At midlife a woman's own self-assertion may be very strong. If she does begin to be domineering, she is likely to slow her husband's progress as he works his way through his midlife crisis. It's a tightrope walk— if she doesn't take charge, then nothing gets done. If she does take charge, he resents her intrusion. "I'll get to it. Just give me some time and space."

It's easy for a wife to slip into a mothering role when

she sees her husband hurting. Part of his little-boy feelings cry out for mothering care. But the wife must be careful she is not viewed by her husband as his "mother." It is possible for her to give loving support as a friend, a lover, and as a wife without becoming his mother. If he identifies her as his mother, he is apt to reject her—because during his midlife crisis he is looking more for a "girlfriend" than a "mother."

*Being Attractive:* As a young adult man thinks of marriage, he looks for a woman who meets his needs for companionship and regular sex, who is willing to combine children and a career, and who in addition is a sensitive, caring spiritual woman. But during his midlife crisis, he may very well be looking for other qualities. Some of the common complaints of men at this age are that their wives aren't attractive, don't turn them on sexually, are old, and don't understand.

Remember that men are more visual than feeling oriented. It's important during her husband's crisis that his wife work on her own physical attractiveness—weight and muscle tone and wardrobe. She can help by temporarily altering her lifestyle a bit to more nearly fit the changing needs her husband is feeling.

Perhaps at no other time in their married life is she so likely to be in competition with other women. So, even though the qualities of companionship and caring are going to be the characteristics a man wants long-range, she must be attractive to him during the short-range crisis period. It's as if the couple are winning each other all over again. Don't ever use the phrase, "Look, Bubba, you made a vow when we were married!" Win him—don't threaten him!

If a wife can swing with the punches and hang onto

her sanity, she'll make it through the midlife crisis *with* her husband. Studies have repeatedly shown that despite their fantasies, men are not dashing off to marry young women.

The wife is stronger than she realizes. In our work with thousands of couples we've found that the growing, flexible wife has a very high probability of not only keeping her husband, but having a stronger marriage.

*Learning to Help:* Dr. Bergler in *The Revolt of the Middle-Aged Man* records part of an interview with a wife who asked how she could help her husband. He said, " 'First, find out what it is all about. Secondly, be patient. Thirdly, don't reproach him.' She interrupted: 'Fourthly, be an angel.' Her voice was heavy with sarcasm."[5]

The wife needs to find ways to gently draw her husband out of his cave of silence. He doesn't like to be alone, but he doesn't know how to share the pain he is feeling. A woman can help her husband during this time by building his self-image, reminding him of the areas in which he is successful. He may outwardly reject her attempts, and she may feel tempted to tell him to quit feeling sorry for himself, but her encouragement will help to maintain his self-esteem.

Encouraging him to attempt new areas of growth will be another positive way in which a wife can assist. Help him think about career alternatives. Suggest he return for more study or training, or encourage him to learn new skills for an entirely different job.

There are times when a man wants to be alone and simply stare out the window. Those times, especially during the depression and withdrawal phases of the crisis, are important and positive for recovery. A wife should allow him those experiences. She can also help by encouraging him to go for a bike ride, take a walk, or go for a ride in the car or boat. Or she may be able to gently involve one or two male friends to keep him in touch with the outside world.

She can help him by keeping herself emotionally strong. Read extensively, keep a good talking relationship with a trusted friend—and talk frequently with God. A small support group can also give perspective on what is happening and encouragement when the bottom seems to drop out.

Perhaps the most effective thing the wife can do is understand his feelings and verbalize them for him. It's not enough for her only to find new ways to look nice or be sexier, she has to recognize the despair he is feeling.

What a wife most needs is perspective from God. Isaiah 43:1-3 says, "Don't be afraid, for I have ransomed you; I have called you by name; you are mine. When you go through deep waters and great trouble, I will be with you. When you go through rivers of difficulty, you will not drown! When you walk through the fire of oppression, you will not be burned up—the flames will not consume you. For I am the Lord your God, your Savior." Sometimes all that will keep a wife going is confidence in God's love and ability. God's presence in the midlife man's life is the ultimate solution.

> Pity me, O Lord, for I am weak. Heal me, for my body is sick, and I am upset and disturbed. My mind is filled with apprehension and with gloom. Oh, restore me soon.
>
> Come, O Lord, and make me well. In your kindness save me.
>
> Psalm 6:2-4

## For Further Reading

*Your Husband's Midlife Crisis* by Jim and Sally Conway (Elgin, IL: David Cook Publishing Co., 1980, 1997).

*When A Mate Wants Out* by Jim and Sally Conway (Grand Rapids, MI: Zondervan Publishing House, 1992).

# 27

# A Man Helps Himself

WHEN I WAS IN MY MID-TEENS, I went on a fishing trip to Canada with my mom, dad, and brother. We were about an hour away from camp on a large, wonderful lake. I sat peacefully in the front of the boat, casting out my line. Suddenly my mother wound up with a giant sidearm cast and buried the hooks of her lure in my back. I felt as if I had been hit with a four-inch steel pipe. The shock was unbelievable—I was totally immobilized.

My reaction some thirty years later to my midlife crises were much the same. I was totally unprepared for what happens to men at midlife. Yes, I had seen other men struggle with similar problems, and I had been involved in helping many of them—but I believed their crises were because of a weakness in their lives. I thought of myself as relatively mature, well educated, growing emotionally, and in a deep relationship with God.

In spite of all these positive assets, the crisis came. It was not until after it hit me that I began an in-depth study about men at midlife. I discovered that other people working in the area of human development were convinced this crisis hits every man to some degree.

As I share with people in their twenties and thirties what I have been through, they emphatically boast, "That will never happen to me." They are sure they'll be able to get around it. Barbara Fried also found this attitude to be widespread. A thirty-two year old, for example, dismissed the idea of the crisis by stating flatly, "But that'll never happen to me, I'm sure of it. I have never been a ladies' man. When I'm that old, I'll know better than to be running around and having affairs. "[1]

It's difficult to convince a twenty year old that a midlife man has romantic fantasies. A man in his twenties is so filled with idealism and so busy beginning his career he simply doesn't have time to think about the developmental problems of midlife. Twenty years for a young adult seems as far away as the moon. Then the man in his thirties is so busy achieving his idealized goals he doesn't take time to stop and think. And if he does pause to reflect, he reasons that if he tries harder, he'll avoid the crisis.

In spite of the fact that men in their twenties and thirties will probably not listen to my tale, I believe it is the obligation of educators and the church to begin preparing men and women for the midlife transitional passage, which could become a midlife crisis.

### Attitudes I Would Need

After the fishhooks had been buried in my back, my father said I had choices to make. One choice we didn't discuss was to pretend I didn't have the hooks in my back. The truth was obvious to everyone—I had a problem. Dad told me I could either endure the agony of an hour's trip back to shore, and then an additional hour driving to find a doctor, or I could allow my dad to cut the hooks there in the boat while my back was still a bit numb. He said all I would need was a little bravery.

That's the way I came to feel about the midlife crisis. I began reading about all of the positive attitudes I needed to make it through. But my question was, "How will I get those attitudes—and what do all those words mean?" Neugarten said I needed "cathectic flexibility," "ego differentiation," "body transcendence," and "sexual integration," among other things.[2] John McLeish in *The Ulyssean Adult* said I should be "emotionally intensely alive."[3] Joel and Lois Davitz in *Making It from Forty to Fifty* said my behavior "is not merely selfish or silly. [The] sometimes astonishing variety of behaviors is part of an overall pattern of personal development."[4] Fried told me it was nothing but a "developmental crisis"—it had a beginning, and it would have an ending.[5] Daniel Levinson cautioned me to do more than simply tough it out. He said, "The fact is that there is something very profound happening here. I mean: Take it seriously, man! Don't just say, 'If I can hold out, I'll be all right.' "[6]

The experts continued their suggestions. Erikson said I needed to move to "generativity."[7] Kenn Rogers said I should not run from my problem but "fight it."[8] Tournier said the struggle was good for me: "Our life, then, has a meaning for us when we have a definite goal, when we struggle to attain it."[9] Sheehy said I needed the crisis and I should "let it happen."[10]

Eda LeShan said a midlife crisis is like the Dark Ages; following would be a renaissance, a time of rebirth, and birth is full of struggle."[11] Hunt said the midlife crisis is like the midcourse correction of a rocket in order to help it reach its goal.[12] For a while I wished I had been a Menomini Indian, because Slotkin told me they had no problems in midlife.[13]

People were giving me all kinds of newspaper and magazine articles. Most of these articles tried to joke me out of my problem—Judith Viorst,[14] Josephine Lowman,[15] and Davis Matheny. Matheny's approach was to show that anyone younger than forty was really dumb. "Never praise the 'vitality' of underaged people. When somebody else does—and those who do are usually trying to show how young-thinking they are—say nothing, but let a look of inexpressible boredom glaze over your features. Our research shows that people under twenty-five usually move about like tree-sloths, and the majority of them, like everyone else, are no more original and fresh in their thinking than rutabagas."[16]

The problem with all of these helpful suggestions is that I was becoming more depressed. It seemed that other people were making it, but I was not. My attitude was clearly one of self-pity. Because I didn't know how to help myself, I wanted to give up. Bergler jumped in and said that "resignation" is not the way out.[17] And yet that was the only way that seemed possible for me.

However, the people who put the most pressure on me were the ones who told me, by subtle remark or direct statement, that if I were a "better Christian" I wouldn't be having these troubles. These people were like Job's comforters, telling me if I'd just confess all my sins to God, I wouldn't be going through all these troubles. I felt like strangling them!

One such comment came from a minister who distributed this idea on a tape. He said people who have a personal relationship with Jesus Christ "have the least amount of problems. They are not threatened really, at any of these levels, because they recognize the purpose of

God in their life and are rounded out at the psyche level with the proper inputs."[18] All of these suggestions were useful after my crisis was past, but for most of the crisis period, their suggestions simply intimidated me and made me feel like a greater failure.

## What Seemed To Help Me

1. *Physical exercise* seemed to clear out my mind and drain off some emotional tension. It was great to get on my daughter's ten-speed bike and head out into the country. It seemed to wash out my personality. I came back physically tired, but the tiredness seemed good. Walking also was helpful—with Sally, but often alone. My office was a mile from our home, and I frequently jogged home at the end of the day. Each of these things seemed to help for brief periods of time.

2. I began to take on some *new challenges*—one was education. I started working on a doctorate at Fuller Seminary. When I got to the first course, I found a large proportion of the men in the program were also obviously wrestling with a midlife crisis. The explosion of adult education indicates that continuing education meets an important need. During the early stages of my crisis I was approached about writing a book. It was good to feel wanted. This new challenge didn't remove the crisis, but it provided an opportunity for personal therapy through research and writing.

3. I began to watch my *diet* and work more seriously on *weight loss*.

The midlife man's weight may be too high, according to an article entitled "In Midlife, the Leanest Men Survive." The author reports a study that shows, "Thin is not just in. For middle-aged men, at least, it is also the route to a longer life, according to a twenty-seven-year study of more than 19,000 graduates of Harvard University. The thinnest men had the lowest death rates.

"We found a direct relationship between weight and mortality, with the heavier men at all ages being more likely to die. . . . . Losing some weight will lower their risk somewhat, but to be at the lowest risk, they really have to be quite thin. . . . An earlier study . . . showed that weight-cycling, or yo-yo dieting, was itself a hazard to health and life."[19]

My physical body became a greater concern to me. As I ate better food, lost weight, and took a high-potency vitamin B complex each day, I began to feel better about my body. I am currently trying to keep my fat intake at ten grams a day, walking three miles a day, eating lots of fresh fruit and vegetables—plus I'm finding a high protein drink at noon really powers me through the afternoon and evening.

4. *A change of scenery* seemed to improve my spirits—even if only for short periods of time. Studying in southern California, conferences in Colorado, weekends away in the woods, and sailing on local lakes all seemed to help lift my spirits. Friends loaned us their recreational vehicles so we could get out into the woods or go to the ocean, and have a warm, dry place when it rained. The woods, the water, and sailing seemed to give me hope for a few more days.

5. *Music was significant* during my midlife crisis. At first, music played a depressive part. I listened constantly to easy-listening stations, heavily oriented toward love songs. I was drawn to that kind of music, but the result was a deeper awareness I no longer was a young man.

As the months went along, some music became extremely helpful to me. One of these songs was "Slow Down." I took the tape to the woods and played it dozens of times. It was as if God was massaging my heart through this song:

> In the midst of my confusion,
> In the time of desperate need,
> When I'm thinking not too clearly,
> A gentle voice does intercede.
>> *Chorus:*
>> Slow down, slow down,
>> Be still, be still and wait
>> On the Spirit of the Lord.
>> Slow down and hear his voice,
>> And know that he is God.
> In the time of tribulation,
> When I'm feeling so unsure,
> When things are pressing in about me,
> Comes a gentle voice, so still, so pure"[20]

6. Gradually I began to open up to Sally and *talk more freely about my midlife anxieties.* At first she was threatened and frightened—so I wouldn't tell her much at a time. You can understand her insecurity when I would say, "I'm not sure the Bible is true, or that God really cares about us." Then I talked about our marriage. "I'm not sure we ever should have gotten married."

But as the months went along, it was easier to share with her even some of the things that were terribly damaging to her self-image. Each time we talked, I seemed to become freer. Over several months our understanding and love for each other seemed to increase.

Most men are unwilling to share with their wives what they really feel. They are afraid they will destroy the marriage. Strangely enough, while men feel the relationship with their wife is bad, they desperately want to protect it. So be brave; talk to your wife.

7. *Rest* became important. I was a workaholic, putting in over one hundred hours a week. During this time I came down with mononucleosis. I was physically exhausted and weak enough that it hit me hard. As a result, I faced the reality that I needed more rest and a drastic change of pace at work. I was totally burned out.

Every spark of creativity had disappeared. I verbally whipped myself because I wasn't more productive and creative. But the more I pushed, the angrier I got at everyone and everything around me. I was like a *Tour-de-France* bicycle racer who decided not to rest at night or eat for twenty-three days. I was obsessively pushing myself.

Christians have not really dealt with leisure. They can't fully understand why God took a day off after He created the world. Certainly it wasn't because He needed the rest. Perhaps He knew that our Christian work ethic needed to be modified.

In one of our worship services a college girl shared what God taught her through her extended sickness. She said, "I learned I glorified God most when I rested and recovered from the sickness. If I had tried to continue carrying my Christian activity, I would have been out of God's will for me." Then she got my attention with these words: "God is not as interested in what we do as—what we are."

As I understood my need for rest during this time, I

also needed to be away from people. At first, aloneness produced guilt. After all, I was a people helper. But I simply couldn't stand the emotional stress of people's problems. During that month of November I saw practically no one other than my family. I took no phone calls. I was in isolation for psychological recuperation.

8. *Physical health.* I was fortunate to have several medical doctors in the church. These men cared deeply for me in more ways than physically. They gave me confidence that I was not having a heart attack and that there was apparently nothing much wrong with my body—other than mono and its effects. They encouraged me to slow down and assured me that I would make it through.

9. *My mental state.* Previously I had not done much to care for my psychological health. I just assumed it would always be good. I wouldn't need to work at it. My attitude changed. I now know it is important for me to be spiritually and emotionally strong for my own benefit as well as for others.

Books have had a powerful impact on me. When you're at a men's retreat buy several; put them in your bathroom and read a little at a time (for suggestions, see the list at the end of various chapters). You don't need to finish a whole chapter—just keep reading.

All of the things I've listed above are important for me to continue to be mentally healthy. I am also planning new adventures and projects which build my mental health.

10. All of my adult life I have regularly *read the Bible and talked to God in prayer.* However, as the ministry years increased, I spent more time looking for material to preach rather than reflecting on the Scriptures for my own nourishment.

My own mental and spiritual well-being are important. It's vital for me to spend personal time in the Bible and in prayer. This time doesn't take hours away from my busy day and lower my productivity. Rather, God contributes directly toward my ability to be more productive by keeping me spiritually and emotionally healthy.

The purpose of the Bible is to give us information about God and ourselves. Hebrews 4:12 (NLT) says, "For the word of God is full of living power. It is sharper than the sharpest knife, cutting deep into our innermost thoughts and desires. It exposes us for what we really are." Timothy adds, "All scripture is inspired by God and is useful to teach us what is true and to make us realize what is wrong in our lives. It straightens us out and teaches us to do what is right. It is God's way of preparing us in every way, fully equipped for every good thing God wants us to do" (2 Timothy 3:16-17 NLT).

My quiet time alone with God is not a duty to impress God—it's a vital necessity for my spiritual and emotional health.

### The Key Role Of God

Beyond any doubt, all of the areas I've mentioned earlier were useful to move me through my midlife crisis. However, the most significant person during this entire time was God. His quiet ministry, through activities as well as through other people, was the most significant factor for my recovery. This subtle work of God within my personality brought great change in me.

Before my midlife crisis I was deeply aware that God

was my ally. I could tell Him anything, even share with Him the contradictory motives within my personality—and He would still love and accept me. As my crisis deepened and I experienced depression and withdrawal, I knew intellectually that God was my friend—but I did not feel it emotionally.

During that time I preached a series of messages on the life of Daniel. The truth God kept bringing to my attention, and which I shared with the congregation, was God's miraculous care for us in every age of our life and through all the stresses of life. God continually confronted me with this truth—yet I did not *feel* that truth.

About nine months earlier God had led me to speak on the emotional and spiritual breakdown of Elijah recorded in 1 Kings 19. It is the story of a prophet of God who was exhausted by the stress of ministry.

Elijah's story has some striking similarities to a man going through a midlife crisis. He had made a great spiritual impact and won a great victory over evil. But his life was threatened. Earlier he might have stood his ground and fought. Now he was simply too tired, so "Elijah was afraid and fled for his life" (vs. 3 NLT).

Then we see "he went on alone into the desert, traveling all day. He sat down under a solitary broom tree and prayed that he might die" (vs. 4 NLT). During a midlife crisis a man often feels desperately alone, wondering what life is all about and even if it's worth living. I understood Elijah's death wish.

Elijah expressed self-pity. " 'I've had enough,' he told the Lord. 'Take away my life. I've got to die sometime, and it might as well be now' "(vs. 4).

## God's Concern—The Whole Man

God wasn't at all frustrated by Elijah's self-pity, but began to restore Elijah *physically* as the first step toward recovery. An angel brought food for him, and he went to sleep. Later, the angel came again with more food to build up Elijah's body.

God also cared by helping Elijah *emotionally*. Elijah was still feeling a great deal of self-pity. "I have worked very hard for the Lord God of the heavens," he said (vs. 10). God sent him on a long journey, which provided an opportunity for him to walk in the fresh air without responsibilities, to unwind for forty days and forty nights. God sent him to a new location, new scenery, a new place for refreshment.

Then God began to build Elijah *spiritually*. The scene is Elijah in a deserted cave. Here God revealed His power as well as His specific concern for the man in the cave. God asked, "Why are you here, Elijah?" (vs. 13). God probed the deep spiritual questions—what are the reasons for man's existence, to whom does he owe allegiance, whom will he serve? In these moments, as Elijah stood at the mouth of his cave, God gently touched him in the depths of his being where no one else could reach.

God continued to build this man and bring him back into usefulness by telling him he had continued service to do. He had work! He was to anoint two kings as well as ordain a new young prophet. He was to prepare this young prophet for spiritual leadership—ultimately to be Elijah's successor.

God cared for all aspects of Elijah's life—physically with food and rest, emotionally with a freedom from responsibility and a change of scenery, and spiritually with a quiet voice deep within. Finally, God restored

Elijah's self-esteem and worth, showing him a continued useful work for years to come.

The message about Elijah's emotional and spiritual breakdown and recovery shows a God who really cares for us—and also shows that our crises are only temporary. We can count on God's care from many different sources to help us again become productive people who enjoy living.

## The Results of God's Work in Me

In the beginning of this book I tried as honestly as possible to share my experiences in my midlife crisis. I stopped on a very despondent note. Now I want to complete that story.

I literally had come to the end of my rope. During the previous months I had often felt very strong urges to leave everything and everyone I knew. Those were my lowest moments. As I walked the cold streets of Urbana, Illinois in November, I was ready to leave everything and run away. I crawled into bed that winter night and hardly slept as I made my plans. I detailed specific steps I would take as I left my present life and ran away to start another.

There were several discussions going on my mind. Part of me would ask, "Where are you going to go?"

The other part would answer, "Probably somewhere south where it's warm, to a small town near the ocean. "

"And what will you do there?"

"I don't know. I'm willing to work at anything—anything just to make a little money to eat and have a place to live. Maybe I'll get a job working on sailboats."

"Will you tell anyone you're a pastor?"

"No! Then they'll want me to help them! I don't want

to help anybody. "

"How do you know everything will work out all right?"

Almost as a reflex response—not really thinking about the meaning of my words, I said, "Well, God has always been faithful to me in the past. I'm sure I can depend on Him to help. "

It was then that God quietly entered the conversation and said, "If you can trust Me to care for you when you run away, why can't you trust Me to care for you *without* running away?"

There was a long silence.

All the voices in my mind were quiet. There was only a quiet new calm. Soon I dropped off to sleep, knowing that I had crossed a line into a new peace.

The next morning I picked up my Bible, reading where I had left off. How did I happen to be at this section? These were the words I read:

> In my distress I screamed to the Lord for his help. And he heard me from heaven; my cry reached his ears.
>
> He reached down from heaven and took me and drew me out of my great trials. He rescued me from deep waters.
>
> You have turned on my light! The Lord my God has made my darkness turn to light. Now in your strength I can scale any wall, attack any troop.
>
> Psalm 18:6, 16, 28-29

I found myself saying with the psalmist, "What a God he is! How perfect in every way! All his promises prove true. He is a shield for everyone who hides behind him"

(Ps. 18:30).

As the days went along, God continued His special ministry to me in my midlife cave as He had with Elijah. I began to sense that I turned a corner.

## Changed Self-Image

I was so glad that the earlier self-pity was gone. I didn't seem to need that anymore. Now there was a new optimism. New goals seemed to be possible. I thought of myself as worthwhile and valuable—I had a contribution to make to the lives of many people. I was far more valuable at midlife than I was when I was younger. Goals and ambitions began to be resurrected in me. I no longer dreaded the future—it seemed to be filled with opportunity.

I was enjoying a deep and pervading peace. Yet at the same time, I had a sensitive awareness of the loneliness in every human being. Part of me wanted to reach out and care for every lonely person. Yet another part of my being cautioned me to let the healing process continue and not to overextend myself.

But I would never be the same. I had a new confidence. Fear faded into the background. That doesn't mean I was never afraid, but my confidence in God gave me new assurance of continued usefulness for the rest of my life—even though the form of that usefulness would change.

God had been working from many different directions, assisting me to change myself—and changing me when I couldn't help myself. He sent books, friends, a gracious wife and family, all with the purpose of moving me through my midlife crisis to a new, settled, and productive era—under God's direction.

It's only a nursery rhyme—but I have to smile now. Humpty Dumpty is together again. All the king's horses and all the king's men had nothing to do with it. I'm not the same Humpty! I'm a new man—more mature, more understanding, more sensitive.

Saint Augustine summed it up when he said, "Our spirits are restless until they find their rest in God."

> For who is God except our Lord? Who but he is as a rock? He fills me with strength and protects me wherever I go.
>
> Psalm 18:31-32

## For Further Reading

*Fight Like a Man* by Gordon Dalbey (Wheaton, IL: Tyndale House Publishers, Inc. , 1995).

*Hope Again* by Charles R. Swindoll (Dallas, TX: Word Publishing, 1996).

*When God Doesn't Make Sense* by James Dobson (Wheaton, IL: Tyndale House Publishers, Inc., 1993).

# Endnotes

## Chapter 1. The Crisis

1. Walter Pitkin, *Life Begins at Forty* (New York: World Publishing Co., 1941).
2. Edmund Bergler, *The Revolt of the Middle-Aged Man* (Madison: International University Press, 1985), 43.
3. Saul Bellow, *Herzog* (New York: Penguin Books, 1988).
4. Barbara R. Fried,*The Middle-Age Crisis* (New York: Harper and Row, 1967), 124.
5. Fred McMorrow, *Midolescence: The Dangerous Years* (NewYork: Quadrangle/New York Times, 1974), 63.
6. Vachel Lindsay, ed. Dennis Camp, *The Poetry of Vachel Lindsay*, Vol. 1 (Peoria, IL: Spoon River Poetry Press, 1984), 134.
7. D. B. Bromley, The *Psychology of Human Aging* (Baltimore: Penguin, 1966), 13.
8. Joel and Lois Davitz, *Making It from Forty to Fifty* (NewYork: Random House, 1976), xvi.

## Chapter 2. Expert Opinions

1. Joseph Campbell, ed., R. F. C. Hull, trans., *The Portable Jung* (New York: Viking, 1971), 12-13.
2. Kenn Rogers, "Mid-Career Crisis," *Saturday Review of Society,* February, 1973, 37-38.
3. Daniel Levinson, "The Normal Crises of the Middle Years," symposium sponsored by The Menninger Foundation at Hunter College, New York City, March 1, 1973, transcript, 9.
4. Gail Sheehy, *Passages* (New York: Dutton, 1976).
5. Cyra McFadden, "Is There Really a Male Menopause?" *New Choices in Retirement Living* (July/August, 1994), Vol. 34, No. 6.
6. Charles M. Sell, *Transitions Through Adult Life*, (Grand Rapids, MI: Zondervan Publishing House, 1991), 125.
7. McFadden, "Is There Really a Male Menopause?"
8. Fred McMorrow, *Midolescence: The Dangerous Years* (New York: Quadrangle/New York Times, 1974), 38.

### Chapter 4. The Cultural Squeeze

1. Harry Levinson, *The Exceptional Executive* (Cambridge, MA.: Harvard University Press, 1968), 79.
2. Peter F. Drucker, *The Age of Discontinuity* (New York: Harper & Row, 1969), x.
3. Robert A. Raines, *Lord, Could You Make It a Little Better?* (Waco: Word, 1972), 135. Used by permission of Word Books, Waco, Texas.
4. Quoted in Martha Weinman Lear, "Is There a Male Menopause?" *The New York Times Magazine,* January 28, 1973.
5. Laura Asric, "Knife Guys Finish First," *Canadian Business*, April 1996, Vol. 69, No. 4, 21.
6. Peter Chew, *The Inner World of the Middle-Aged Man*, (New York: Macmillan, 1976), 33.
7. Ralph Barton Perry, *Plea for an Age Movement* (Stamford, CT: The Overbrook Press, 1942).
8. Maggie Scarf, "Husbands in Crisis," *McCall's*, June 1972, Vol. 99, No. 9, 76.

### Chapter 5. Second Adolescence

1. Brian O'Reilly, "Men at Midlife: Crisis? What Crisis?" *Fortune*, September 18, 1995, 72.
2. *Ibid.*
3. *Ibid.*
4. Barbara R. Fried, *The Middle-Age Crisis* (New York, NY: Harper and Row, 1967), 59.
5. *Ibid.*

### Chapter 6. The Enemy Horde

1. Avery Corman, *The Old Neighborhood* (Avery Corman Inc., 1980). Corman is also the author of *Kramer vs. Kramer*, *Prized Possessions*, and *The Big Hype.*

### Chapter 7. Depression

1. Dian Stafford, "The New Face of Depression," *Orange County Register*, March 6, 1996.
2. *Ibid.*
3. Jim and Sally Conway, *Women in Midlife Crisis* (Wheaton, IL: Tyndale House Publishers, 1983, 1998), 224-227.
4. Lewis Smedes, *Forgive and Forget* (San Francisco: Harper & Row, 1984).

5. Archibald D. Hart, *Dark Clouds, Silver Linings* (Colorado Springs: Focus on the Family, 1993), ix.

## Chapter 8. A New Shell
1. Marilyn Elias, "More Men Go for the Nip and Tuck," *USA Today*, March 1995, Vol. 6, No. 2.
2. Justin Martin, "Men Giving Plastic Surgery a New Look," *Fortune*, October 1995, Vol. 132, 46.
3. Joyce Brothers, *Better Than Ever* (New York: Simon & Schuster, 1975), 19-20.
4. Bernice and Morton Hunt, *Prime Time,* (New York: Harper & Row, 1965), 164.
5. Joel and Lois Davitz, *Making It from Forty to Fifty* (New York: Random House, 1976), 93.
6. Alan Farnham, "You're So Vain," *Fortune*, September 9, 1996, 66-69.
7. Robert Manry, *Tinkerbelle* (New York: Harper & Row, 1965), 218.
8. Edwin E. "Buzz" Aldrin, *Return to Earth* (New York: Random, 1973), 308-309.

## Chapter 9. Early Retirement
1. Gene Tharpe, "Stressed Out in Midlife," *Atlanta Constitution*, July 22, 1996.
2. Rust L. Hills, *How to Retire at Forty-One* (Garden City, NY: Doubleday, 1973), 3.
3. Hills, *How to Retire,* 98.
4. Quoted in Hills, *How to Retire,* 122. Perhaps Thoreau's most famous work is *Walden*. Written in 1854, this book is still available.

## Chapter 10. The Affair
1. Peter Chew, *Inner World of the Middle-Aged Man* (New York: Macmillan, 1976), 58.
2. Barbara Fried, *The Middle-Age Crisis* (New York: Harper and Row, 1967*)*, 6.
3. Morton Hunt, *The Affair* (New York: New American Library, 1969), 29.
4. Reid Kanaley, "Internet Infidelity," *Wichita Eagle*, February 25, 1996, 14.
5. Giuseppe Mantovani, "Virtual Reality as a Communication Environment: Consenual Hallucination, Fiction, and Possible Selves," *Human Relations*, Vol. 48, No. 6, June, 1995, 699.

6. Maia Szalavitz, "Virtual Liaisons," *Orange County Register*, December 12, 1995.

7. See Bill and Pam Farrel and Jim and Sally Conway, *Pure Pleasure: Making Your Marriage a Great Affair*, (Downers Grover, IL: InterVarsity Press, 1994).

8. William Braden, "Study: 15 Percent of Spouses Cheat," *Chicago Sun Times*, October 18, 1994, 14.

9. *Ibid.*

10. Harry J. Johnson, *Executive Life-styles* (New York: Crowell, 1974), 19.

11. Gail Sheehy, *Passages* (New York: Dutton, 1976), 471.

12. Bernice Neugarten, *Personality in Middle and Late Life* (New York: Atherton Press, 1964), 72.

## Chapter 11. Escaping the Affair

1. Jim Conway, *Adult Children of Legal or Emotional Divorce* (Downers Grove, IL: InterVarsity Press, 1990), 34.

2. Cotton Ward, "Confessions of an Internet Widow," *net,* Spring 1996, 62.

3. Judith Viorst, *How Did I Get to Be 40 and Other Atrocities* (New York: Simon & Schuster, 1973), 39.

4. David R. Mace, *Success in Marriage* (Nashville: Abingdon, 1958), 100.

5. Barbara Fried, *The Middle-Age Crisis* (New York: Harper and Row, 1967), 114.

## Chapter 13. Adults Keep Developing

1. Shirley Braverman and Joel Paris, "The Male Midlife Crisis in the Grown-up Resilient Child,"*Psychotherapy* (Winter 1993), Vol. 30, No. 4, 655.

2. Braverman and Paris, 651.

3. Braverman and Paris, 652.

4. Braverman and Paris, 656.

## For Further Reading about Adult Development

Buhler, Charlotte, "The Curve of Life as Studied in Biographies," *Journal of Applied Psychology* (1935), 405-409.

Chiriboga, D., Lowenthal, M. F., Thurnher, M. *et al, Four Stages of Life: A Comparative Study of Women and Men Facing Transitions* (San Francisco: Jossey-Bass, 1975).

Commons, Michael, Jack Demick, and Carl Goldberg, *Clinical Approaches* to *Adult Development* (Norwood, NJ: Ablex Publishing Corp, 1996).

Conway, Jim, *Adult Children of Legal or Emotional Divorce* (Downers Grove, IL: InterVarsity Press, 1990).

Conway, Jim and Sally, *Women in Midlife Crisis* (Wheaton, IL: Tyndale House Publishers, 1983, 1998).

Gruen, Walter, "Adult Personality: An Empirical Study of Erikson's Theory of Ego Development" in B. Neugarten, Ed., *Personality in Middle and Late Life: Empirical Studies* (New York: Atherton, 1964).

Knox, Alan B. *Adult Development and Learning* (San Francisco: Jossey-Bass Publishers, 1977).

Levenson, Michael R and Crumpler, Cheryl A., "Three Models of Adult Development," University of California Human Development and Family Studies, David, CA, *Human-Development*, May-June 1996, Vol. 39, No. 3, 135-149.

Levinson, Daniel, *Seasons Of a Man's Life* (New York: Knopf, 1978).

**For Further Reading about the Resilient Child**
Cohler, Ball, "Adversity, Resilience, and the Study of Lives" in E. J. Anthony and B.J. Cohler, eds., *The Invulnerable Child* (New York: Guilford, 1987).

Pollact, W. S., "Men's Development And Psychotherapy: A Psychoanalytic Perspective," *Psychotherapy,* 1990, 316-321.

Sameroff, A. J. and Seifer, R. "Early Contributors to Developmental Risk" in J. Rolf, A. S. Masten, D. Ciicchetti, K. H. Nuechterlein and S. Weintraub, eds., *Risk and Protective Factors in the Development of Psychopathology.* (New York: Cambridge University Press, 1990), 52-66.

**Chapter 14. This Crisis Came to Pass**
1. Elisabeth Kubler-Ross, *On Death and Dying* (New York: Macmillan, 1969).

**Chapter 15. Bewildered at Thirty-Five**
1. Barbara Fried, *The Middle-Age Crisis*, (New York: Harper and Row, 1976), 70-71.

2. Fried, *Middle-Age Crisis,* 39.

### Chapter 16. Barren at Fifty

1. Frank and Mary Alice Minirth, Brian and Deborah Newman, Robert and Susan Hemfelt, *Passages of Marriage* (Nashville, TN: Thomas Nelson Publishers, 1991), 232-260.
2. Quoted in Gail Sheehy, *Passages* (New York, NY: Dutton, 1976), 337.
3. Judith Viorst, *How Did I Get to Be Forty and Other Atrocities* (New York: Simon & Schuster, 1973), 45.

### Chapter 17. The Marriage Knot

1. Eda J. LeShan, *The Wonderful Crisis of Middle Age* (New York: Warner Books, 1985), 148-149.
2. Jim and Sally Conway, *Traits of a Lasting Marriage* (Downers Grove, IL: InterVarsity Press, 1991), 25.
3. David L. Cohn, *Love In America* (New York: Simon & Schuster, 1943), 86.
4. Conway, *Traits of a Lasting Marriage*, 60.
5. Conway, *Traits of a Lasting Marriage*, 127-136.

### Chapter 18. In Love Again

1. Daniel Goldstine and others, *The Dance-Away Lover* (New York: Morrow, 1977).
2. Les and Leslie Parrot, "The Boomerang Effect," *Partnership*, Summer 1997, Vol. 14, No. 2, 65.
3. Robert Lee and Marjorie Casebier, *The Spouse Gap* (Nashville, TN: Abingdon, 1971), 40.

### Chapter 19. A Sexy Marriage

1. Bill McCartney, *What Makes a Man?* (Colorado Springs: Navpress, 1992), 61-68.
2. Jim and Sally Conway, *Sexual Harassment No More* (Downers Grove, IL: InterVarsity Press, 1993), 38-42.
Tracy D. Bostwick and Janice L. Decuia, "Effects of Gender and Specific Dating Behaviors on Perception of Sex Willingness and Date Rape," *Journal of Social and Clinical Psychology* 1992), Vol. 11, 22.
Derrick R. Holcomb, Linda C. Holcomb, K. Sondag and Nancy Williams, "Attitudes About Date Rape: Gender Differences Among College Students," *College Student Journal* 1991, Vol. 25, 437.
3. Orie Pocs and others, "Is There Sex After 40?" *Psychology Today,* June 1977, Vol. 11, 54.

4. Fred McMorrow, *Midolescence: The Dangerous Years* (New York: Quadrangle/New York Times, 1974), 13.

5. Bernice and Morton Hunt, *Prime Time,* (New York: Harper & Row, 1965), 79.

6. Gail Sheehy, *Passages* (New York: Dutton, 1976), 461.

7. Henry Still, *Surviving the Male Midlife Crisis* (New York: Crowell 1977), 82-83.

8. Stanley Frank, *The Sexually Active Man Past Forty* (New York: Macmillan, 1968), 74.

9. Bill and Pam Farrel and Jim and Sally Conway, *Pure Pleasure: Making Your Marriage a Great Affair,* (Downers Grover, IL: InterVarsity Press, 1994), 99.

10. Frank, *Sexually Active Man*, 222.

11. Robert Lee and Marjorie Casebier, *The Spouse Gap* (New York: Warner Books, 1985), 112.

12. Lee and Casebier, *Spouse Gap*, 117.

**Chapter 20. Work That's Fun**

1. Justin Martin, "Men Giving Plastic Surgery a New Look," *Fortune*, Oct. 1995, Vol. 32, 46.

2. Alan Farnham, "You're So Vain" *Fortune*, Sept. 1996, Vol. 134, 66.

3. Smiley Blanton, *Now or Never* (Englewood Cliffs, NJ: Prentice Hall, 1959), 86.

4. Jan Halper, "Male Mystique," *American Way* (American Airlines), Aug. 1989, 42.

5. Peter Chew, *The Inner World of the Middle-Aged Man,* (New York: Macmillan, 1976), 138.

6. Eda J. LeShan, *The Wonderful Crisis of Middle Age* (New York: Warner Books, 1985), 80.

7. Arthur Miller, *Death of a Salesman* (New York: Viking, 1949), 82.

8. Ruth Simon, "When You're Too Damn Old," *Money*, July 1996, Vol. 25, No. 7, 118-126.

9. Simon, "Too Damn Old," 120.

10. Robert Peterson, *New Life Begins at Forty* (New York: Trident, 1967), 35-46, 48-89.

11. Richard N. Bolles, *What Color is Your Parachute?* (San Francisco: Ten Speed, 1997).

12. Bernice and Morton Hunt, *Prime Time,* (New York: Harper & Row, 1965), 104, 108.

13. "Employment and Earnings," *Bureau of Labor Statistics,* January 1977, Vol. 24, No. 1.

14. Alan Knox, *Adult Development and Learning,* (San Franciso: Jossey-Bass Publishers, 1977), 405-469.

15. Peterson, *New Life*, 94.


## Chapter 21. Aging with Finesse

1. Bernice and Morton Hunt, *Prime Time,* (New York: Harper & Row, 1965), 39.

2. Hunt, *Prime Time,* 38.

3. Thomas C. Desmond, "America's Unkown Middle-Agers," *The New York Times Magazine,* July 29, 1956.

4. Anne W. Simon, *The New Years: A New Middle Age* (New York: Knopf, 1968), 167-168.


## Chapter 22. Children in Transition

1. Teresa Julian, "Men's Well-Being at Mid-life," *Mental Health Nursing*, 1992, Vol. 13, 295.

2. Earl Henslin, *Man to Man* (Nashville, TN: Thomas Nelson Publishers, 1993).

3. Bergler, *The Revolt of the Middle-Aged Man* (Madison: International University Press, 1985), 281.

4. Ross Campbell, *How to Really Love Your Children* (Wheaton, IL: Victor Books, 1977).


## Chapter 23. Parenting the Parents

1. Peter Chew, *The Inner World of the Middle-Aged Man*, (New York: Macmillan, 1976), 123.

2. US Bureau of the Census, *Resident Population by Age and State: 1995*, 33.

3. Ruth Shonle Cavan, "Family Tension Between the Old and the Middle-Aged," *Marriage and Family Living,* November 1956, 323-327.

4. Quoted in Eda J. LeShan, *The Wonderful Crisis of Middle Age* (New York: Warner Books, 1985), 275.

5. Evelyn Duvall, *In-Laws—Pros and Cons* (Chicago: Wilcox and Follett, 1954).

6. Tim Stafford, *As Our Years Increase* (Grand Rapids, MI: Zondervan Publishing House, 1989), 12-13.

### Chapter 24. Creative Retirement

1. Ken Dytchtwald and Joe Flower, *Age Wave: The Challenges and Opportunities of an Aging America* (Los Angeles, CA: Jeremy P. Tarcher, 1989), 4.
2. Dan McGraw, "Business and Technology: Old Executives Never Die," *US News and World Report*, October 14, 1996, Vol. 121, No. 15, 61-62.
3. Barbara Deane, *CreativeRetirement* (Colorado Springs: Navpress, 1992), 9.
4. Anne W. Simon, *The New Years: A New Middle Age* (New York: Knopf, 1968), 72-73.

### Chapter 25. Sooner or Later

1. Quoted in Peter Chew, *The Inner World of the Middle-Aged Man* (New York: Macmillan, 1976), 6.
2. Paul Tournier, *Learn to Grow Old* (New York: Harper & Row, 1972), 218.
3. Anne W. Simon, *The New Years: A New Middle Age* (New York: Knopf, 1968), 155.
4. Ernest Becker, *The Denial of Death* (New York: The Free Press, 1973), ix.
5. Simon, *New Years*, 217.
6. Quoted in Rollo May, *Love and Will* (New York: Norton, 1969), 99.

### Chapter 26. We Can Help

1. Paul Robbins, "Must Men be Friendshipless?" *Leadership*, Fall 1984, 27.
2. Jim Conway, *Friendship* (Grand Rapids, MI: Zondervan Publishing House, 1989).
3. Teresa Julian, Patrick McKenry and Mary W. McKelvey, "Components of Men's Well-Being at Mid-life," *Mental Health Nursing*, 1992, Vol. 13, 285-299.
4. Julian, McKenry and McKelvey, 285.
5. Edmund Bergler, *The Revolt of the Middle-Aged Man* (Madison: International University Press, 1985), 104.

### Chapter 27. A Man Helps Himself

1. Barbara Fried, *The Middle-Age Crisis* (New York: Harper & Row, 1967), 13.
2. Bernice Neugarten, *Personality in Middle and Late Life* (New York: Atherton Press, 1964), 16-19.
3. John A. B. McLeish, *The Ulyssean Adult* (New York, NY: McGraw-Hill Ryerson, 1976).

4. Joel and Lois Davitz, *Making it From Forty to Fifty* (New York: Random House, 1976).

5. Fried, *The Middle-Age Crisis*, ix.

6. Quoted in Peter Chew, *The Inner World of the Middle-Aged Man* (New York: Macmillan, 1976), 13.

7. Quoted in Gail Sheehy, *Passages* (New York: Dutton, 1976), 405.

8. Kenn Rogers, "Mid-Career Crisis," *Saturday Review of Society*, February 1973, 38.

9. Tournier, *Learn to Grow Old* (New York: Harper and Row, 1972), 93.

10. Sheehy, *Passages*, 364.

11. Eda LeShan, *The Wonderful Crisis of Middle Age* (New York: Warner Books, 1985), 240.

12. Bernice and Morton Hunt, *Prime Time,* (New York: Harper & Row, 1965), 148, 151.

13. J. S. Slotkin, "Life Course in Middle Age," *Social Forces,* December 1954, Vol. 33, 171-177.

14. Judith Viorst, "How Do You Know When You're 40?" *The New York Times Magazine,* February 6, 1977, 66.

15. Josephine Lowman, "Don't Think 'Middle Age,'" *The Champaign-Urbana News-Gazette,* September 13, 1977, 10-A.

16. Davis F. Matheny, "Is There Life After Forty?" *Minneapolis Star*, September 24, 1977, 8-9.

17. Edmund Bergler, *The Revolt of the Middle-Aged Man* (Madison: International University Press, 1985), 297.

18. Gerald B. Hall, "What Happens to the Man over Forty?" tape for Renewing Love Alumni Seminar, Annandale, VA, 1975.

19. Jane E. Brody, "In Midlife, the Leanest Men Survive," *The New York Times*, December 15, 1993, 17.

20. "Slow Down" by Chuck Gerald ©1974 Dunamis Music. All rights reserved. Used by permission.

# Additional Help for You

If you need more help recovering from an affair or any aspect of midlife crisis, write to us at Midlife Dimensions—P.O. Box 3790, Fullerton, CA 92834, or look at the additional help on our web site—www.midlife.com)

Also available from ChariotVictor Publishing—*Your Husband's Midlife Crisis*, by Sally Conway.